50 WALKS IN
Gloucestershire

50 Walks in Gloucestershire

Published by AA Publishing (a trading name of AA Media Limited, whose registered office is Grove House, Lutyens Close, Lychpit, Basingstoke, Hampshire RG24 8AG; registered number 06112600)

© AA Media Limited 2024
Fourth edition
First published 2002

Mapping in this book is derived from the following products:
OS Landranger 149 (walk 47)
OS Landranger 150 (walks 22–24, 27, 35, 41)
OS Landranger 151 (walks 2, 7, 11–14)
OS Landranger 162 (walks 36–39, 42, 43, 46, 48–50)
OS Landranger 163 (walks 1, 3–6, 8–10, 15–21, 25–26, 28–34, 38)
OS Landranger 172 (walks 44, 45)
OS Landranger 173 (walk 40)

© Crown copyright and database rights 2024 Ordnance Survey. 100021153.

Maps contain data available from openstreetmap.org © under the Open Database License found at opendatacommons.org

ISBN: 978-0-7495-8372-9
ISBN: 978-0-7495-8382-8 (SS)

A CIP catalogue record for this book is available from the British Library.

AA Media would like to thank the following contributors in the preparation of this guide:
Clare Ashton, Tracey Freestone, Lauren Havelock, Nicky Hillenbrand, Lin Hutton, Graham Jones, Ian Little, Richard Marchi, Nigel Phillips, Victoria Samways.

Cover design by
berkshire design company.

Printed and bound in the UK by Oriental Press, Dubai.

A05851

We would like to thank the following photographers, companies and picture libraries for their assistance in the preparation of this book. Abbreviations for the picture credits are as follows:
Alamy = Alamy Stock Photo
Trade Cover, Dee Cresswell/Stockimo/Alamy
Special Cover, Martin Bache/Alamy
Back Cover Advert, SolStock/istockphoto; 9, Dave Porter/Alamy; 12/13, Margaret Clavell/Alamy; 23, Cotswolds Photo Library Creative/Alamy; 48/49, Alan Skipp/Alamy; 71, imageBROKER.com GmbH && Co. KG/Alamy; 84/85, paul weston/Alamy; 95, John Corry/Alamy; 105, Tim Wright/Alamy; 130/131, Wolstenholme Images/Alamy; 153, Cotswolds Photo Library Creative/Alamy; 169, Ashley Cooper pics/Alamy; 176, SolStock/istockphoto

The contents of this book are believed correct at the time of printing. Nevertheless, the publishers cannot be held responsible for any errors or omissions or for changes in the details given in this book or for the consequences of any reliance on the information it provides. This does not affect your statutory rights. We have tried to ensure accuracy in this book, but things do change and we would be grateful if readers would advise us of any inaccuracies they may encounter by emailing walks@aamediagroup.co.uk

We have done our best to make sure that these walks are safe and achievable by walkers with a basic level of fitness. However, we can accept no responsibility for any loss or injury incurred while following the walks. Advice on walking safely can be found on pages 10–11.

Some of the walks may appear in other AA books and publications.

Discover and book AA-rated places to stay at www.RatedTrips.com.

AA

50 WALKS IN
Gloucestershire

CONTENTS

How to use this book	6
Exploring the area	8
Walking in safety	10

The walks

WALK		GRADIENT	DISTANCE	PAGE
1	Adlestrop	▲	5 miles (8km)	14
2	Todenham	▲	4.75 miles (7.7km)	17
3	Windrush Valley	▲	6.5 miles (10.4km)	20
4	Sherborne	▲	2.5 miles (4km)	24
5	Lechlade	Negligible	5.75 miles (9.2km)	27
6	Eastleach	▲	4 miles (6.4km)	30
7	Sezincote	▲	3 miles (4.8km)	33
8	Bourton-on-the-Water	▲	5 miles (8km)	36
9	Bourton-on-the-Water	▲	4 miles (6.4km)	39
10	Fairford	Negligible	3.75 miles (6km)	42
11	Blockley	▲▲	5 miles (8km)	45
12	Mickleton	▲▲	5 miles (8km)	50
13	Chipping Campden	▲▲	4.75 miles (7.7km)	53
14	Chipping Campden	▲	4.5 miles (7.2km)	56
15	Condicote	▲	9 miles (14.5km)	59
16	Northleach	▲	4 miles (6.4km)	62
17	Guiting Power	▲	5.75 miles (9.2km)	65
18	Bibury	▲▲	6.25 miles (10.1km)	68
19	Coln St Aldwyns	▲	3 miles (4.8km)	72
20	Hazleton	▲	4.5 miles (7.2km)	75
21	Ampney	▲	10 miles (16.1km)	78
22	Cutsdean	▲	6 miles (9.7km)	81

WALK		GRADIENT	DISTANCE	PAGE
23	Snowshill	▲▲▲	7 miles (11.3km)	86
24	Stanton	▲	3.75 miles (6km)	89
25	Chedworth	▲	4.5 miles (7.2km)	92
26	South Cerney	Negligible	5 miles (8km)	96
27	Hailes Abbey	▲	5 miles (8km)	99
28	Winchcombe	▲▲	4 miles (6.4km)	102
29	Belas Knap	▲▲	5.5 miles (8.8km)	106
30	Brockhampton	▲▲	7.75 miles (12.5km)	109
31	Prestbury	▲	3.25 miles (5.1km)	112
32	Brimpsfield	▲	4 miles (6.4km)	115
33	Sapperton	▲	6 miles (9.7km)	118
34	Bisley	▲▲	5.5 miles (8.8km)	121
35	Tewkesbury	Negligible	4 miles (6.4km)	124
36	Painswick	▲▲	7.5 miles (12.1km)	127
37	Slad Valley	▲▲	3.75 miles (6km)	132
38	Chalford	▲▲▲	6 miles (9.7km)	135
39	Gloucester	▲	7 miles (11.3km)	138
40	Tetbury	▲	3.5 miles (5.7km)	141
41	Deerhurst	▲	3.25 miles (5.3km)	144
42	Ashleworth	Negligible	7.25 miles (11.7km)	147
43	Uley	▲▲	3 miles (4.8km)	150
44	Dyrham Park	▲	6 miles (9.7km)	154
45	Horton	▲	3.75 miles (6km)	157
46	Arlingham	▲	7.5 miles (12.1km)	160
47	Kempley to Dymock	▲	9.25 miles (14.9km)	163
48	Brockweir	▲▲	4.5 miles (7.2km)	166
49	Brockweir	▲▲	4.25 miles (6.8km)	170
50	Forest of Dean	▲▲	6.25 miles (10.1km)	173

HOW TO USE THIS BOOK

Each walk starts with an information panel giving all the information you will need about the walk at a glance, including its relative difficulty, distance and total amount of ascent. Difficulty levels and gradients are as follows:

Difficulty of walk
- 🟢 Easy
- 🟠 Intermediate
- 🔴 Hard

Gradient
- ▲ Some slopes
- ▲▲ Some steep slopes
- ▲▲▲ Several very steep slopes

Maps
Every walk has its own route map. We also suggest a relevant Ordnance Survey map to take with you, allowing you to view the area in more detail. The time suggested is the minimum for reasonably fit walkers and doesn't allow for stops.

Route map legend

Symbol	Meaning	Symbol	Meaning
──▶──	Walk route	▭	Built-up area
❶	Route waypoint	▭	Woodland area
─ ─ ─ ─	Adjoining path	🚻	Toilet
•	Place of interest	🅿	Car park
⌂	Steep section	▭	Picnic area
☀	Viewpoint	)(	Bridge
▬▬▬	Embankment		

Start points
The start of each walk is given as a six-figure grid reference prefixed by two letters referring to a 100km square of the National Grid. More information on grid references can be found on most OS Walker's Maps.

Dogs
We have tried to give dog owners useful advice about how dog friendly each walk is. Please respect other countryside users. Keep your dog under control, especially around livestock, and obey local by-laws and other dog control notices.

Car parking

Many of the car parks suggested are public, but occasionally you may have to park on the roadside or in a lay-by. Please be considerate about where you leave your car, ensuring that you are not on private property or access roads, and that gates are not blocked and other vehicles can pass safely.

Walks locator map

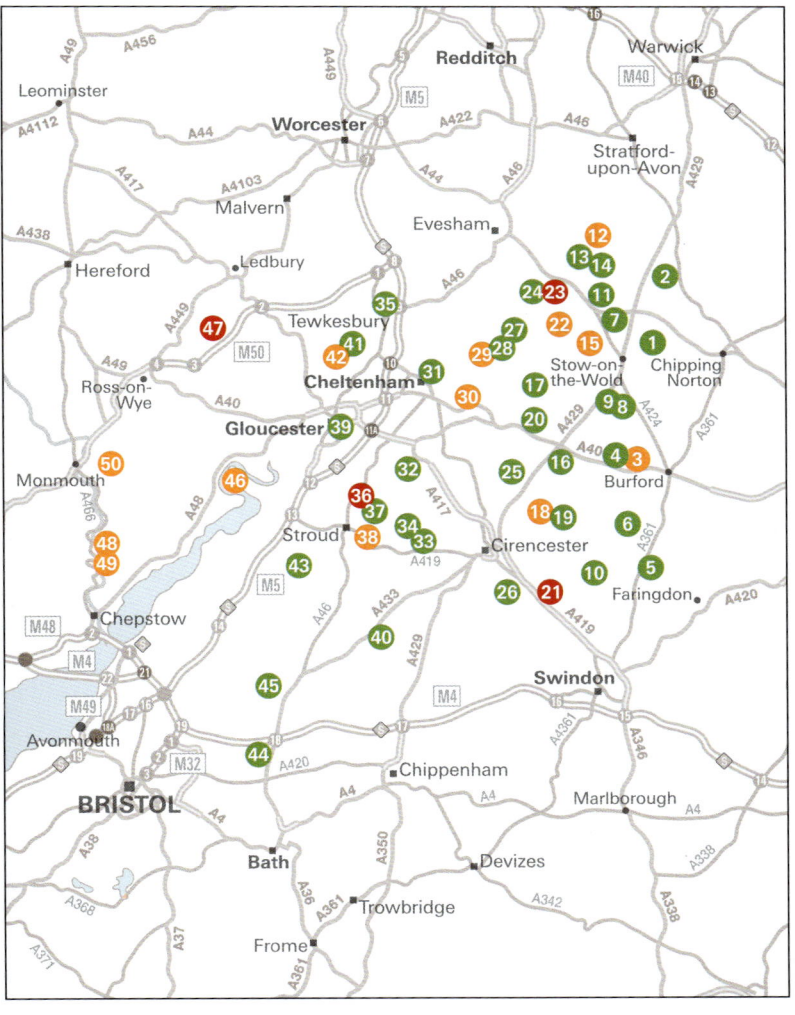

EXPLORING THE AREA

Gloucestershire has almost everything to make it a delightful county for discovering on foot. Within its boundaries are exceptionally varied landscapes. The Cotswolds, a region of gentle hills, valleys and gem-like villages, roll through the county. To their west is the Severn Plain, watered by Britain's longest river, and characterised by orchards and farms marked out by hedgerows that blaze with mayflower in the spring. Beyond the Severn are the Forest of Dean and the Wye Valley – this border country is a distinctive mix of Celtic and Anglo-Saxon traditions. All of these have been an inspiration to some of England's finest writers and composers. Together, they combine to create a notion of mellow rosiness that epitomises rural southern England.

GOLDEN VILLAGES

Gloucestershire doesn't have any real mountains: this is not a rugged county and will not suit the seekers of wilderness and rocky grandeur. The hills – though there are plenty of them – rise no higher than about 1,000ft (305m). What you do get from these hills, however, is a particular intimacy with the countryside. Climb out of Stanton, for example, and the views behind you, westward across the vale towards the Malverns and the Forest of Dean, are spectacular but never dizzy. Below you are fields of poppies and strings of golden villages, but you are never high enough to be isolated from their warmth.

What Gloucestershire lacks in rock it makes up for with an abundance of stone. Best known is the limestone of the Cotswolds, much of it a golden hue, which gives the villages of the region their widely admired charm. But there are also the standing stones of the Forest of Dean and the fossils in the Severn mud. Stone walls are everywhere on the hills, and even on the vale, stone has found its way into the fabric of some fine buildings, from churches to tithe barns.

DISCOVER THE PAST

In Gloucestershire you are never far away from tangible remains of the past. There is something remarkable to see and touch from almost every era of British history, right up to our own time. Neolithic burial chambers are widespread, and so too are the remains of Roman villas, many of which retain the fine mosaic work produced by Cirencester workshops. There are several examples of Saxon building, including a chapel amazingly still intact, an array of medieval manor houses, and hundreds of villages visually unchanged for five centuries. In the Stroud valleys abandoned mills and canals are the mark left by the Industrial Revolution.

Gloucestershire has always been known for its abbeys, but most of them have disappeared or lie in ruins. However, few counties can equal the churches that remain. These are many and diverse, from the 'wool' churches in Chipping Campden and Northleach, to the cathedral at Gloucester, the abbey church at Tewkesbury or remote St Mary's, standing alone near Dymock.

CASTLES AND A QUEEN

If there is a shortage of anything in Gloucestershire, it is of castles. Well, you can't have it all; and yet even so, there are a couple of them. There is Sudeley Castle, where Catherine Parr is buried, and if you seek the real medieval article there is Berkeley, down on the vale.

Battles, with the exception of that at Tewkesbury, were usually fought elsewhere, leaving Gloucestershire to carry on being beautiful. Perhaps that is what makes walking here a singular experience. Gloucestershire's natural advantages have been made use of, but never transformed into something ugly – on the contrary, people and nature have got together and created something that suits them both.

PUBLIC TRANSPORT

The main railway stations in Gloucestershire are Gloucester, Stroud, Cheltenham and Moreton-in-Marsh, all of which are served directly from London's Paddington Station. There is also a line running along the west bank of the Severn. Cheltenham is well located for trains serving the north and the southwest. For all local transport information see www.travelinesw.com.

Walk 15

WALKING IN SAFETY

All these walks are suitable for any reasonably fit person, but less experienced walkers should try the easier walks first. Route-finding is usually straightforward, but you will find that an Ordnance Survey walking map is a useful addition to the route maps and descriptions; recommendations can be found in the information panels.

Risks

Although each walk here has been researched with a view to minimising the risks to the walkers who follow its route, no walk in the countryside can be considered to be completely free from risk. Walking in the outdoors will always require a degree of common sense and judgement to ensure that it is as safe as possible.

- Be particularly careful on cliff paths and in upland terrain, where the consequences of a slip can be very serious.
- Remember to check tidal conditions before walking on the seashore.
- Some sections of route are by, or cross, busy roads. Take care, and remember that traffic is a danger even on minor country lanes.
- Be careful around farmyard machinery and livestock, especially if you have children with you.
- Be aware of the consequences of changes in the weather, and check the forecast before you set out. Carry spare clothing and a torch if you are walking in the winter months. Remember that the weather can change very quickly at any time of the year, and in moorland and heathland areas, mist and fog can make route-finding much harder. Don't set out in these conditions unless you are confident of your navigation skills in poor visibility.
- In summer remember to take account of the heat and sun; wear a hat and carry water.
- On walks away from centres of population you should carry a whistle and survival bag. If you do have an accident that means you require help from the emergency services, make a note of your position as accurately as possible and dial 999.

Countryside Code
Respect other people:

- Consider the local community and other people enjoying the outdoors.
- Co-operate with people at work in the countryside. For example, keep out of the way when farm animals are being gathered or moved, and follow directions from the farmer.

- Don't block gateways, driveways or other paths with your vehicle.
- Leave gates and property as you find them, and follow paths unless wider access is available, such as on open country or registered common land (known as 'open access land').
- Leave machinery and farm animals alone – don't interfere with animals, even if you think they're in distress. Try to alert the farmer instead.
- Use gates, stiles or gaps in field boundaries if you can – climbing over walls, hedges and fences can damage them and increase the risk of farm animals escaping.
- Our heritage matters to all of us – be careful not to disturb ruins and historic sites.

Protect the natural environment:
- Take your litter home. Litter and leftover food don't just spoil the beauty of the countryside; they can be dangerous to wildlife and farm animals. Dropping litter and dumping rubbish are criminal offences.
- Leave no trace of your visit, and take special care not to damage, destroy or remove features such as rocks, plants and trees.
- Keep dogs under effective control, making sure they are not a danger or nuisance to farm animals, horses, wildlife or other people.
- If cattle or horses chase you and your dog, it is safer to let your dog off the lead – don't risk getting hurt by trying to protect it. Your dog will be much safer if you let it run away from a farm animal in these circumstances, and so will you.
- Everyone knows how unpleasant dog mess is and it can cause infections, so always clean up after your dog and get rid of the mess responsibly – bag it and bin it.
- Fires can be as devastating to wildlife and habitats as they are to people and property – so be careful with naked flames and cigarettes at any time of the year.

Enjoy the outdoors:
- Plan ahead and be prepared for natural hazards, changes in weather and other events.
- Wild animals, farm animals and horses can behave unpredictably if you get too close, especially if they're with their young – so give them plenty of space.
- Follow advice and local signs.

For more information visit www.gov.uk/government/publications/the-countryside-code

EXPLORING ADLESTROP AND DAYLESFORD

DISTANCE/TIME	5 miles (8km) / 2hrs
ASCENT/GRADIENT	450ft (137m) / ▲
PATHS	Track, field and road
LANDSCAPE	Rolling fields, woodland and villages
SUGGESTED MAP	OS Explorer OL45 The Cotswolds
START/FINISH	Grid reference: SP242272
DOG FRIENDLINESS	Some livestock and one busy roadside
PARKING	Village Hall car park in Adlestrop (donation requested)
PUBLIC TOILETS	None on route

You may not know the name Warren Hastings but he played a prominent role in the British Empire. Born in the nearby village of Churchill in 1732, he spent much of his childhood in Daylesford, where his grandfather was rector. When debt forced the sale of the manor, Hastings was sent to London for a career in commerce. He joined the East India Company, which had become the de facto ruler of India, and by 1773 he was Governor-General of Bengal with the specific remit of cleaning up the corruption that was rife among the ruling classes. His methods were draconian but considered effective. Upon his return to England, he used his savings to repurchase Daylesford, where he died in 1818. The years before his death were bitter. A change in attitude to harsh colonialist methods meant that Hastings was impeached for corruption. The seven-year trial ruined him and his health, although he was eventually made Privy Councillor to George III.

Daylesford House was rebuilt by Hastings to the design of the architect Samuel Cockerell, a colleague at the East India Company. The building is in a classical style with Moorish features. The parkland around Daylesford House was laid out in 1787 by the landscape gardener Humphrey Repton in the spacious style of the day, made popular by Lancelot 'Capability' Brown. The village grew out of a need for cottages for estate workers. Similarly, Daylesford church was rebuilt by Hastings in 1816 as a place of worship for the estate workers. By 1860 the congregation had outgrown the church, so it was redesigned to accommodate it. Inside there are monuments to the Hastings family, while Warren Hastings' tomb lies outside the east window.

This small rural village has come to be associated the poem by the war poet, Edward Thomas (1878–1917). Called simply 'Adlestrop', the poem captures a single moment as a train halts briefly at the village's station. Its haunting evocation of the drowsy silence of a hot summer day is all the more poignant when it is borne in mind that Thomas was killed by an exploding shell at Ronville near Arras in April 1917. Though trains still run on the line, the station was closed in 1964. The station sign now decorates a bus shelter, and the station bench has the poem inscribed upon it.

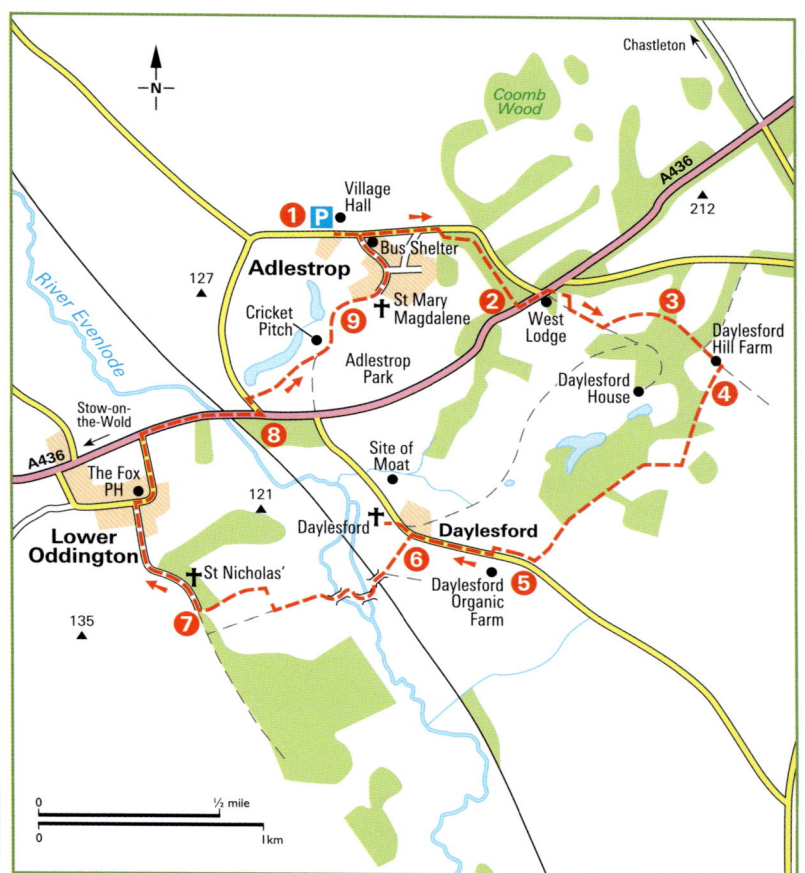

1. From the car park at the village hall turn left along the road. Pass a road on the right, the bus shelter bearing the Adlestrop sign, and some houses. Some 200yds (183m) after another road, turn right over a stile. Follow a woodland path to the left. Continue on this path until it meets a gate at a road.

2. Cross the road with care and turn left along the verge. Before a road on the right, and after West Lodge, turn right through a wooden gate onto a path in the Daylesford Estate. The path curves left to a post-and-rail fence. Turn right alongside it as it curves to the drive. Turn left onto the drive, flanked by poplar trees, and after 100 paces, turn left between post-and-rail fences.

3. Follow these to cross a bridge and follow a tree-lined avenue towards buildings. Traverse the farmyard and then turn right at Daylesford Hill Farm Cottage, passing the estate office.

4. Walk along the drive between paddocks, which soon begins following the estate wall. Pass the gardens office gate and, as the wall goes sharp right, stay on the drive to reach a road. Turn right at a gate.

5. Don't go out onto the road but turn right and walk along a short fenced section beside a hedge to emerge opposite Daylesford Organic Farm. Turn right and walk along the road to Daylesford estate village. Opposite the drive to Daylesford House is a path leading to Daylesford church. After visiting the church, return to the road, turn right and retrace your steps. About 95 paces beyond the phone box, turn right through a kissing gate.

6. Cross this field to a gate. Turn right onto a track and cross a railway footbridge. Curve along the track to cross an iron lattice-sided footbridge over the stream. In 75yds (69m), turn right off the track through a kissing gate, and then left by the hedge to walk parallel to the track. At the end of the field turn left through a gate back onto the track, through another gate and then right, beyond the hedge. The path follows two sides of the field to a gate into a copse in the far corner.

7. At a track through the trees turn right and pass Oddington Church. Continue, now on tarmac, to a junction in the village, and turn right. Pass The Fox pub and go to another junction. Turn right and walk on the pavement. Where it ends, cross the road carefully to the pavement opposite.

8. Beyond the railway bridge, turn left along the Adlestrop road and turn immediately right through two kissing gates. Walk through Adlestrop Park, skirting to the right of the cricket pitch and head for a kissing gate to its right, which is in a tree gap.

9. Follow the track through a kissing gate and past Adlestrop's St Mary Magdalene Church. At the next junction, turn left through the village until you reach the bus stop. Turn left here to return to the car park where you began your walk.

Where to eat and drink
Daylesford Farm's award-winning organic Farm Shop is well stocked with a range of tasty fare, much of it locally sourced. It also has a café that is open seven days a week, year round, for snacks and meals.

What to see
As you walk around Daylesford Park, try to catch a glimpse of the house – it's very cleverly concealed behind ornamental parkland, designed to preserve privacy while creating a harmonious landscape.

While you're there
Bledington church, about 3 miles (4.8km) south of the Oddingtons, has an outstanding series of beautiful medieval stained glass windows. North of Adlestrop is the handsome Stuart manor house of Chastleton.

TODENHAM AND THE LOST DITCHFORDS

DISTANCE/TIME	4.75 miles (7.7km) / 1hr 45min
ASCENT/GRADIENT	271ft (82m) / ▲
PATHS	Track and field, quiet lanes, ford or bridge, several stiles
LANDSCAPE	Rolling fields, with good views at some points
SUGGESTED MAP	OS Explorer OL45 The Cotswolds
START/FINISH	Grid reference: SP240362
DOG FRIENDLINESS	On lead around livestock
PARKING	Lay-bys on Todenham's main street, south of village hall
PUBLIC TOILETS	None on route

There are cases of so-called 'lost villages' all over England, and almost as many theories and explanations for their demise. The principal culprit is said to be the Black Death sweeping through the countryside in the 14th century. However, in the case of the Ditchfords, there appear to be other reasons for their disappearance. Ditchford is a name that was widespread in this area (perhaps because of their proximity to the Fosse Way – fosse meaning 'ditch' in Old English). Remnants of this, in the form of the house and farm names, are still evident on detailed maps, but of the three villages – Ditchford Frary, Lower Ditchford and Upper Ditchford – there is almost no trace.

A priest from Warwickshire called John Rouse wrote in 1491 that the Ditchfords had been abandoned during his lifetime. Changes in agricultural practices are thought to be the principal reason for this abandonment. As farming gradually became more efficient there was a disinclination to cultivate the stony soils of the more exposed and windswept upland areas.

At the same time, in the Cotswolds, the wool trade was rapidly supplanting arable farming as the wolds were given over to sheep. Much of the land was owned by the great abbeys who, deriving a third of their income from wool, turned vast tracts of land over to summer pasture in the uplands and winter pastures on the more sheltered lower slopes. The result was that the villagers, mostly farm labourers who depended on access to arable land for their livelihood, lost access. They simply had to move elsewhere in search of work.

Today there are no solid remains of any of the three villages. What you can see, however, is a series of regular rolls and shapes in the land that indicate settlement. Upper Ditchford, which stood on the slope near Neighbrook Farm, is the least obvious, but you can see banked enclosures and terraces that probably supported buildings. The site is somewhat clearer in the case of Lower Ditchford, where there are terraces and the site of a manor house and moat. Ditchford Frary has left its name to a nearby farmhouse.

Todenham survived the rigours of depopulation, and today is a quiet and unspoilt village situated on the edge of the Cotswolds. It's really a long, single road flanked by an assortment of houses and their leafy gardens. The manor house dates from the end of the Georgian period, while St Thomas à Becket Church, with its tall steeple, towers over the village, and is worth a visit for its decorated and Gothic interior. Other notable features include its 13th-century font with the names of 18th-century churchwardens inscribed upon it.

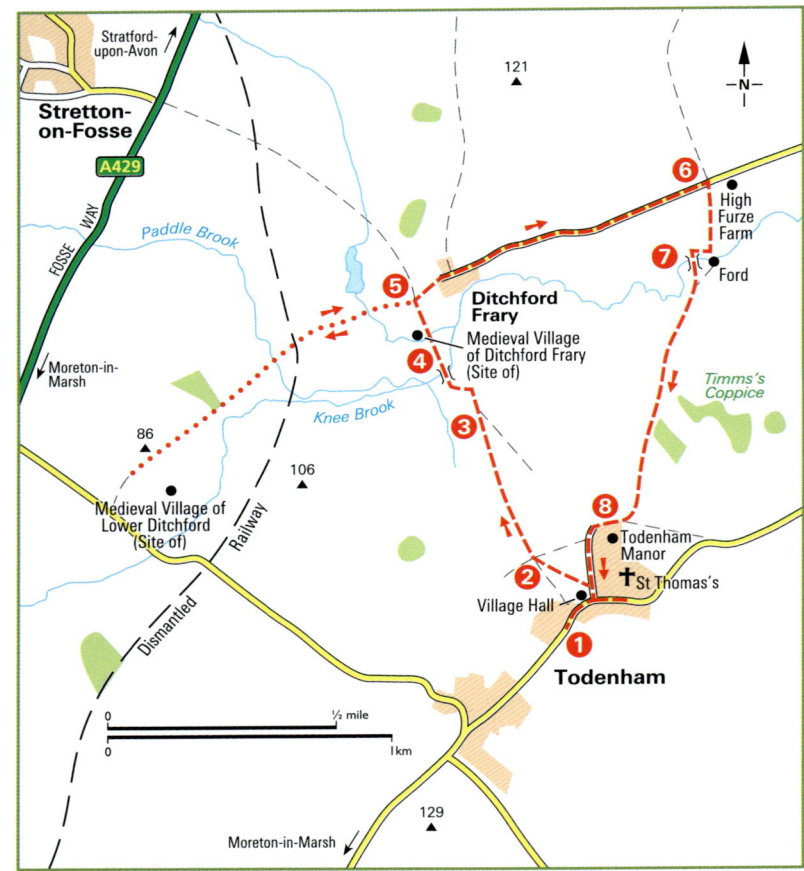

1. From a lay-by below Todenham village hall, walk up to turn left onto a wide track just after the hall, signposted 'public path'. Just before Ash House, go left through a kissing gate in the corner of the hedge, then diagonally right across the open field to the gate opposite.

2. Go through a kissing gate in the hedge on the far side, into a field of undulations indicating medieval ploughing. Go straight ahead to a stile, cross into the neighbouring field and, staying on its upper part, go straight ahead in the direction of a large house.

3. Cross another stile and join a grassy farm track. Where the track goes into a field on the right, bear left to pass to the right of a brick ruin, and cross a footbridge with gates at each end.

4. Cross this bridge and then go straight ahead, crossing a field (amid the earthworks of the site of Ditchford Frary) with a farmhouse ahead to the right. On the other side, go through a field gate, cross another field and pass through a field gate to join a farm track.

5. If you wish to see the site of Lower Ditchford, turn left here onto the metalled track and keep going across the former railway line until you approach a road – the remains are to your left. Then return along the track. Otherwise turn right on the track and pass behind the farmhouse. The track becomes a metalled lane.

6. After 0.5 miles (800m), turn right through a gate just before High Furze farm into a field. Follow its left margin until it dips down to a ford across Knee Brook. Turn right here, and after 70 paces find a bridge on your left.

7. Cross this ancient stone bridge and head uphill to the faint, grassy track that rises from the ford. Staying on this line, with the brook now to your right, you will come to a gate in the top corner. Go through onto a track that rises between tree lines and copses. After 0.5 miles (800m) you reach a junction opposite an entrance to Todenham Manor.

8. Turn first right here and then follow this track as it curves left, around the manor between post and rail fences and beech hedges, and finally brings you back to the village. Turn left for the church, or turn right to return to your car.

Where to eat and drink
The market town of Moreton-in-Marsh, 3 miles (4.8km) southwest, has plenty of pubs, cafés and restaurants catering for all tastes. Alternatively The Plough Inn in Stretton-on-Fosse is a free house serving food seven days a week.

What to see
As you're crossing the fields at the start of the walk, look for the pleats in the fields that indicate medieval ridge and furrow ploughing techniques. These are common all over central England, though many have been ploughed out by modern machinery. The furrows were created by ox-drawn ploughs; the ridges separated different farmers' workings in the same open field. Each furrow would originally have been about a furlong (201m) in length, the distance being about as far as the ploughing beast could pull before it needed a rest.

While you're there
Tuesday is market day in Moreton-in-Marsh; it's the largest – indeed, practically the only – weekly market left in the Cotswolds. Full of bustling bargain hunters, it gives a hint, at least, of how village life must have once been.

THE LIMESTONE BUILDINGS OF THE WINDRUSH VALLEY

DISTANCE/TIME	6.5 miles (10.4km) / 2hrs 45min
ASCENT/GRADIENT	520ft (158m) / ▲
PATHS	Fields, tracks and pavement, many stiles
LANDSCAPE	Streams, fields, open country and villages
SUGGESTED MAP	OS Explorer OL45 The Cotswolds
START/FINISH	Grid reference: SP192131
DOG FRIENDLINESS	Some care required but can probably be off lead for long stretches without livestock
PARKING	On-street parking in Windrush
PUBLIC TOILETS	None on route

The Cotswolds, characterised by villages of gilded stone, lie mainly in Gloucestershire. Stone is everywhere here – walk across any field and shards of oolitic limestone lie about the surface like bits of fossilised litter. This limestone, for so long an obstacle to arable farming, is a perfect building material. In the past almost every village was served by its own quarry, a few of which are still worked today. Golden hue limestone is a sedimentary rock, made largely of material derived from living organisms that thrived in the sea that once covered this part of Britain. The rock is therefore easily extracted and easily worked; some of it will actually yield to a handsaw. However, it is for its golden hue, due to the presence of iron oxide, that it is most famous.

The composition of the stone dictates the use to which it will be put. Some limestone, with a high proportion of grit, is best suited to wall building or to hut building. Some outcrops are in very thin layers and are known as 'presents' because they provide almost ready-made material for roof-slates. When the stone needs a little help it is left out in the winter so that frost freezes the moisture trapped between layers, forcing them apart. The stone can then be shaped into slates and hung on a wooden roof trellis by means of a simple nail. The smallest slates are placed at the top of the roof, the largest at the bottom. Because of their porous nature they have to overlap, and the roof is built at a steep pitch so that the rain runs off quickly.

There are four basic types of traditional stone construction to be seen in the Cotswolds – dry-stone, mortared rubble, dressed stone and ashlar. Dry-stone, without any mortar, is used in the many boundary walls you'll see as you walk around the region. Mortared rubble, on the other hand, depends on the use of lime pointing in order to stay upright. You'll see its use in many of the simpler buildings or as a cheaper backing to buildings faced with better stone. Dressed stone refers to the craft of chopping and axing stone to give it a more polished and tighter finish. This is used in higher order buildings and houses. Ashlar is the finest technique, where the best stone is expertly sawn and shaped into perfectly aligned blocks that act either as a facing on rubble, or, more rarely, make up the entire wall. Ashlar was used in the region's finer houses and, occasionally, in barns. The quarries here, to the west of Burford, provided building material for London's St Paul's Cathedral and several Oxford colleges.

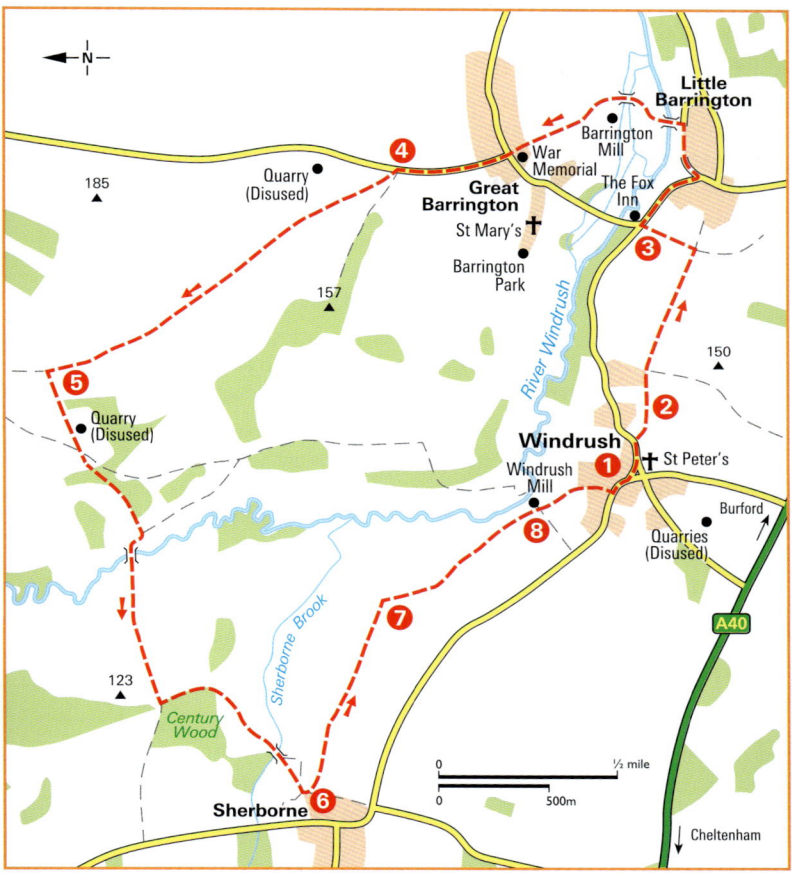

1. Walk out of the village, keeping to the left of the church. After about 100yds (91m), turn right opposite No. 27 through a gate into a field. Go across this field to the other side, keeping to the left.

2. Go through the right-hand gate and continue across three fields until you emerge in a large field at a wide grass strip (careful here, as it is used by horses and their riders with the houses of Little Barrington opposite. Cross two-thirds of the field, then turn left and head for the hedge at the bottom to the right of the cricket field.

3. Go through a gap on the left for a short path to the road. Ahead is The Fox Inn. Turn right, with the pub car park on your left, enter Little Barrington and turn left along a 'No Through Road'. Pass Sundial Cottage on your left, the lane soon narrowing to a path. Where the path becomes a lane again, go left across a bridge, then further on cross three footbridges as you pass around the right-hand boundary of Barrington Mill. Walk up a hedged lane, eventually

emerging in Great Barrington at a war memorial cross. Take the road in front of you, signed 'Little Rissington and Bourton-on-the-Water'.

4. Where the stone park wall to Barrington Park on your left ends, go left onto a track and immediately right through a gate. Stay on this track for a little over 1 mile (1.6km) until, after climbing out of a dry valley, you come to a junction of tracks with large hedges and a waymark post before you.

5. Turn sharp left and follow this track to the valley bottom. Where it turns hard left, go straight on and enter scrubby woodland. Follow the waymarks onto a path through trees. Cross the bridge over the River Windrush and follow a grassy track for two fields (ignoring waymarked paths off left and right) until, just before Century Wood, you turn left over a bridge with a stile at each end into a field. Follow the margin of the woods. Go through a kissing gate into a field and turn slightly right to the far corner. Through a gate, cross a footbridge and, after 50 paces, go through a gate on the right and bear left.

6. Go through a gate on the far side. Cross the track straight ahead and after a few paces turn left at a gate. Go over into the next field and cross it, going straight ahead, with a hedge close on your right. Go through several fields.

7. Go through a kissing gate and on the far side of an open field go through a gap into another field, with a stone wall on your right. Continue over a stone stile and through several fields, passing a stone barn on the way. Finally, pass a derelict farm building to your left-hand side, shortly before you arrive at a gate by a lane.

8. Opposite, go up and over a stone stile. Follow the perimeter of the next field as it goes right, ignoring a footpath into a field at the corner immediately on your left. Walk instead beside a stone wall and go over a stone stile onto a narrow track which leads into Windrush village.

Where to eat and drink

The Fox Inn at Great Barrington is charmingly located by the River Windrush. In the summer you can eat in the garden, which is very helpful if you are with children.

SHERBORNE AND THE SHERBORNE ESTATE

DISTANCE/TIME	2.5 miles (4km) / 1hr 15min
ASCENT/GRADIENT	238ft (72m) / ▲
PATHS	Fields, tracks and pavement
LANDSCAPE	Village and landscaped estate
SUGGESTED MAP	OS Explorer OL45 The Cotswolds
START/FINISH	Grid reference: SP175144
DOG FRIENDLINESS	No stiles and some clear stretches without livestock
PARKING	On-street parking in Sherborne
PUBLIC TOILETS	None on route

Sherborne was always an estate village, originally belonging to Winchcombe Abbey. Huge flocks of sheep were gathered here for shearing, with much of the wool exported to Flanders and Italy. In the 14th century, the tenants of the Abbot of Winchcombe had to work for a fortnight washing and shearing the abbey's sheep. A century later Sherborne, because of the plentiful water supply provided by the river (essential for washing the wool) and because it was the largest of the abbey's manorial possessions, had become the principal shearing station for all the abbey's flocks. In 1485, drovers brought in 2,900 sheep from the surrounding villages. Quarters were provided for all the shearers while the Abbot of Winchcombe rode up to supervise and inspect the weighing of the fleeces in a room set aside for the purpose. He bought as much of the tenants' wool as he required and then sold it on. The abbot, of course, wanted to ensure that he made as much money as possible; and indeed in 1341 local tenants were fined by their abbot for attempting to set up a fulling mill in competition with his own.

After the Dissolution, the estate was purchased by the Dutton family, who built themselves a fine house with the help of the eminent local quarryman, Valentine Strong. In the 19th century the house, said to be haunted by the hunchback and gambler known as 'Crump' Dutton, was rebuilt using estate stone, but eventually it became a boarding school and is now luxury flats. Today, the estate, and much of the village, belongs to the National Trust.

The village of Sherborne has some very pretty cottages – one of which, in the eastern part, has somehow acquired a Norman arch that originally graced a 12th-century chapel that apparently stood in the grounds of one of the nearby farms. From the road near the church are sweeping rustic views across Sherborne Brook and its water meadows, where once the medieval flocks of sheep would have grazed.

South of Sherborne, near the village of Aldsworth, is Lodge Park, originally part of the Sherborne Estate. This was created in 1634 by 'Crump' Dutton and is a unique survival of a deer course, park and grandstand, which has been painstakingly reconstructed using archaeological evidence. Sherborne was also the birthplace of an eminent scientist. James Bradley, born here in 1693, was appointed the third Astronomer Royal in 1742, and is remembered as the first person to calculate the speed of light, in 1729. He is also responsible for establishing the meridian line at Greenwich.

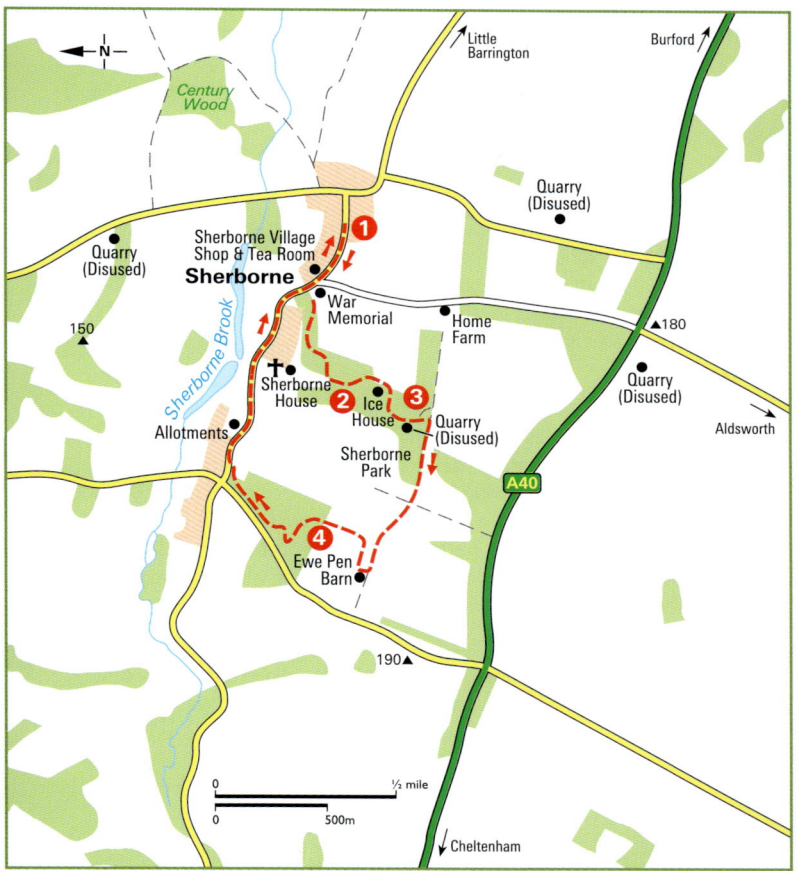

1. From the main part of the village, east of the church, walk back towards Sherborne House. Continue to a road on the left beside the war memorial. Enter the Sherborne Estate through a doorway beside the telephone box and follow the main path. The house will appear to the right. The path bends left and after 150yds (137m) and turns right at a bench into woodland. After a further 100yds (91m), bear left onto another gently ascending path.

2. Stay left of a tree surrounded by a metal seat on a mound and continue for a few paces to a waymarked T-junction. Turn right and go through a wrought-iron gate to pass the old Ice House. Keep right at the waymark and head for another gate.

3. Follow the main path through the trees. Join another path and, at a gate, go through onto a farm track and turn right. Follow this, passing a sports field on the left, to a gate at Ewe Pen Barn. Go through this and turn right straight

away to pass through another gateway. Just beyond it and immediately past a right-hand gate, turn right into a field to follow the right-hand margin. Follow this as it bears left at the corner and descend to the bottom corner where the path will take you into conifer woodland. Follow this wide path down past a bench until you come to a fork by a second bench.

4. Stay left and keep to the path as it skirts the woods, bearing right to flatten out at the bottom. Stay on it all the way to an opening in a wall. Emerge at a road and turn right. Follow the pavement through the village, passing the church on the right, and return to your starting point.

Where to eat and drink
Sherborne Village Shop & Tea Room on the main street is open daily for snacks and light refreshments. The nearest pub is The Fox Inn, just outside Great Barrington, about 2.5 miles (4km) away to the east in the Windrush Valley. It has a lovely riverside location, a good range of locally brewed real ales and an extensive menu.

What to see
Sherborne Park is a typical example of 18th-century estate design, where the intention has been to bring order to unruly nature without undermining its exuberance. The estate is now owned and managed by the National Trust. In the church, look out for the sculpture to the Dutton family by Flemish-born John Michael Rysbrack (1694–1770), a respected sculptor and best known for his monument to Sir Isaac Newton in Westminster Abbey. There is also a memorial in the village church to the locally born Astronomer Royal, James Bradley.

While you're there
The walk can easily and briefly be extended by walking a little way east of Sherborne to a point east of Century Wood, where the old water meadows have been restored to become a haven for wildlife once again.

LECHLADE AND THE THAMES

DISTANCE/TIME	5.75 miles (9.2km) / 2hrs 30min
ASCENT/GRADIENT	Negligible
PATHS	Fields, tracks and road; many stiles
LANDSCAPE	Water-meadows, river and village
SUGGESTED MAP	OS Explorer 170 Abingdon
START/FINISH	Grid reference: SU214995
DOG FRIENDLINESS	On lead at locks; much birdlife beside rivers
PARKING	Memorial Hall and sports complex off A361 north
PUBLIC TOILETS	On Burford Street in Lechlade

At different stages of this walk the high, slender spire of Lechlade's majestic parish church is seen on the horizon, even as the route strays into Wiltshire and Oxfordshire. The church was the inspiration for Percy Shelley's *Summer Evening Meditation*, which includes these lines:

Clothing in hues of heaven thy dim and distant spire
Around whose lessening and invisible height
Gather among the stars the clouds of night

The church has a panelled chancel roof decorated with 40 exquisitely carved bosses and stone corbels. The exterior is parapeted with two rich tiers of quatrefoils. Pinnacled buttresses bear the weight. On the last leg of the walk there's another interesting church, at Buscot. It contains a striking east window by the pre-Raphaelite artist Edward Burne-Jones, a pulpit partly made from a Flemish triptych, and some delightful paintings.

Lechlade was the upper limit for navigation on the Thames, and is the only town within the county of Gloucestershire to be found on the river. In 1789, when the Thames and Severn Canal was completed, it became possible to move cargoes from ship to barge for the 29-mile (46.5km) journey across Gloucestershire. Cotswold stone for the dome of Wren's St Paul's Cathedral was loaded into barges at Lechlade and at one time Gloucestershire cheeses also began their journey to London from here.

With both the River Coln and the River Leach flowing into the River Thames hereabouts, it is no surprise that there are a number of bridges on this walk. Beneath the bridges, crowds of river pleasure craft have replaced the trading vessels of the past while, above, the bridges continue their function, bearing modern-day road traffic. Near the start, the walk crosses Ha'penny Bridge, a late 18th-century toll bridge. The toll house still stands.

St John's Bridge, the last bridge before Ha'penny Bridge on the walk back to Lechlade, dates from the 14th century and takes its name from a former priory nearby. This, like Ha'penny Bridge, was also a toll crossing. Nearby St John's Lock includes the statue of 'Father Thames'. It was built for the Great Exhibition of 1851, and moved here from its original site at Thames Head near Cirencester.

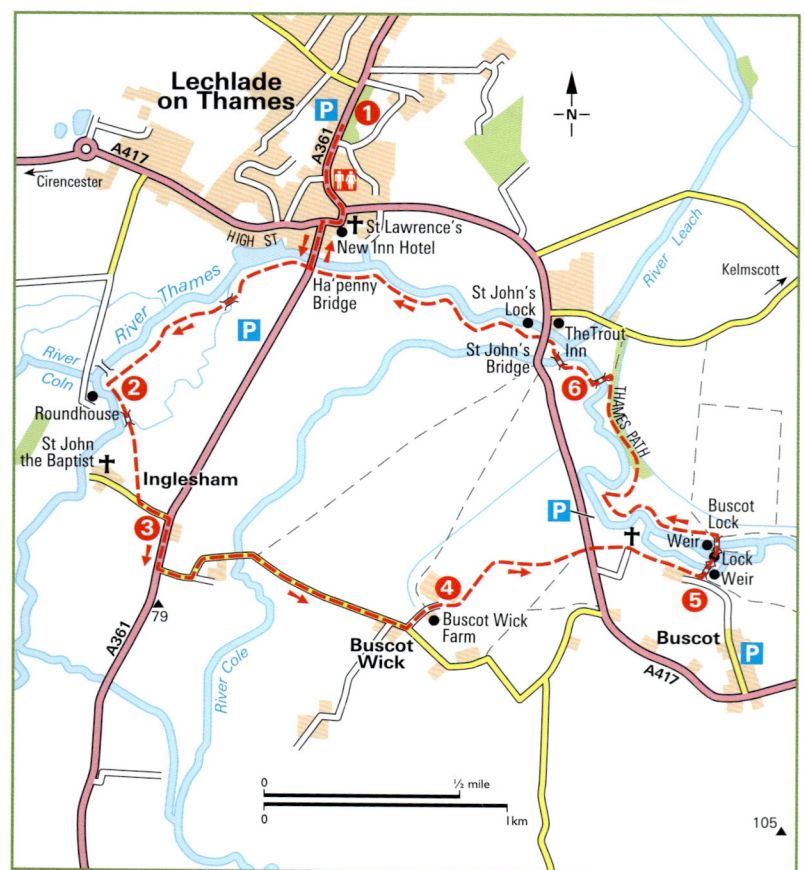

1. From the car park in Lechlade go south to the Market Place, then walk west along the High Street, and then left along Thames Street. Cross Ha'penny Bridge and on the far side drop down some steps on the right to the riverbank. Walk ahead, with the river to your right, for just over 0.5 miles (800m). After passing a bridge across the Thames, draw level with an old roundhouse among the trees on the far bank.

2. Here the River Coln joins the Thames, alongside the now silted-up Thames and Severn Canal. Continue along the riverbank, cross a footbridge over a stream, and head across the field to find a kissing gate to the left of Inglesham House. The walk continues by turning left along the lane, but to visit Inglesham Church turn right. This charming medieval building, much admired by William Morris, contains an exceptionally beautiful 13th-century stone carving of a Madonna and Child.

3. At the end of the lane turn right along the main road, using the verge. After 200yds (183m) turn left towards Buscot. In 0.75 miles (1.2km) turn left along the drive of Buscot Wick Farm. Just before the farmyard and cottages turn right along a drive and then go across some grass to a gate.

4. Look for near and distant black gates across extensive pasture and use them to guide you. Keep to the right of a copse, passing through three gates to reach the road. Go through a gate on the far side, cross two fields to a stile and turn left into the churchyard. Leave by the lychgate and follow the riverbank to emerge at Buscot Weir.

5. Follow the concrete track here if you want to visit the estate village of Buscot, which now belongs to the National Trust. Otherwise turn left, then right to pass Lock Cottage and make your way across a succession of bridges at Buscot Lock, following a sign for 'Lechlade 2 miles (3.2km)'. Continue to a galvanized gate by a large sign indicating the lock ahead. Follow the river's meanderings, with the spire of St Lawrence's Church seen in the distance, and remain on the tow path to a wooden bridge just beyond a three-way post.

6. Cross this and turn right to continue along the riverbank, and soon pass over the River Cole just before St John's Bridge. Walk beneath the bridge, pass St John's Lock, then enter a wide meadow to return to Ha'penny Bridge and Lechlade. Turn right at the High Street and walk back through Lechlade to return to the Memorial Hall car park.

Where to eat and drink
Lechlade has several venerable pubs to tempt the walker. Try the New Inn Hotel on the Market Place, a traditional coaching inn serving bar food and real ale. By the Thames, on the Faringdon road, is the Trout Inn, which traces its origins to the 13th century.

What to see
At Buscot Lock, look for plaques that compare the January 2003 flood level with those of 1947 and 1894. In Lechlade spend time exploring the streets that run off from the market square. You will see some handsome buildings dating from the 17th to the 19th centuries.

While you're there
Just over 2 miles (3.2km) to the east of Lechlade is Kelmscott. The poet and craftsman William Morris, the leading light of the Arts and Crafts Movement, lived in the Elizabethan manor house here from 1871 until his death in 1896. Morris is buried in the churchyard, and there is a charming carving of him on the village's Memorial Cottages.

RIVERSIDE IN THE EASTLEACHES

DISTANCE/TIME	4 miles (6.4km) / 2hrs
ASCENT/GRADIENT	300ft (91m) / ▲
PATHS	Tracks and lanes, valley paths and woodland
LANDSCAPE	Villages, open wold, narrow valley and streams
SUGGESTED MAP	OS Explorer OL45 The Cotswolds
START/FINISH	Grid reference: SP200052
DOG FRIENDLINESS	Sheep country – dogs on lead at all times
PARKING	On-street parking in Eastleach Turville
PUBLIC TOILETS	None on route

Eastleach Turville and Eastleach Martin, sitting cheek by jowl in a secluded valley, carry an air of quiet perfection. And yet these two Cotswold villages are quite distinctive, and each has a parish church (though one is now redundant). St Andrews in Eastleach Turville faces St Michael and St Martin's across the narrow River Leach. Their origins lie in the development of the parish system from the earliest days of the Anglo-Saxon Church.

The English parish has its origins in the shifting rivalries of Saxon England, for the one thing that united the various Saxon kingdoms was the Church. The first 'parishes' were really the Anglo-Saxon kingdoms. Christianity, the new power in the land, not only saved souls but also secured alliances.

The Pope's aim was to invest more bishops to act as pastors who would try to convert people, but at the same time their appointments were useful politically, helping to smooth the way as larger kingdoms absorbed their smaller neighbours. The number of appointments would also depend on local factors. Wessex, for example, was divided into shires and so a bishop was appointed for each one. Later the Normans appointed archdeacons, whose job was to ensure that church buildings were maintained for worship.

Over the centuries the assorted conventions and appointments that had accumulated through usage coalesced into a hierarchical English Church. For a long time, however, control was not tight. Missionaries, for example, would occasionally land from Ireland and found their own churches, quite independently of anyone else. Rulers and local landholders were certainly influential in the development of the parish system, but many parishes also derived from the gradual disintegration of the local 'minster', a central church on consecrated ground that controlled a group of client chapels. As population and congregations grew, the chapels themselves became new parish churches, with rights equal to those of the minster. This included the right to bury the dead in their own graveyard, and the administration of births and marriages.

With the passage of time and the establishment of a single English kingdom, the parish diminished to something akin to its modern size. By the 10th century, the parish had become the accepted framework for enforcing the payment of tithes, the medieval equivalent of an income tax. By the 12th century, much of the modern diocesan map of England was established. So, in the Eastleaches all these developments mean you find two parish churches virtually side by side. With politics, power and bureaucracy all playing a part, it's likely that the pastoral needs of the community were quite low on the list.

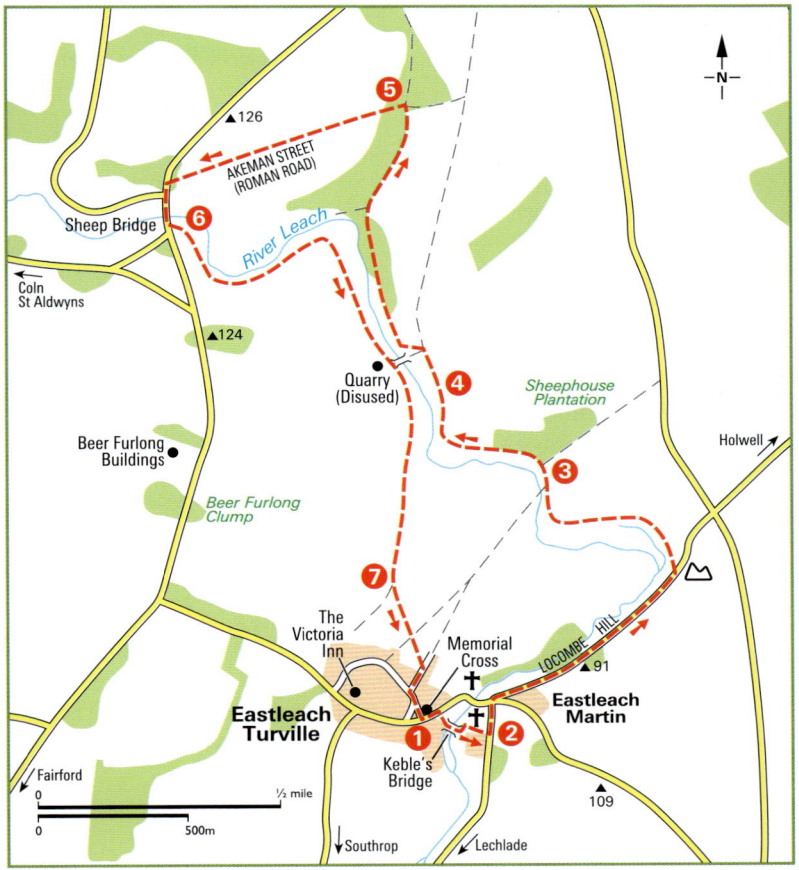

1. From the memorial cross in Eastleach Turville, walk along the road with the river on your right. After a few paces, locate a path on your right to cross the clapper bridge and follow the path into the churchyard of Eastleach Martin. Pass to the right of the church and emerge at a road.

2. Turn left and then turn right at a junction, finally taking the lower road in the direction of Holwell. Walk on for perhaps 600yds (549m) to where the road begins to rise steeply. Turn left here, pass through a gate into a field, and follow an obvious grassy track at the base of a slope for 0.5 miles (800m).

3. This will bring you to a gate at the corner of Sheephouse Plantation. Go through the gate and continue ahead, with the woods to your right. Continue to a gate at a field – do not go through this, but veer left with the field and a dry-stone wall to your right. Soon you will reach a small area of scrubby trees; turn right here over a stile into a field and turn left.

4. Continue, passing through gates, until you come to a gated bridge on your left. Do not cross this, but continue forward towards a small gate at the edge of woodland. Go through and follow a woodland path until you reach a crossroads of tracks.

5. Turn left and follow the track up out of the woods and across a field until you come to a road at the bottom of the slope. Turn left here, cross Sheep Bridge opposite the cattle grid on your right and, just before a turning to the right, go left into a field.

6. Bear right along the valley bottom, then left and right again. This will bring you to a gate. Go through it onto a track, and soon pass the gated bridge again. Go through a gate and follow the wall on your right as it curves up to another gate, then stay on the same line through gates until you reach the gate into the last field bordering Eastleach Turville.

7. Walk diagonally across this field, heading for a gate just to the right of a prominent horse chestnut tree. Join the lane here, and keep left at the fork to return to the starting point at the memorial cross.

Where to eat and drink
Eastleach Turville has a lovely little pub, The Victoria Inn, in the western part of the village (closed Mondays and Tuesdays). Nearby Southrop has The Swan, a creeper-clad pub with real fires in winter and a wide choice of food. In Coln St Aldwyns, to the west, you'll find The New Inn, everybody's idea of a classic Cotswold pub.

What to see
The little clapper bridge linking the two parishes is known locally as Keble's Bridge, after a family who were eminent in the area. John Keble, for whom Keble College in Oxford is named, was nominal curate for the two parishes in the 19th century. In the middle part of the walk the straight track to a road is part of Akeman Street, the Roman road that linked Cirencester with St Albans.

While you're there
There are two places nearby worth visiting while you are in the area. To the south is Lechlade, Gloucestershire's only settlement on the River Thames. There is a handsome market square, an idyllic riverside and some fascinating old streets to wander through. To the west is Fairford, a handsome village noted for its fine church, which contains one of the only sets of medieval stained glass in the country.

FROM BOURTON-ON-THE-HILL TO SEZINCOTE

DISTANCE/TIME	3 miles (4.8km) / 1hr 30min
ASCENT/GRADIENT	85ft (26m) / ▲
PATHS	Tracks, fields and lanes; many stiles
LANDSCAPE	Hedges, field and spinney on lower part of escarpment
SUGGESTED MAP	OS Explorer OL45 The Cotswolds
START/FINISH	Grid reference: SP175324
DOG FRIENDLINESS	Under close control – likely to be a lot of livestock
PARKING	Street below Bourton-on-the-Hill Church, parallel with main road
PUBLIC TOILETS	None on route

Bourton-on-the-Hill's church owes its impressive features to the fact that the village was formerly owned by Westminster Abbey. The abbey's income was handsomely supplemented by sales of wool from its vast flocks on the surrounding hills. There is a fine 15th-century clerestory, lighting an interior notable for its substantial nave columns, and a rare bell-metal Winchester Bushel and Peck (8 gallons/35.2 litres and 2 gallons/8.8 litres respectively). These particular standard English measures date from 1816, but their origins go back to the 10th century when King Edgar (reigned AD 959–75) decreed that standard weights be kept at Winchester and London. They were used to settle disputes, especially when they involved tithes. Winchester measures finally became redundant in 1824 when the Imperial system was introduced, though many Winchester equivalents remain in the US.

For anyone with a fixed idea of the English country house, Sezincote will come as a surprise. It is, as the poet John Betjeman said, 'a good joke, but a good house, too.' Built on the plan of a typical large country house of the era, in every other respect it is thoroughly unconventional. A large copper onion dome crowns the house, while at each corner of the roof are finials in the form of miniature minarets. The walls are of Cotswold stone, but the Regency windows and decoration owe a lot to Eastern influence.

Sezincote is a reflection of the fashions of the early 19th century. Just as engravings brought back from Athens had been the inspiration for 18th-century Classicism, so the colourful aqua-tints brought to England from India by returning artists such as William and Thomas Daniell, were a profound influence on architects and designers. Sezincote was one of the first results of this fashion. Sir Charles Cockerell was a 'nabob', the Hindi-derived word for a European who had made their wealth in the East. On his retirement from the East India Company he had the house built by his brother, Samuel Pepys Cockerell, an architect. The eminent landscape gardener

Humphry Repton helped Cockerell to choose the most picturesque elements of Hindu architecture from the Daniells' drawings.

Some modern materials, like cast iron, were thought to complement the intricacies of traditional Mogul design. The garden buildings took on elements from Hindu temples, with a lotus-shaped temple pool, Hindu columns supporting a bridge and the widespread presence of snakes, sacred bulls and lotus buds.

The Prince of Wales was an early visitor. The experience obviously made some impression as the intensely Mogul-influenced Brighton Pavilion arose not long after. Betjeman was a regular guest at Sezincote during his undergraduate days. 'Stately and strange it stood, the nabob's house, Indian without and coolest Greek within, looking from Gloucestershire to Oxfordshire.'

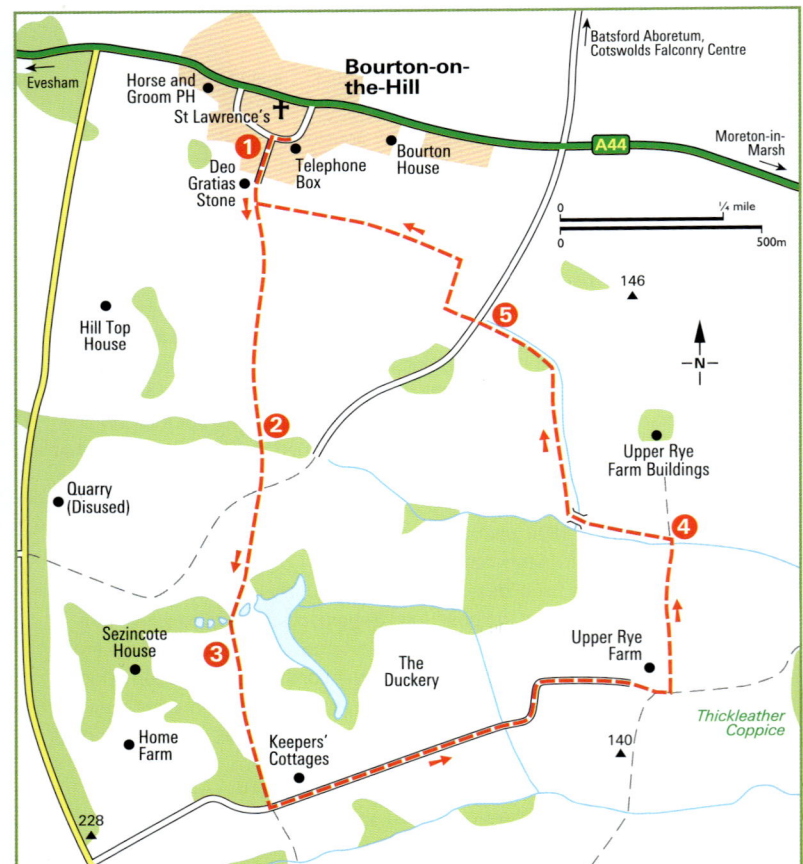

1. Walk up the road from the telephone box, with the church to your right. Turn left down a track between walls, signed for the Heart of England Way. Go through a gate into a field and then continue ahead to pass through two more field gates.

2. Continue to two stiles, followed by two kissing gates amid a tree belt. This is the Sezincote Estate – go straight ahead, following markers and crossing a drive. Dip down, following the path through a gate and between fencing and woodland to the next gates, with ponds on either side. Go ahead into a field, from where Sezincote House is visible to the right.

3. Keeping the fence on your right, go right to the end, aiming for the top, right-hand corner. Pass through a kissing gate to a narrow road and turn left. Walk down this road, passing the keepers' cottages to your left. The road bottoms out, curves left then right and brings you to Upper Rye Farm. Avoid a left turning to the farm, but pass well to the right of the farmhouse. Immediately before a barn, turn left along a track and a road.

4. After a second cattle grid, go left over a stile. Follow the left edge of the field across three stiles to a footbridge between step-through stiles. Go over it and turn right. Now follow the right-hand margin of the field across two stiles, to a stile in the far corner. Cross this to follow a path through woodland until you come to step-through stiles on each side of a footbridge and a field and continue on the same line to another stile.

5. Cross a track to another stile into Sezincote's Millennium Oak Plantation and walk on. After a few paces, with Bourton-on-the-Hill plainly visible before you, bear right to a stile and follow the path to the next corner. Turn left and cross four stiles. After the fourth one, walk on for 60 paces and turn right through a gate to return to the start.

Where to eat and drink

At the top of Bourton-on-the-hill is a handsome old pub called The Horse and Groom that serves good lunches. In nearby Moreton-in-Marsh there are several pubs and restaurants to choose from.

What to see

As you start the walk, about 60yds (55m) after the first gate, look for an inscription in the stone wall on the right. It reads 'Deo Gratias AD 1919' and is thought to be in gratitude for the end of World War I. After Sezincote, as you walk down the road towards the farm, look for the buildings of the Fire Service College, the main training centre for firefighters in the country, on the far side of Moreton-in-Marsh.

While you're there

Both Sezincote House and Bourton House Garden are open to the public but have a limited season, so check their opening hours in advance. Batsford Arboretum and Garden Centre and The Cotswold Falconry Centre are only a mile (1.6km) away, just off the road to Moreton-in-Marsh.

LAKES AND RIVERS AT BOURTON-ON-THE-WATER

DISTANCE/TIME	5 miles (8km) / 2hrs 30min
ASCENT/GRADIENT	230ft (70m) / ▲
PATHS	Track and field, can be muddy and wet in places, several stiles
LANDSCAPE	Sweeping valley views, lakes, streams, hills and villages
SUGGESTED MAP	OS Explorer OL45 The Cotswolds
START/FINISH	Grid reference: SP169208
DOG FRIENDLINESS	Some stiles may be awkward for dogs; occasional livestock
PARKING	Pay-and-display car park on Station Road signposted Bourton Vale Car & Coach Park
PUBLIC TOILETS	At car park

Despite Bourton-on-the-Water's popularity, the throng is easily left behind by walking briefly eastwards to a chain of redundant gravel pits. In the 1970s these were landscaped and filled with water and fish. As is the way of these things, for some time the resulting lakes looked every inch the artificial creations they were, but now they have bedded into their surroundings and seem to be an integral part of the landscape.

The fish and water have acted as magnets for a range of wetland birds, whose populations rise and fall with the seasons. During the spring and summer you should look out for the little grebe and the splendidly adorned great crested grebe, as well as the more familiar moorhens and coots, and mallard and tufted ducks. Wagtails will strut about the water's edge, swans and geese prowl across the water, and kingfishers, if you are lucky, streak from bush to reed. Come the autumn, the number of birds will have increased significantly. Above all there will be vast numbers of ducks – pintail, shoveler, widgeon and pochard among them – as well as occasional visitors like cormorants. Either around the lakes or by the rivers you may also spy dippers and, in the hedgerows, members of the finch family.

Should you get drawn into the village – as you surely will – keep listening for birdsong and you will hear some improbable 'visitors'. There's a large bird sanctuary in Bourton-on-the-Water that houses, among many other birds, one of the largest collections of penguins in the world. The reason for the presence of so many penguins in the Cotswolds is that the sanctuary's founder was also the owner of two small islands in the Falklands.

Penguins aside, Bourton-on-the-Water has a long history. The edge of the village is bounded by the Roman Fosse Way and many of its buildings are a pleasing mix of medieval, Georgian and Victorian. Although the village can become very crowded during the summer months, with the river banks like green beaches, strewn with people picnicking and paddling, it can still be charming. Arrive early enough in the morning, or hang around in the evening until the daytrippers have gone and you will find the series of bridges spanning the Windrush (one from 1756) and the narrow streets beyond them enchanting. They retain the warm honeyed light that attracts people to the Cotswolds. You'll see far fewer visitors in little Clapton-on-the-Hill, which overlooks Bourton. Make the detour just before Point 5 to see its tiny church.

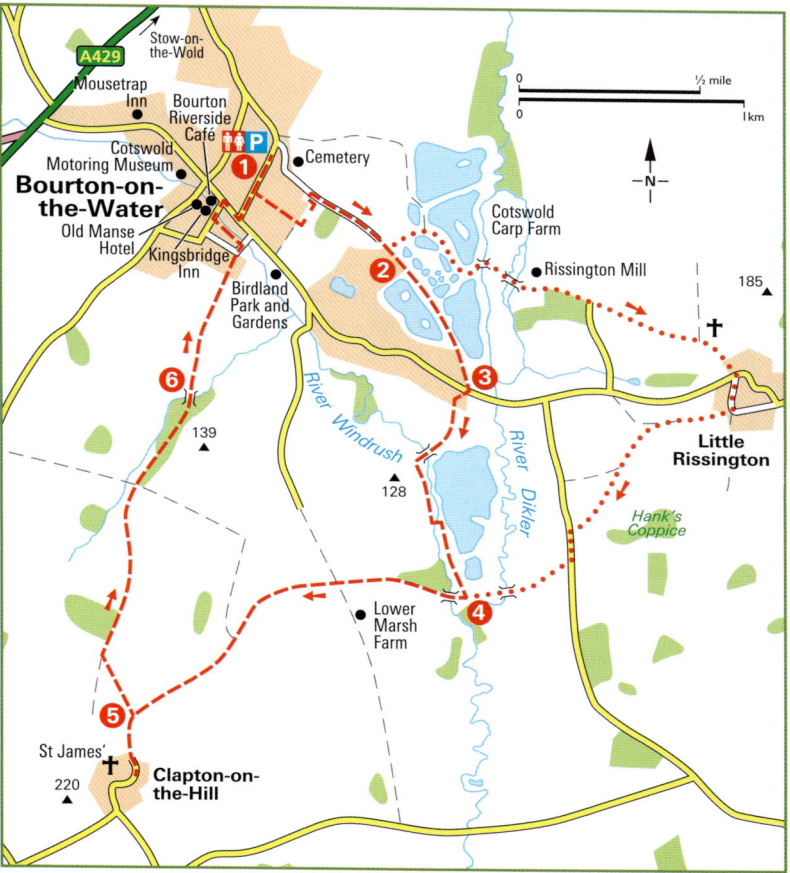

1. Turn right out of the main pay-and-display car park in Bourton-on-the-Water and then turn left on a public footpath and continue to a junction, turn left again and continue to a junction opposite the village cemetery. Bear right to follow a lane until it bends left by two gates on the right. Take the right-hand gate to join a path by the entrance to Cotswold Carp Farm.

2. Follow the path between lakes to where it curves right. Leave the track to go left and over a bridge and through a gate into a field. Go across the field, curving right, to come to a kissing gate at a road.

3. Cross the road, turn right and immediately left onto a track. After 100yds (91m), go left through a kissing gate into a field and continue parallel to the track. Through another kissing gate, return to the track with a lake to your left.

Approaching a gate, cross a bridge to turn left through a kissing gate onto a path alongside the River Windrush. Continue until the path comes to a gate at a field. Turn left, go through another kissing gate and go left over a bridge before turning right beside another lake.

4. Where this second, smaller lake ends, bear right to a gate, followed by a bridge and another bridge and a stile at a field. Keep to the right side of fields until you come to a track after a footbridge and stile. Continue straight ahead on this track. At a house, continue straight on, leaving the track, and continue to a gate. In the next field, after 25yds (23m), turn left through a gate and then sharp right. Continue to a gate and then go slightly left across a field to another gate. Continue on the same line across the next field to a kissing gate, footbridge and gate. Cross this and follow the right margin of a field, to climb slowly to a junction of tracks. Turn left to visit Clapton-on-the-Hill, or turn right to continue.

5. Follow a track to a field. Go forward then slightly right (round the field edge if ploughed) to a gateway and descend to pass to the right of woodland. Past this, continue alongside a hedge on your left to two gates followed by a field. Go straight on to a hedge gap; after a stile, a stream appears to the left. Keep on this side of the stream and pass through a copse, crossing two stiles. The path then turns left over a footbridge.

6. Cross the bridge and then go slightly right across a field to a bridge. Continue across farmland to a stile. Walk along a grassy track between conifers. Go through one more gate and follow a path between fences to a road in Bourton. Walk ahead to the river and turn left, then right past Bourton Riverside Café, then right again, and left to return to the start.

Extending the walk You can extend this walk to include the pretty village of Little Rissington. As you leave Bourton on the lane after the cemetery, at Point 2, follow a path to the left, past lakes and meadows to Rissington Mill. Field paths take you into the village and you can meet up with the main route again across the bridge near Point 4.

Where to eat and drink
Bourton-on-the-Water provides the best opportunity for refreshment, with a choice of pubs, cafés and restaurants catering to most tastes. Try The Kingsbridge Inn by the River Windrush, or The Mousetrap Inn on Lansdowne for reliable pub food. The Old Manse Hotel, near the river, serves a good lunch and dinner.

What to see
Bourton-on-the-Water has many attractions. The pick of these are probably Birdland Park and Gardens with its penguins, and the Cotswold Motoring Museum and Toy Collection, which has lots of pre-1950s cars, as well as a few novelty items.

BOURTON-ON-THE-WATER

DISTANCE/TIME	4 miles (6.4km) / 2hrs
ASCENT/GRADIENT	200ft (61m) / ▲
PATHS	Tracks, paths, some road walking
LANDSCAPE	Pleasant walking by the rivers Windrush and Eye, with good Cotswold views from higher ground
SUGGESTED MAP	OS Explorer OL45 The Cotswolds
START/FINISH	Grid reference: SP169208
DOG FRIENDLINESS	Lead required in and close to Bourton and Lower Slaughter
PARKING	Pay-and-display car park on Station Road
PUBLIC TOILETS	At car park

The spectacle of a tall redbrick chimney rising above a delightful river and a waterwheel adjacent to picturesque houses and cottages gladdens the eye at the northernmost point of this walk, but it might also come as something of a surprise. The idea of using flowing water to turn machinery has, of course, been around for centuries, but perhaps stumbling on it in a picture-postcard village in the Cotswolds is unexpected.

The Romans introduced the process when they invaded Britain in AD 43. However, Britain's mills went into decline when the Roman Army eventually withdrew from this country in the 4th century. Mills were subsequently re-introduced 300 years later from Europe, during the Anglo-Saxon period, and by 1086 there were more than 6,000 mills recorded in the Domesday Book. In reality the number was probably far greater, as many mills were not documented. However, a mill on the Rive Eye at Lower Slaughter was recorded in the survey.

In its later years the mill was run by the Wilkins family, whose cousins also ran a mill at nearby Bourton-on-the-Water (now the Cotswold Motoring Museum and Toy Collection). From World War I until 1958 the flour mill at Lower Slaughter was in the hands of Joseph Morris Wilkins – known to all his friends as Morris. He was the last of the four generations to mill here, and died in 1958.

Morris had two daughters, and so there was no prospect of the Wilkins family continuing to run the business. The bakery part of the mill changed hands that year, passing into the ownership of Alfred and Edith Collett. They converted part of the mill house into a village post office and shop. Alfred and Edith's two sons, Toby and Stephen, together with their daughter Linda, also helped to turn the mill at Lower Slaughter into a successful bakery. So well did it do that they moved to larger premises in neighbouring Upper Slaughter.

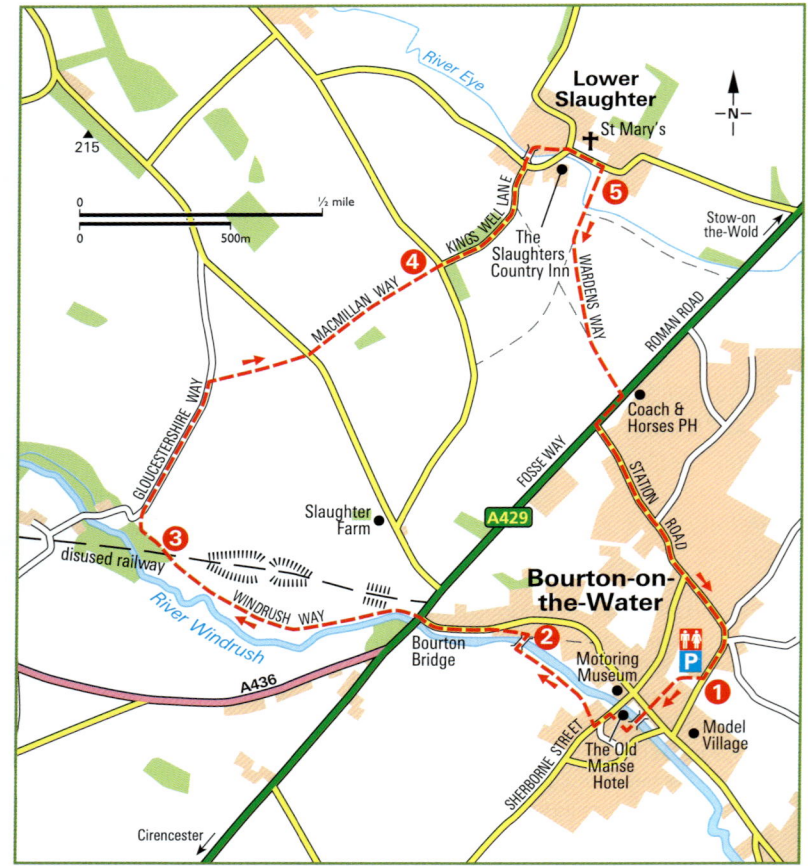

1. Facing the road, leave the car park by turning right and following the broad path signposted to the village. Cut between stone walls to emerge in the centre of Bourton-on-the-Water. Cross the stone bridge over the River Windrush, turn right to The Old Manse Hotel, then immediately left, passing the Duke of Wellington pub. Shortly the road divides; take the path on the right (the Windrush Way) and follow the twisting path to a meadow. Take the riverside path, crossing the river at one point to reach the road.

2. Turn left and walk to the junction with the A429. Cross over the A429 and continue on the Windrush Way, keeping to the right of the river. Pass through meadows to a gate, and in the next field keep to its left boundary, all the way to a gate beside trees in the corner. Follow the path along a brief stretch of the former Cheltenham–Chipping Norton railway, and when it forks, keep right on the bridleway.

3. Continue beside farmland and through trees, and at the next path junction turn right to follow the Gloucestershire Way. Head uphill through trees, go through a gate and continue between fields. Some 50yds (46m) beyond the next gate, look for a gap in the hedge on the right and follow the path across farmland to the road. Cross over and follow the Macmillan Way between fields to a road junction.

4. Go straight over and down the lane between trees, following it into Lower Slaughter. At the junction cross the stone bridge over the River Eye, and then turn right, alongside the river. At the next road bridge, with The Slaughters Country Inn on your right and the church to the left, continue beside the river. After about 75yds (69m) take the path on the right, Wardens Way, towards Bourton-on-the-Water.

5. Follow the shaded riverside path, pass a path on the left and keep ahead. Continue towards the Fosse Way when the path runs alongside a stony track. On reaching the road, almost opposite the Coach and Horses pub, turn right to the traffic lights. Cross over and take the road for Bourton-on-the-Water. Disregard turnings left and right, pass an Oxfordshire Way sign and follow the road as it bends right. The car park where the walk began is on the right.

Where to eat and drink

Bourton-on-the-Water has plenty of pubs, cafés and tea rooms. The Slaughters Country Inn at Lower Slaughter serves morning coffee, lunches, tea and dinner and has an outdoor seating area alongside the River Eye.

What to see

Have a look at St Mary's Church in Lower Slaughter, which dates back to 1867. It is designed in the Early English style and has an impressive spire. Many of the memorials inside are to members of the Whitmore family, who lived in the Manor House for 300 years. There is also a tablet in memory of Sir Anthony Milward, once Chairman of British European Airways.

While you're there

Visit Bourton-on-the-Water's famous model village. It took craftsmen five years to build it out of Cotswold stone, and reflects the village as it was when built in the 1930s. It is now protected by a Grade II listing.

FAIRFORD AND THE RIVER COLN

DISTANCE/TIME	3.75 miles (6km) / 1hr 30min
ASCENT/GRADIENT	15ft (4.5m) / Negligible
PATHS	Fields, tracks, riverside, can be muddy after rain; several stiles
LANDSCAPE	Water-meadows, river and village
SUGGESTED MAP	OS Explorer 169 Cirencester & Swindon
START/FINISH	Grid reference: SP152011
DOG FRIENDLINESS	Good, but lots of swans and ducks along riverside
PARKING	On High Street or car park near church
PUBLIC TOILETS	On the High Street

Fairford, like so many other small towns in the Cotswolds, owes its original importance to the medieval wool trade, and to one family in particular – the Tames. They were wool merchants, and it was their money that embellished St Mary's Church, one of the great Cotswold wool churches. The 16th-century writer and antiquary John Leland wrote, 'John Tame began the fair new chirche of Fairforde, and Edmund Tame finished it.' John Tame bought the manor, and rebuilt the church on the foundations of its predecessor.

The church's best feature is the near-complete set of medieval stained-glass windows. They were made in the late 15th century, probably by the Flemish craftsman Barnard Flower (who also worked on Westminster Abbey and at King's College, Cambridge.) The idea behind the windows in St Mary's is to explain the Christian faith as if the onlooker were turning the pages of a picture book. They are arranged symmetrically. On one wall are windows depicting 12 prophets, opposite which are depicted the 12 Apostles. The journey around the church, bathed in the magical light thrown down by the windows, is memorable.

There are other things to admire here: John Tame's tomb, the amusing misericord seats in the chancel, and the gravestone of Tiddles the cat in the churchyard.

The walk follows the Coln – one of Gloucestershire's prettiest rivers – at different stages, and it provides the perfect setting for peaceful riverside strolling. Along this stretch you might spot swans, kingfishers, brown trout and possibly elusive water voles. While Fairford lies on the banks of the River Coln, where it meanders peacefully across a flat landscape of meadows and woodland, the town has an association with noise. Concorde was tested at the nearby airbase, and over recent decades it has served as a base for various military campaigns around the world. Every summer the Royal International Air Tatoo is held here.

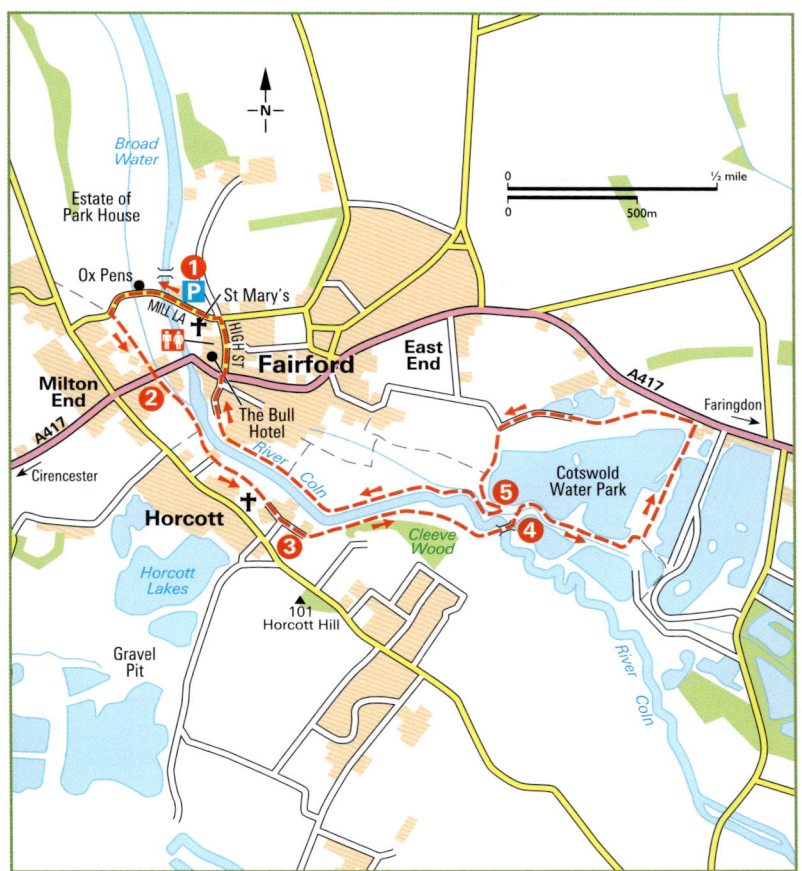

1. From the car park turn right along Mill Lane, to the old mill and bridge. Beyond the bridge reach a small garden flanked on two sides by an ancient shelter consisting of a stone slate roof supported by weathered wooden pillars – these are restored ox-pens. Continue along the road, and after 150yds (137m) turn left over a stile into a meadow. Go straight across to the other side to reach the buildings of Fairford, pass through a gate and cross a stile to a road.

2. Cross the road and join Waterloo Lane, staying on this as it becomes a footpath. Avoid a path and bridge on the left and keep ahead. Where the football pitches come to an end, bear left along a footpath behind some houses. Stay on the path, cross a drive to pass beside a garden dotted with trees and a secluded bungalow, and soon reach a junction.

3. Turn left to enter a farmyard, and then turn right, aiming for a point to the left of a cottage. Pass the cottage and cross a double stile into a field. Bear left to the right of the river, to meet a stile at the edge of woodland. Cross onto a wide grassy track and continue close to the woodland, the river easing away to your left. Where the woods come to an end, pass beneath electricity cables and keep ahead to a gate and bridge in the far corner of the field, among bushes and trees. Enter the woodland, and beyond the trees follow the footpath across a marshy area to a bridge over the river.

4. Beyond the bridge is a conveniently placed seat. Follow the riverbank to the left for 40yds (37m), and cross a footbridge on the right. Now the route enters an area of former gravel pits, part of the Cotswold Water Park. Walk anti-clockwise around the first lake, approaching but avoiding a road just across a meadow. On reaching a path junction at its northwest corner, turn left. At the next junction keep left, avoiding a path running into a field. Follow the path to a bridge on the right, cross it and turn right.

5. Keep to the riverbank and make for the outskirts of Fairford. Houses can be seen near by. Follow the route into Gas Lane and then left into Back Lane. In the town centre, cross over the A417, passing The Bull Hotel on the left. St Mary's Church and the car park where the walk began lie a short distance beyond.

Where to eat and drink

There is a choice of several pubs and cafés in Fairford. The Bull Hotel, on the High Street, is a pleasant old pub and convenient for this walk. The writers C S Lewis and J R R Tolkien spent a walking weekend at Fairford in 1945, exploring the town and its surroundings and staying at The Bull.

What to see

As you pass the mill at the start of the walk look to the right and you will see what is left of the estate of Park House, which was demolished in 1955. The most obvious reminder is the elegant bridge beyond the mill pool. Keble House, on London Road, was the birthplace of poet and theologian, John Keble (1792–1866).

While you're there

It's difficult to avoid the presence of the military, with the United States Air Force's (USAF) making RAF Fairford its European base. Make the most of it and take in the Royal International Air Tattoo, usually held in July, at RAF Fairford.

BLOCKLEY AND BATSFORD ARBORETUM

DISTANCE/TIME	5 miles (8km) / 2hrs 15min
ASCENT/GRADIENT	800ft (243m) / ▲▲
PATHS	Lanes, tracks and fields, many stiles
LANDSCAPE	Woodland, hills with good views and villages
SUGGESTED MAP	OS Explorer OL45 The Cotswolds
START/FINISH	Grid reference: SP164349
DOG FRIENDLINESS	Some good long stretches without livestock
PARKING	On-street parking near church
PUBLIC TOILETS	In Blockley on edge of churchyard, just off main street
NOTES	There is no public access to the arboretum from Batsford village, but you will cross the entrance road on this walk. Vehicles can approach via the A44 between Moreton-in-Marsh and Bourton-on-the-Hill.

England seems to be a country of trees. Walking through Gloucestershire you are surrounded by many native species, but when you visit Batsford Arboretum, you will encounter 50 acres (20.3ha) of woodland containing over 1,000 species of trees and shrubs from all over the world, including 90 species of Japanese magnolia, maples, cherry trees and conifers.

The arboretum was originally a garden created in the 1880s by the traveller and diplomat Bertie Mitford, 1st Lord Redesdale and grandfather to the renowned Mitford sisters. Posted as an attaché to the British Embassy in Tokyo, he became deeply influenced by the Far East. Throughout the park there are bronze statues, brought from Japan by Bertie Mitford, and a wide range of bamboos. Not long after his death, Batsford was sold to 1st Lord Dulverton and his son who transformed the garden into the arboretum we see today.

Batsford village is comparatively recent, having grown up at the gates of Batsford Park, a neo-Tudor house built between 1888 and 1892 by Ernest George for Lord Redesdale. Batsford Church was constructed earlier, in 1862, in a neo-Norman style. It has several monuments to the Mitford family and a fine work by the sculptor Joseph Nollekens from 1808.

This walk starts in the unspoilt village of Blockley. It was originally owned by the bishops of Worcester, but it didn't really begin to prosper until the 19th century. At one time no fewer than six silk mills, with more than 500 employees, were driven by Blockley's fast-flowing stream. Their silks went mostly to Coventry for the production of ribbon. Blockley was one of the first villages in the world to have electric light – in the 1880s, Dovedale House was illuminated through Lord Edward Spencer-Churchill's use of water to run a dynamo. Blockley's church tower predates the silk boom by about 100 years, and inside the large church are several imposing monuments, at least two of them by the eminent sculptor John Michael Rysbrack (1694–1770).

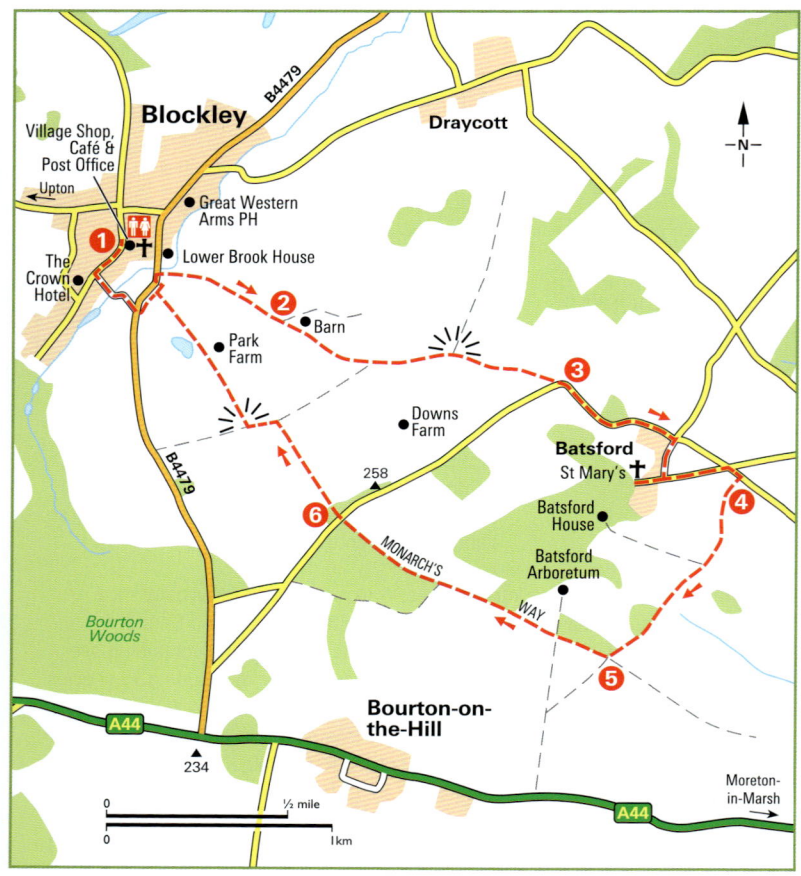

1. Keep the church and post office on your left and walk through the village, turning left at School Lane. Follow this down across a stream and up to the main road. Cross over and turn left on a short path signposted Quiet Lanes Footpath. Re-join the road at the bottom of the hill. Just before Lower Brook House turn right onto a lane, walking up for 0.25 miles (400m) until the lane bears left.

2. Continue ahead to pass to the right-hand side of a barn. In the next field, follow its right-hand boundary to another gate. Pass through to walk between pastures. Pass into yet another field, and after passing through the next gate go slightly right to a gate leading out to a road.

3. Go straight on and follow the road down to a crossroads. Turn right to pass through Batsford, to a junction from where you can visit the church on the right. After visiting the church retrace your steps to the junction and walk down the lime tree avenue. At the next junction turn right.

4. After 100 paces turn right onto a footpath and follow this through a succession of fields, negotiating stiles and gates where they arise. Batsford House will be visible above you to the right.

5. Eventually, go through a gate into a large field at a signposted junction of tracks, then turn right to a gate just left of a lodge at a drive. Cross this (the entrance to Batsford Arboretum), pass through a gate and follow the path up the field to a stile. Cross and continue to a track. Follow this up until it bears left. Keep right here (Monarch's Way) to continue the ascent with the park wall on your right. Keep going until you reach a stile onto a road.

6. Cross the road to join a track, then go through a gate and pass through two fields until you come to a path among trees. Turn left, follow this downhill, then turn right over a stile into a field with Blockley below you. Continue down to a stile at the bottom. Cross into the next field and pass beneath Park Farm on your right. Cross a drive and descend to a stile. Keep ahead on a field path to a gate and stile, then follow a lane until you come to a road. Turn left at the Quiet Lanes Footpath and then, where this ends, cross the road carefully and return to your starting point in the village.

Where to eat and drink
The Crown Hotel in Blockley serves excellent lunches of all sorts. There is also the Great Western Arms on Station Road, named after the railway service, which in fact came no closer than Paxford. The lovely café next to the village shop is open for lunch every day. It has an impressive menu and is open for dinner reservations Wednesday to Saturday (no booking needed for other times).

What to see
An unusual feature of Blockley is its raised footpaths running along the main street. It was noted in the 19th century that 'many dangerous accidents were occurring'. Richard Belcher, a parish waywarden of the day, added iron posts and railings, 'setting the unemployed to work in January and February'. At the southwestern end of the High Street is Rock Cottage, where the self-proclaimed prophetess Joanna Southcott once lived.

While you're there
A short distance to the west of Blockley is Upton, the site of a medieval village that has since disappeared. Although the village was recorded in the Domesday Book in 1086, it is likely that Upton's inhabitants were forced out by the bishops of Worcester who sequestered the land for sheep pastures. While there isn't a lot to see on the ground, this is one of the few abandoned villages that have been excavated.

MICKLETON AND HIDCOTE MANOR GARDEN

DISTANCE/TIME	5 miles (8km) / 2hrs 15min
ASCENT/GRADIENT	660ft (201m) / ▲▲
PATHS	Fields, firm tracks, possibly some muddy woodland
LANDSCAPE	Woodland, open hills and villages
SUGGESTED MAP	OS Explorer 205 Stratford-upon-Avon & Evesham
START/FINISH	Grid reference: SP162434
DOG FRIENDLINESS	On lead in livestock fields, good open stretches elsewhere; dogs not allowed in Kiftsgate Court
PARKING	Car park at church, Mickleton
PUBLIC TOILETS	None on route

This walk takes you within striking distance of two of the finest planned gardens in the country. The first, Kiftsgate Court, is the lesser known of the two, but nonetheless demands a visit. The house itself is primarily Victorian, but the garden was created immediately after World War I by Heather Muir, who was a close friend of Major Johnston, the creator of the nearby Hidcote Manor Garden. Kiftsgate's gardens are designed around a steep hillside overlooking Mickleton and the Vale of Evesham, with terraces, paths, flower beds and shrubs. The layout is in the form of rooms and the emphasis is more on the plants themselves, rather than on the overall design.

The second horticultural treat is Hidcote Manor Garden. This garden is the fruit of more than 40 years of work by Major Lawrence Johnson, an East Coast American who purchased the 17th-century manor house in 1907 and gave it to the National Trust in 1948. Many people consider it be the greatest of English gardens, and certainly it is one of the most influential. Hidcote grew from almost nothing – when Major Johnson first arrived there was a just a cedar tree and a handful of beeches on 11 acres (4.5ha) of open wold.

To some extent it reconciles the formal and informal schools of garden design; Hidcote is not one garden but several. Like Kiftsgate, it is laid out in a series of 'outdoor rooms', with walls of stone and of hornbeam, yew and box hedge. These rooms are themed, having names such as the White Garden and the Fuchsia Garden. There is also a wild garden growing around a stream, as well as lawns and carefully placed garden ornaments.

This walk begins in Mickleton, at the foot of the Cotswold escarpment, below these two fine gardens. It's clearly a Cotswold village, with its mixture of stone, thatch and timber. The church has a 14th-century tower and a monument to Thomas Woodward, the 18th-century quarry owner from Chipping Campden. Near the hotel in the village centre is a Victorian memorial fountain designed by William Burges, the architect behind Cardiff Castle.

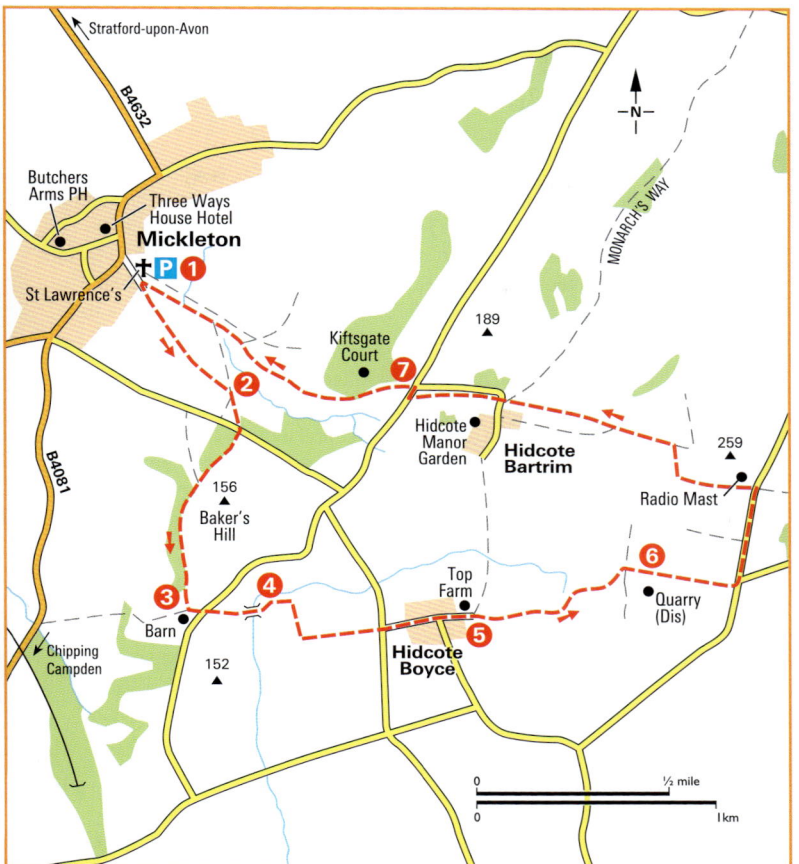

1. With your back to the church, turn right up a bank to reach a kissing gate to the left of Cowland Orchard. Continue diagonally right across a field to a kissing gate at a thicket. Follow a path through trees and go through another kissing gate to emerge into a field. Follow its left margin to reach a kissing gate at the end.

2. In the next field, go slightly right to a gate in the top corner. Cross a road and go up some steps to a gate. Turn right to walk around the edge of the field as it bears left. After 250yds (229m), take a path among trees, a steep bank eventually appearing down to the right. The path brings you to a field and then a Dutch barn.

3. At the barn turn left, briefly joining a semi-surfaced track to the left. On the far side of a hedge, turn right and follow the edge of a field to the bottom corner. Go through a gap to a bridge with a stile on each side over a stream, cross and turn left.

4. Follow the margin of the field as it goes right and then right again. Continue until you come to a gateway on the left. Go through this and walk until you reach a field gate at a road. Walk ahead through Hidcote Boyce. Where the road goes right, stay ahead to pass Top Farm.

5. Beyond a kissing gate, take a rising track along the edge of successive fields. Nearing the top, follow the track through a gate, and bear left and then right around a hedge and head for a field gate at the top of the slope. In an area of grassy mounds, stay to the left of a barn and head for a gate in the top-left corner.

6. Follow the path to a road. Turn sharp left to follow the lesser road. Immediately before a radio mast, turn left onto a track and follow this all the way down to pass through Hidcote Manor Garden's car park entrance. Go straight on for 30 paces to turn left through a gate, and then immediately right to walk a path parallel to the road with Hidcote's trees on your left. Walk through a beech copse, enter a field through a kissing gate and cross it to a gate on the far side.

7. At the road, turn right and then, before Kiftsgate Court, turn left through a gate and descend through a field. Pass through some trees and follow the left-hand side of the next field, through a gate and left around another field, until you come to a stile on the left. Ignore a footbridge to your left. Follow the edge of the next field to a gate. Go through this and head towards Mickleton Church and a path between walled graveyards to return to the start via a gate.

Where to eat and drink
In Mickleton, the Butchers Arms serves good pub food, and the Three Ways House Hotel is the home of the famous 'Pudding Club', where you can taste the finest in traditional English desserts. There is also a restaurant at Hidcote Manor Garden (Winthrop's Café) and a tearoom at Kiftsgate Court.

What to see
In Hidcote Boyce some of the houses, though built of stone broadly in the Cotswold style, are unusually tall. The style is almost unique to the village.

While you're there
It would be a shame to miss the two fine gardens, but note that dogs are not allowed at Kiftsgate Court. Up the road, Hidcote Manor Garden is owned by the National Trust. There is a good restaurant and plant sales centre. Visit the websites for specific opening times.

CHIPPING CAMPDEN AND DOVER'S HILL

DISTANCE/TIME	4.75 miles (7.7km) / 2hrs
ASCENT/GRADIENT	733ft (223m) / ▲▲
PATHS	Fields, woodland paths, one busy road, several stiles
LANDSCAPE	Open hillside, fields, woodland and village
SUGGESTED MAP	OS Explorer 205 Stratford-upon-Avon & Evesham
START/FINISH	Grid reference: SP151391
DOG FRIENDLINESS	Suitable in parts but livestock in many fields, where dogs should be kept on leads
PARKING	Market Square car park; Chipping Campden School car park available at weekends and school holidays only
PUBLIC TOILETS	A short way down Sheep Street

The Cotswold Olimpicks bear only a passing resemblance to their more famous international counterpart. What they lack in grandeur and razzmatazz, however, they make up for in local passion. Far from being held in a multi-million-pound stadium, the stadium here is a natural amphitheatre – the summit of Dover's Hill. It's on the edge of the Cotswold escarpment, with spectacular views westwards over the Vale of Evesham. Established with the permission of James I, the Olimpicks were dubbed 'royal' games, and indeed have taken place during the reign of 14 monarchs. Dover's Hill is named after its founder of the Cotswold Olimpicks, Robert Dover. Dover was born in Norfolk in 1582, educated at Cambridge and became a barrister in London. His profession took him to the Cotswolds, but he had memories of the plays and spectacles that he had seen in the capital.

It is accepted that the first games took place in 1612, but they may well have begun at an earlier date. It is also possible that Dover was simply reviving an existing ancient festivity. Initially, at least, the main events were horse racing and hare-coursing, with the prizes being, respectively, a silver castle ornament and a silver-studded collar. Other competitions in these early games were for running, jumping, throwing, wrestling and staff fighting. The area was festooned with yellow flags and ribbons, and there were dancing events as well as pavilions for chess and other cerebral contests.

The Olimpicks soon became an indispensable part of the local Whitsuntide festivities, with mention of them even being made in Shakespeare's work. Robert Dover managed the games for 30 years, and he died in 1652. The games continued in a variety of forms throughout the following centuries, surviving several attempts to suppress them when they became more rowdy and seemed to present a threat to public order and safety. They finally became an established annual event once again in 1966. Nowadays, the games are more like a carnival, but they have retained their atmosphere of local showmanship. At the end of the evening's events, all the spectators, holding flaming torches, file down into Chipping Campden, where the festivities continue with dancing and music along the main street and in the square.

It's worth lingering in Chipping Campden, before or after the walk. Possibly the most beautiful of all the Cotswold towns, it was once famous throughout Europe as the centre of the English wool trade. A leisurely stroll along its high street is a must. The church, too, is particularly fine, and it's also worth searching out the Ernest Wilson Memorial Garden on the High Street. Wilson was one of the great plant hunters of the early 20th century.

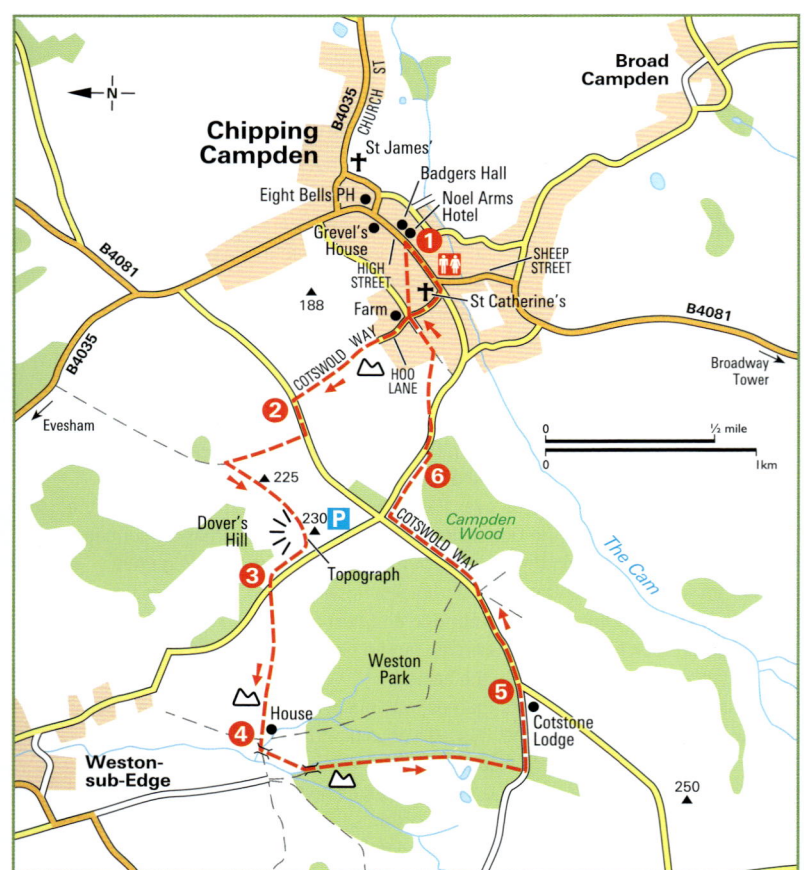

1. With your back to the Noel Arms Hotel, turn left and walk past Sheep Street, then turn right by St Catharine's Church, following the Cotswold Way markers. Where the road bears right, go straight ahead on Hoo Lane. Follow this to some farm buildings, and keep going straight on a continuation path to a road.

2. Turn left, then very shortly cross the road on a path to the right, still following Cotswold Way signs. Go between hedges to a kissing gate. Through this turn left into open access land and onto Dover's Hill, with extensive views from the escarpment edge that drops away to your right. Pass a trig point and

then further along a topograph. Immediately beyond this, take a gap in the upper scarp slope and follow a grassy ramp down towards the bottom left of the field, passing one kissing gate then exiting via a second lower down.

3. Cross the road and go through a kissing gate. Turn right, then in the next field go left. After another kissing gate, veer right by a fence through two fields. Go over a grassy strip, then two kissing gates either side of a hedge, and continue downhill across two wide fields. Head steeply down the next field, cross a track just to the right of a house, then find a pair of sleeper bridges with stiles in the lower left corner of the field.

4. Cross the leftmost one and continue straight ahead under power lines and up the centre of the field to reach a small bridge with stiles. Cross this and turn left, following a rising woodland bridleway alongside the stream. Enter parkland through a gate and continue ahead, keeping just to the right of the woodland. Go through a wide gate and continue uphill to reach a small gate leading to a country lane. Go through this and turn left.

5. Reach a busier road by Cotstone Lodge. Turn onto this, taking care as the verge is narrow. Immediately after the road curves left, drop to the right and over a stile onto a field path parallel with the road. Turn right at the far end of the field and continue downhill, running parallel to a country lane on a woodland path beyond the field.

6. Join the lane downhill and roughly 110yds (100m) further on, cross the road to a footpath. Head diagonally down the field to the far corner. Pass through a gateway, cross a road among houses and continue down an alley into Birdcage Walk. Turn right then left to return to the centre of Chipping Campden.

Where to eat and drink
Chipping Campden has plenty of pubs, cafés and restaurants. Badgers Hall on the High Street does exceptionally fine tea and home-made cakes, while the Eight Bells on Church Street is a very relaxing pub.

What to see
Spend a little time poring over the topograph on Dover's Hill – on a clear day there is much to identify. In Chipping Campden, look out for the 14th-century Grevel's House, opposite Church Street. William Grevel is thought to have been the inspiration for the Merchant in Chaucer's *The Canterbury Tales*.

While you're there
Broadway Tower, with its associations with William Morris, stands about 4 miles (6.4km) southwest of Chipping Campden. A Gothic folly built in Portland stone in 1798, it contains an interesting small museum and offers fine views across the vale.

FROM CHIPPING CAMPDEN TO BROAD CAMPDEN

DISTANCE/TIME	4.5 miles (7.2km) / 2hrs
ASCENT/GRADIENT	295ft (90m) / ▲
PATHS	Field paths, tracks and some road walking
LANDSCAPE	Gently undulating farmland
SUGGESTED MAP	OS Explorer OL45 The Cotswolds
START/FINISH	Grid reference: SP151391
DOG FRIENDLINESS	Lead required in villages
PARKING	Chipping Campden High Street or main square
PUBLIC TOILETS	A short way down Sheep Street

One of this walk's great points of interest is reserved for the end of the route as you approach Chipping Campden's glorious wool church, its splendid tower looking out over the Cotswold landscape. Just a few yards from it lies Court Barn Museum, which tells the story of the Arts and Crafts Movement from the beginning of the 20th century to the present day. For it was here in Chipping Campden that some of the movement's greatest craftspeople gathered. These were figures of national and international renown and reputation in their day – people such as C R Ashbee, Gordon Russell and Robert Welch. The displays illustrate examples of the different design styles and explain how they came to be created.

Ashbee, a radical figure and a noted designer and writer, was an architect who specialised in church restoration. In 1902 he moved the Guild of Handicraft from his East End of London workshops, where he employed more than 100 workers, to the village of Chipping Campden, the intention being to draw the various creative threads together in one place. Many of the outstanding designers and architects he had teamed up with lived locally, so it made obvious sense to settle in Gloucestershire. Ashbee also believed that the rural setting and the harmonious atmosphere of the Cotswolds would be conducive to producing craftwork of the finest quality.

Katharine Adams bound books for the printer Emery Walker, who regarded her work highly and wanted her acknowledged as the finest artist binder in the country. The Court Barn Museum collection also includes engravings of Chipping Campden by the architect F L Griggs – who completed his most important work here – as well as silverwork by Robert Welch and examples of Gordon Russell's radio cabinets.

The time these designers spent working together at Chipping Campden was short but productive and very rewarding. The failure of the Guild of Handicraft in 1908 resulted in many of the craftspeople returning to London, but by then some of their best work had been created. The name and the reputation of the movement had been forged.

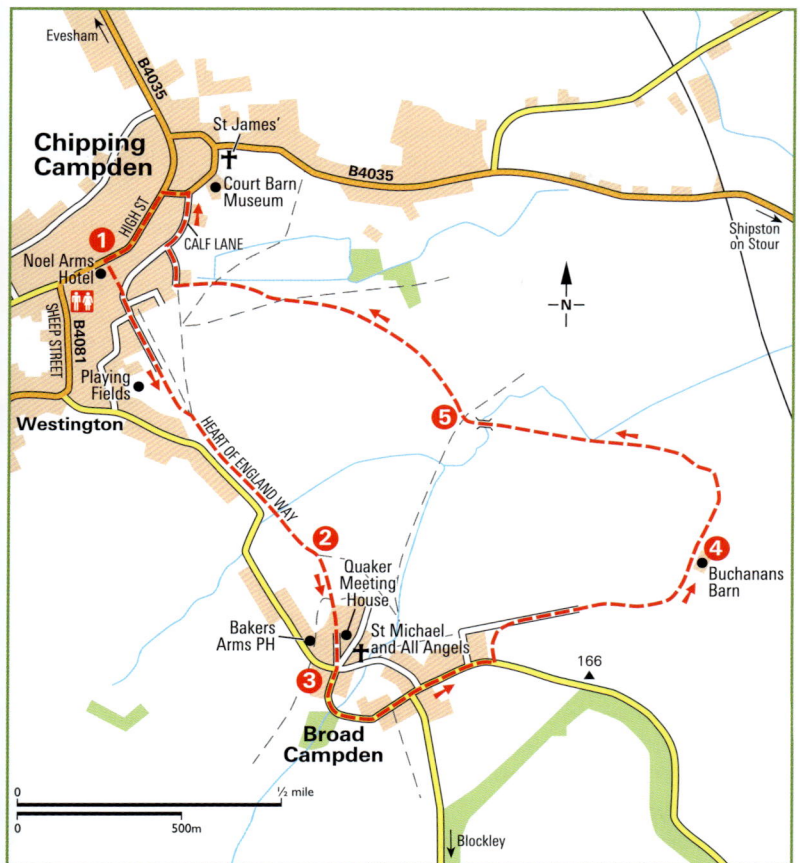

1. From the High Street, walk through the arch next to the Noel Arms Hotel near the Market Hall, and continue ahead through the car park and beside a sign for Coldicotts Close. Pass Badgers Field to join a path as the road bends right into Pear Tree Close. Pass playing fields to reach a junction with a road. Go left here, into a field, then immediately right, to follow the field-edge parallel with the road. This is part of the Heart of England Way.

2. After 500yds (457m), fork right to a gate. Pass Maidenwell Cottage, then leave the drive to walk ahead to a gate. Pass through into an alley and follow it to pass the Quaker Meeting House in Broad Campden. Emerge at the green, with the church to your left.

3. At a junction continue ahead for 400yds (366m) through the village. The road bears left and straightens. Pass a turning for Blockley and continue through Broad Campden to the edge of the village. Turn left at a gate and sign for Buchanans Barn, and after 100yds (91m) swing right at a waymarker. Follow the track up the slope, and from the brow of the hill enjoy glorious views across Gloucestershire and the Cotswolds. Continue on the track, descending to a stile and cattle-grid, and follow it as it bends left to a converted barn and outbuildings.

4. Some 60yds (55m) beyond the buildings go through a gate and keep ahead by a hedge on the right. Follow the field boundary as it sweeps left to reach a kissing gate in the corner. Go diagonally left across the next pasture and drop down to a gate in the far corner. Once through it, look for two gates either side of a footbridge in the right-hand boundary. Cross the field, looking for a gate in the line of trees on the far side. Cross the footbridge beyond it and turn left for 40yds (37m) to a path junction.

5. Turn right, crossing the field on the obvious path through the crops. At the top go through a kissing gate, cross a broad grassy track and follow a path between paddocks. St James' Church edges into view on this stretch. Draw level with the church and pass through two gates with a paddock in between. Head for the bottom corner of the next paddock and make for the houses of Chipping Campden. Pass a stone arch on the right in the field and look for a gate about 100yds (91m) beyond it, also on the right. Go through this and follow the path, turning left onto a drive. Turn right and head up to Calf Lane. Turn right, and at the top turn left into Church Street to reach the main street, or right to visit Court Barn Museum and the church.

Where to eat and drink
Chipping Campden has plenty of pubs, tea rooms and restaurants. If you want to stop along the way, try the Bakers Arms in Broad Campden, which offers morning coffee, light fare and a hearty Sunday lunch.

What to see
The Broad Campden Quaker Meeting House in the centre of the village is directly on the route of the walk. The building dates back to 1663, making it the oldest meeting house in the country still in use.

While you're there
St Michael and All Angels in Broad Campden has an eye-catching round bellcote with an unusual conical roof. The church is small and dates back to 1867. In Chipping Campden take a look at the almshouses and the Market Hall, both landmarks created by the first Viscount Campden and regarded as impressive works of architecture.

AROUND CONDICOTE

DISTANCE/TIME	9 miles (14.5km) / 3hrs 30min
ASCENT/GRADIENT	263ft (80m) / ▲
PATHS	Track, field, estate road and country lanes; several stiles
LANDSCAPE	Long views across high wolds, estate land, villages
SUGGESTED MAP	OS Explorer OL45 The Cotswolds
START/FINISH	Grid reference: SP151282
DOG FRIENDLINESS	Nice long stretches of track; lead required around livestock
PARKING	Roadside parking in Condicote village
PUBLIC TOILETS	None on route

During the first portion of this walk you will be following the unmistakable line of a Roman road, Ryknild Street. This extended northwest from the Fosse Way near Bourton-on-the-Water, crossed Watling Street near Lichfield, and turned northeast to terminate at Templeborough, near Rotherham. The stretch you will be walking along may not have changed much in 2,000 years, even if the ordered landscape that rolls away on either side would not, perhaps, be immediately recognisable to travellers of the era.

It is well known that the Romans built remarkably straight roads throughout Britannia, with a total length of about 10,000 miles (16,000km). Most of these were built during the first 100 years of occupation, which equates to a mile (1.6km) of road every four days. Later roads were not as well built as the earlier ones – road building has always been an expensive business and the Romans sometimes found it expedient not to insist on straight lines.

Roman roads differed from their predecessors in the quality of the road building and the comprehensive coverage of the road network. The basic aim was to link sites with water supplies, which were located a day's march apart (10–15 miles/16–24km). Alignments were laid out from hilltop to hilltop and then with intermediate points between. Some zig-zagging was permitted, but only for good reasons – hill cuttings, for example, were rarely used, and perhaps only as early military roads. Marshes were not considered an obstacle and roads were built across them by the copious use of brushwood. Fording was preferred to bridges, presumably for reasons of cost and longevity.

The procedure for the construction of the road itself might consist initially of woodland clearance to the tune of a 90ft (27.4m) line, marked by ploughed outer ditches, followed by two more drainage ditches about 30ft (9m) apart that provided the outer limits of the road itself. Material from around about would be dug up and used to build up the roadway. On top of this would go local stone, followed by rubble or gravel, which would then be cambered.

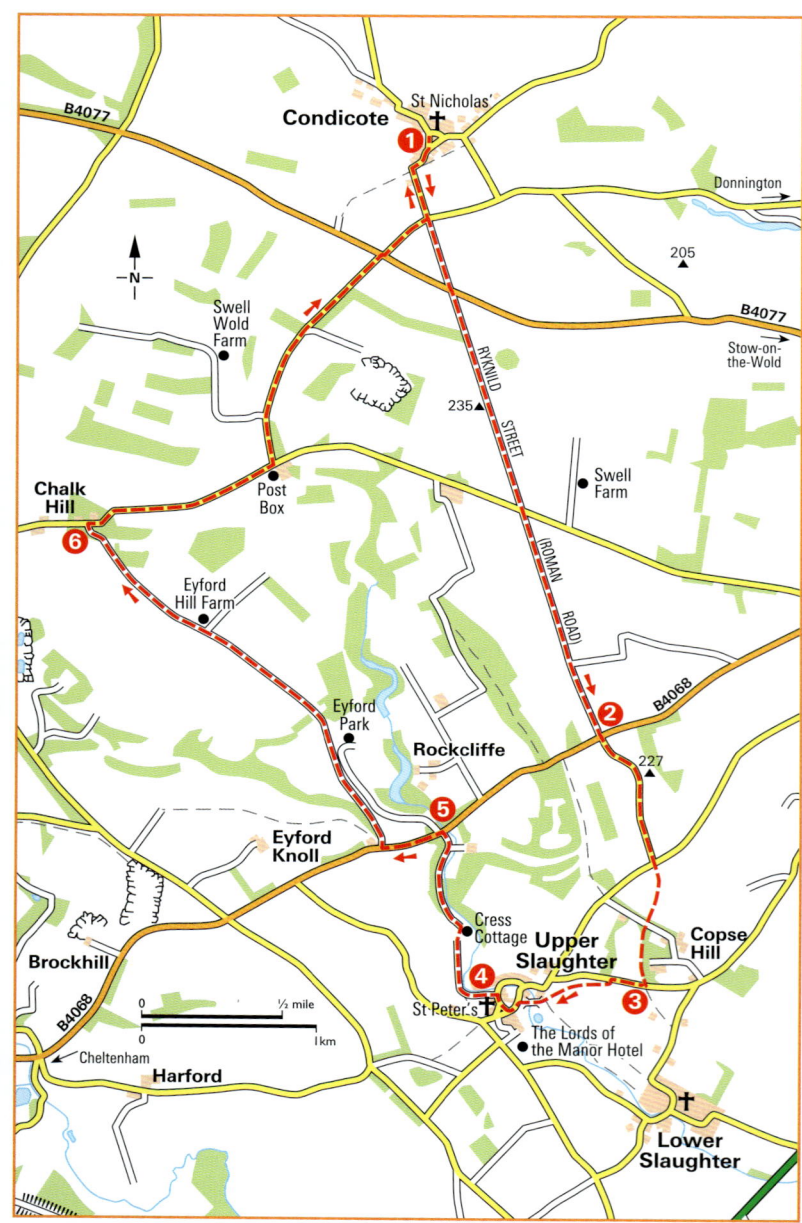

1. From Condicote village green, with your back to the church, take the road south out of the village. Beyond the houses of Condicote bend left where a footpath leads straight on at a gate and follow the lane to a junction. Go straight ahead onto a track at a sign 'Unsuitable for Motors' and follow what is in effect all that remains of Ryknild Street. As you might expect, the route is clear – follow this track for just under 2 miles (3.2km) to the B4068, crossing two roads by further 'Unsuitable for Motors' signs.

2. The views are good from this stretch, with distant glimpses of Cotswold hills, combes and farmland, and either side of the track is a landscape divided by fields and dotted with woodland. The section after the B4068 is a surfaced road, which will bring you to a T-junction. Cross to a gate and stile, and then cross a field to a stile. In the next field, curve right to a stile at the edge of woodland. Cross an estate road to follow a woodland path across a staggered junction to a kissing gate at the edge of a field. Curve left to follow a fence down the field to a gate in the bottom corner.

3. Turn right along the road. After 100yds (91m) go left and turn immediately right through a gate. Pass through a succession of fields, finally dipping down to a gate and a bridge over a stream. Follow a path up to Upper Slaughter and turn left at the road. At the village triangle turn right and head back towards the river.

4. Pass the church, then bear left at a Wardens Way sign and follow the bridleway track with the river to your right, passing a house to enter trees. Pass through a gate and cross grassland to gates by Cress Cottage. Walk in woodland for 700yds (640m), eventually descending to the B4068.

5. Turn left and walk along the road for about 350yds (320m), using the verge where possible. Just before cottages turn right onto a metalled drive rising up between trees. This will take you past Eyford Park. Stay on the drive for 1.5 miles (2.4km), crossing a series of cattle grids, to eventually reach a road.

6. Turn right for 0.75 miles (1.2km) to a junction where a George VI letterbox is seen on the right, built into the wall of a barn. Turn left, signposted 'Condicote', and follow the road to the B4077. Cross over and continue until you come to the road on your left leading back into Condicote. Return to the village green where the walk began.

Where to eat and drink
The only place on the route is The Lords of the Manor Hotel in Upper Slaughter. This is a luxurious hotel with an excellent restaurant and prices to match, so you may prefer to head into Stow-on-the-Wold, where there's a wide choice of pubs and tea rooms.

What to see
Halfway through the walk you will pass through the domain of Eyford Park. You may be able to catch glimpses of this elegant house, built in 1910 in Queen Anne style by Sir Guy Dawber on the site of an earlier mansion.

While you're there
Southeast of Condicote lies Donnington and, not far from it, is the Donnington Brewery. This small concern, offers tours on Fridays and you can buy beer direct from the brewery. You can taste their excellent brews at The Fox in nearby Broadwell as well as numerous other pubs in the area.

A STROLL AROUND NORTHLEACH

DISTANCE/TIME	4 miles (6.4km) / 1hr 45min
ASCENT/GRADIENT	165ft (50m) / ▲
PATHS	Fields, tracks and pavement, muddy after rain
LANDSCAPE	Valley track, wolds and villages
SUGGESTED MAP	OS Explorer OL45 The Cotswolds
START/FINISH	Grid reference: SP113145
DOG FRIENDLINESS	Some clear stretches without livestock, few stiles
PARKING	Northleach Market Place
PUBLIC TOILETS	In Market Place

Northleach as a settlement dates back to approximately 1200 AD, its fine church was built and subsequently restored with money gained from the wool trade of the late Middle Ages. More recently, the House of Correction opened in the last few years of the 1700s, but only lasted for 60 years before closure.

An important wool town in the Middle Ages, Northleach still just about manages to take you back to that period. The atmosphere of antiquity comes from the fact that one of the finest wool churches in the Cotswolds overlooks the market square. This mighty fine example of the English Perpendicular style dates from the 15th century – its magnificent south porch is one of the finest in the country. The interior is quite stark, but beautifully proportioned. The church contains the grandest collection of monumental brasses in the Cotswolds, commemorating the medieval wool merchants who brought prosperity to Northleach and passed some of it along to the church.

To the west of Northleach, at a corner of a Fosse Way crossroads, lies the Old Prison café. It is housed in an 18th-century house of correction, built by the prison reformer and wealthy philanthropist Sir Onesipherous Paul. He was a descendant of a family of successful clothiers from Woodchester, near Stroud, who were also responsible for the construction of what is now the King's house at Highgrove. Paul's intentions were surely good, but conditions in the prison were still harsh and the treadmill was still considered effective as the unrelenting instrument of slow punishment. As well as a restored 18th-century cell block, you'll find the Lloyd-Baker Rural Life Collection, an interesting collection of agricultural implements and machinery which displays plenty of fascinating photographs showing what rural life in the Cotswolds was once like.

Northleach itself, like Cirencester and Chipping Campden, was one of the key medieval wool trading centres of the Cotswolds. Though once on a crossroads of the A40 and the Fosse Way, neither now passes through the town, the completion of the A40 bypass in the mid-1980s left the town centre a quiet and very attractive place to visit. The main street is lined with houses, some half-timbered, dating from the 16th to 19th centuries. Many of these retain their ancient 'burgage' rear plots that would have served as market gardens. Above the market square is a tiny maze of narrow lanes, overlooked by the Church of St Peter and St Paul, the town's impressive 15th-century Perpendicular 'wool church'.

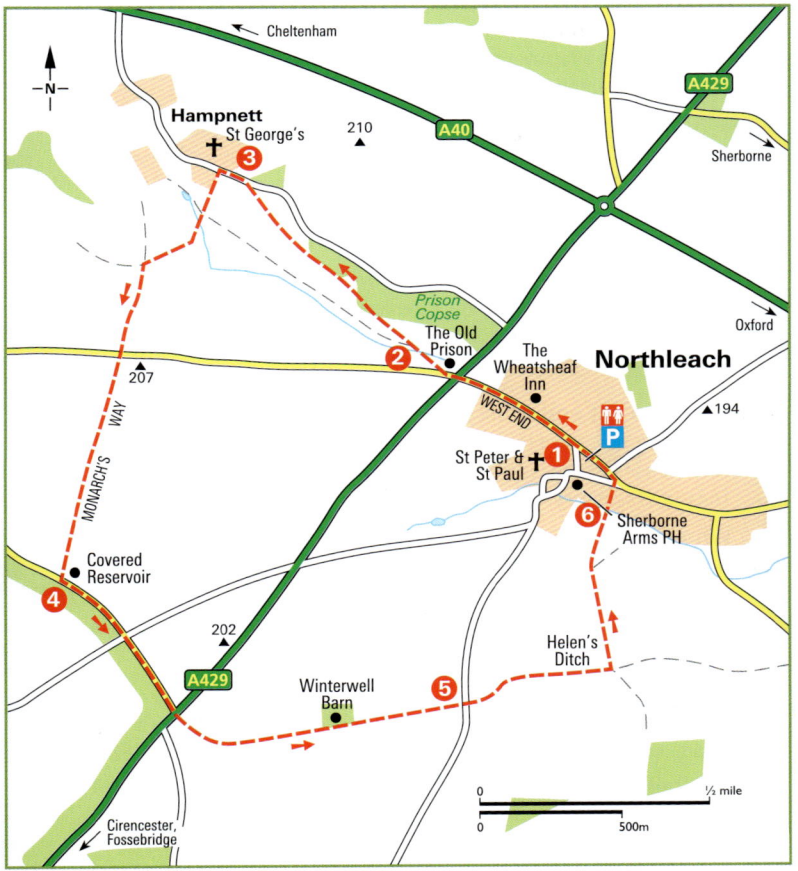

1. From Northleach Market Place, with the church behind you, turn left and walk along the main street to the traffic lights at the A429. Cross the road with care, keep left of The Old Prison and, immediately after passing the centre, turn right through a gate into a field. Go half right to cross a stream by a field corner and walk on into the next field.

2. Aiming for a church tower, go diagonally right up the field to a gate. Pass through this into the next field and, keeping fairly close to the field's right-hand margin, head for a kissing gate on the far side. Pass into the next field and walk around the right-hand perimeter in the general direction of St George's Church in Hampnett. This will bring you to a kissing gate at a road.

3. Turn left and almost immediately come to a concrete track on your left. To visit the church walk ahead and then return to this track. Otherwise, turn left down the track and follow it as it descends to pass farm buildings. Where the track begins to bear right, turn left to climb a track towards a gate. Go through it and continue to follow the track, eventually striking a road. Cross this to walk along another track (Monarch's Way) all the way to another road by a reservoir.

4. At this road turn left and walk until you reach the A429. Cross with great care to a gap in the hedge at a marker post and then walk along a grassy track until you come to a farmyard. Walk through the yard and out the other side along a track to another road.

5. Cross to a track and follow this for about 330yds (300m). Turn left through a gate to enter a field and follow the left margin with a stone wall to your left. Northleach is ahead of you. Where the field comes to an end, go through a kissing gate and go straight down the field to a kissing gate beside a playground.

6. Go through and, bearing right, walk between the tennis courts and the playground to cross a stream. Walk the length of an alley and, at the top, turn left to return to the starting point.

Where to eat and drink
Although small, Northleach has two pubs – the Sherborne Arms and the Wheatsheaf Inn; the latter has an covered outdoor area. The café within The Old Prison serves tasty food daily from 9am to 4pm.

What to see
Leaving Northleach, look for some interesting old houses. Walton House, for example, was formerly the King's Head, an important inn on the old London to Gloucester route. Further on, set back from the road, are the buildings of the former brewery.

While you're there
Close by is the National Trust's 4,000-acre (1,620ha) Sherborne Park Estate (see Walk 4). This was bequeathed by Lord Sherborne in 1982 and includes the estate village and richly planted parkland. The highlight is Lodge Park (guide dogs only), a 17th-century deer course with an ornate grandstand boasting spectacular views. The grandstand has been extensively restored.

ALONG THE WINDRUSH FROM GUITING POWER

DISTANCE/TIME	5.75 miles (9.2km) / 2hrs
ASCENT/GRADIENT	570ft (173m) / ▲
PATHS	Fields, tracks and country lanes, several stiles
LANDSCAPE	Woodland, hill and village
SUGGESTED MAP	OS Explorer OL45 The Cotswolds
START/FINISH	Grid reference: SP094246
DOG FRIENDLINESS	Fairly clear of livestock but look out for horses on roads
PARKING	Village hall car park
PUBLIC TOILETS	None on route

Looking from the village green, surrounded by stone cottages, with its church and secluded manor house, it is easy to imagine that very little has changed in Guiting Power in 1,000 years. The name comes from the Saxon word gyte-ing, or 'torrent', and indeed the name was given not only to Guiting Power but also to neighbouring Temple Guiting, which in the 12th century was owned by the Knights Templar. Guiting Power, however, was named after the pre-eminent local family of the 13th century, the Le Poers. Over the years the village was variously known as Gything, Getinge, Gettinges Poer, Guyting Poher, Nether Guiting and Lower Guiting. Its current name and spelling date only from 1937.

In 1086, the Domesday Book noted the inhabitants as 'four villagers, three Frenchmen, two riding men, and a priest with two small-holders'. Just under 100 years later the first recorded English fulling mill was in operation at the nearby hamlet of Barton, to the northeast. In 1330, permission was given for a weekly market to be held at Guiting Power, which may explain the current arrangement of the houses about the green. The village had its share of the prosperity derived from the 15th-century wool trade, as the addition of the tower to the church testifies.

In other ways history was slow to catch up with small villages like Guiting Power. Its farmland, for example, was enclosed only in 1798, allowing small landowners such as a tailor called John Williams, who owned 12 acres (4.86ha) in the form of medieval strips scattered throughout the parish, to finally consolidate their possessions. Local rights of way were enshrined in law at this time. By the end of the 19th century the rural depression had reduced the population to 431, and it continued to decline throughout the 20th century. Nonetheless, it is recorded that apart from public houses (there were at least four), there were two grocers, two bakers, two tailors, two carpenters, two policemen and a blacksmith. There are still two pubs in Guiting Power but everything else, apart from The Old Post Office café, has disappeared. The village is unusual in that it hasn't succumbed to the inflationary effects of second-homeowners from the cities pushing housing beyond the reach of locals. Much of this is down to the far-sightedness of Moya Davidson, a resident in the 1930s who purchased cottages to be rented out locally. Today, these are managed by the Guiting Manor Amenity Trust. It has meant that younger people can stay in the village to live and work, and there are a few local families who can trace their roots back for several generations.

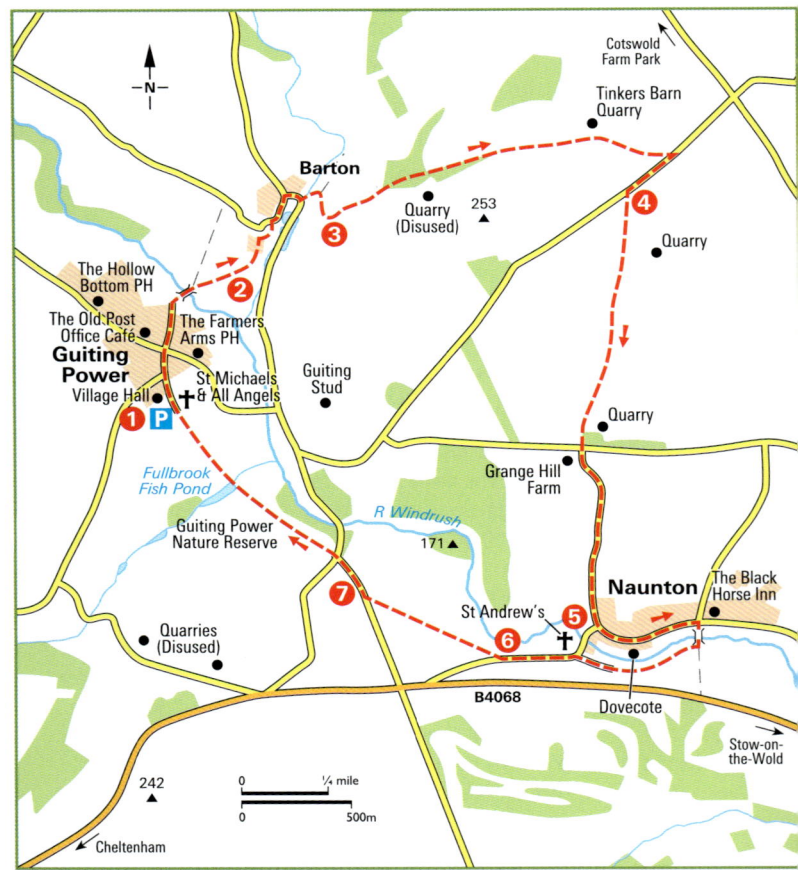

1. From the village hall car park walk down the road to the village green. Cross the road to walk down a lane, passing the Guiting Manor Amenity Trust Estate Office on the right. At the bottom go through a kissing gate into a field and ahead onto a path alongside a stream. Through a gate and over a footbridge, the path climbs towards a kissing gate. Don't take the one in front of you, but go through the one to your right into a field.

2. Turn left and walk straight across this field to a kissing gate. Go through this and over two stiles to pass a farmhouse in Barton village. Follow the lane down to a larger road and turn right. Cross a bridge and turn left up a track. After 100yds (91m), turn right up another track.

3. Follow this as it bears left and walk along this track for about a mile (1.6km), until you reach another road after passing a working quarry called Tinkers Barn. Turn right, walk along the road for about 250yds (229m) and turn left onto a stony track.

4. Follow this to a road junction, passing more quarries as you go. Cross the road and enter a lane descending past Grange Hill Farm. This quiet lane will bring you all the way into the village of Naunton.

5. At the junction, turn left and walk along the village street for 500yds (457m) to The Black Horse Inn. Just before you get to it, turn right into Close Hill, a narrow lane. Over a bridge turn right to cross a stone slab stile and walk alongside the stream, the young River Windrush. Go through two gates. The path becomes a village lane emerging near Naunton Church. Turning left, follow the lane up out of the village.

6. After 0.25 miles (400m), turn right through a kissing gate into a field. Turn slightly left, walk to a stile and go into the next field. Cross this field, enter the next one and follow the path to the right of a wood to a gate at the road.

7. Turn right along the road and continue to a junction at the bottom. Cross the road to enter a field via a gate and walk straight across, aiming to the left of Guiting Power church. At the end go through a kissing gate and down some steps to pass to the right of a pond. Go through a kissing gate, walk across the next field, then go through another kissing gate to walk to the left of the church via two further kissing gates and return to the start.

Where to eat and drink
Guiting Power's two pubs are The Farmers Arms, just off the village green, and The Hollow Bottom, on the Winchcombe side of the village. There's also The Old Post Office café, open Thu-Tue, 9am-4pm. In Naunton, there is the very pleasant Black Horse Inn.

What to see
The Norman doorway in Guiting Power church is an exceptionally rich golden hue. In Naunton, if you stroll back from The Black Horse Inn towards the church on the opposite side of the river, you will be rewarded with a view of a large but charming 17th-century dovecote, which is occasionally open to the public. Many villages had dovecotes for the supply of eggs and winter meat.

While you're there
Located between Guiting Power and Stow-on-the-Wold is the Cotswold Farm Park, specialising in rare breeds of British farm livestock including the Cotswold Lion. This breed of sheep was the foundation of the medieval wool trade and has fortunately been pulled back from the brink of extinction in recent years. There's plenty for animal lovers of all ages to enjoy – and you might see Adam Henson, the farm's owner, of BBC *Countryfile* fame.

BIBURY, ARLINGTON AND ABLINGTON

18

DISTANCE/TIME	6.25 miles (10.1km) / 2hrs 30min
ASCENT/GRADIENT	380ft (115m) / ▲▲
PATHS	Fields, tracks and lane, may be muddy in places
LANDSCAPE	Exposed wolds, valley, villages and streams
SUGGESTED MAP	OS Explorer OL45 The Cotswolds
START/FINISH	Grid reference: SP113068
DOG FRIENDLINESS	Lead required throughout – lots of sheep and horses
PARKING	Off-road parking area in Bibury village opposite Trout Farm
PUBLIC TOILETS	Near post office

Arlington Row is the picturesque terrace of cottages that led William Morris to refer to Bibury as the most beautiful village in England. It was originally built, it is thought, in the late 14th century, to house sheep belonging to Osney Abbey in Oxford. The wool was washed in the river and then hung out to dry on Rack Isle, the marshy area in front of the cottages. Following the Dissolution of the Monasteries, the land was sold off and the sheep houses converted to weavers' cottages. Before mechanisation transformed the wool-weaving industry, most weaving took place in the houses of the poor. Firstly, women and children spun the wool either at home or at the workhouse. Then it was transferred to the houses of the weavers, who worked on handlooms at home at piece rates. A typical weaver's cottage might have had four rooms, with a kitchen and workshop downstairs and a bedroom and storeroom upstairs. There were very few items of furniture in the living rooms, while the workroom would have contained little more than a broadloom and the appropriate tools. The woven cloth was then returned to the clothier's mill for fulling and cutting.

Work on cloth was often a condition of tenure imposed by landlords. The merchant landlord fixed a piecework rate, and provided that the work was satisfactory, the cottage could stay in the weaver's family from generation to generation. Weaving went on this way for some 200 years, until the introduction of steam power in the 18th century, after which it tended to take place in the Stroud Valley mills. Despite their unfavourable conditions, the cottage weavers resisted the change, but to no avail.

Apart from Arlington Row, there is plenty to enjoy in the village, especially the church, which has Saxon origins and is set in pretty gardens. Nearby Ablington has an enchanting group of cottages, threaded by the River Coln. *A Cotswold Village* (1898), which describes local life in the late 19th century, was written by J. Arthur Gibbs who lived at Ablington Manor. You pass the walls of the manor on the walk.

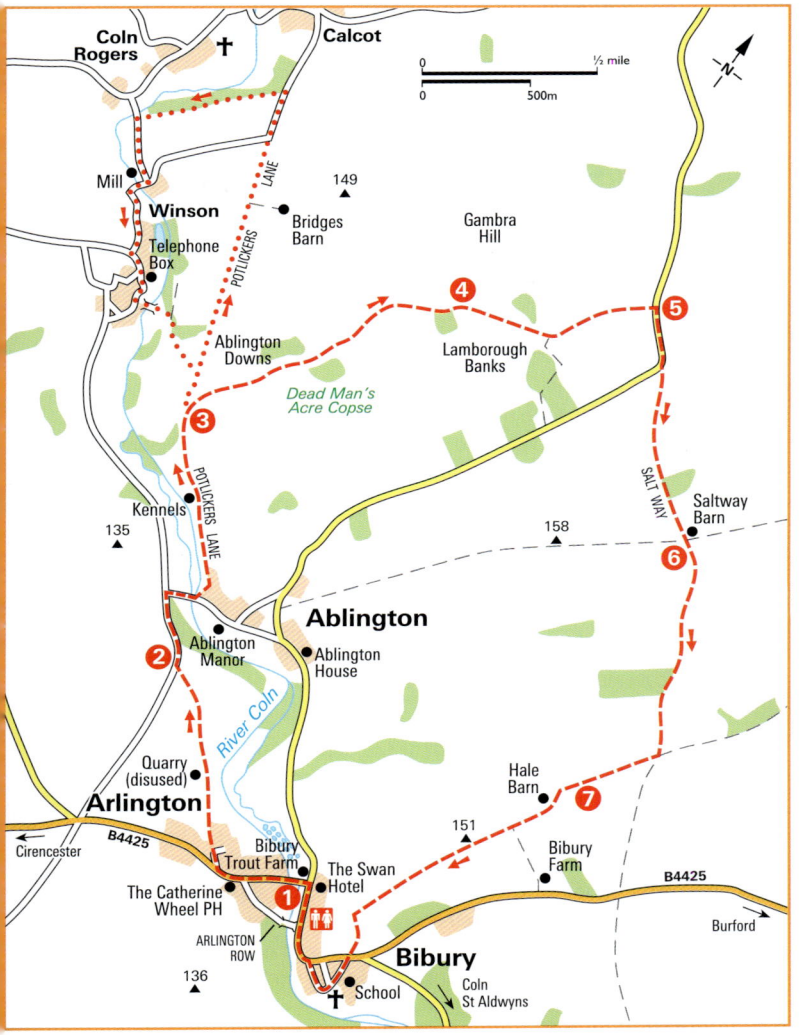

1. From the entrance to the trout farm, walk away from Bibury along Cirencester Road. Opposite the telephone box, after The Catherine Wheel pub, turn right along a lane and then keep left at a fork. Go through a wooden gate, past some cottages and through another gate into a field. On the same path, curve left and then right through fields and past a farm building until you come to a road.

2. Turn right and walk down to a junction. Turn right into Ablington and cross the River Coln on a bridge. After about 33yds (30m), turn left along a track with houses on your right and a stream to your left. Continue to a gate and then follow the track, veering to the right and heading slightly uphill, arriving at another gate after 0.3 miles (500m).

3. Go into a field and turn sharp right along the valley bottom. Follow a twisting route along the bottom of the valley. When you reach the next gate continue into a field, still following the contours of the valley. The route will eventually take you through a gate at the far end of the field beyond a row of ash trees, just before a barn and with another gate immediately after.

4. Keep to the track as it bears into the right-hand valley and gently ascends a long slope, with woodland to your left. When the track goes sharp right just beyond the end of a conifer plantation, with a gate before you, turn left through a gate onto a track. Follow it all the way to a road.

5. Through a gate turn right. After 250yds (229m), where the road goes right, continue straight on through a gate to enter a track (the Salt Way). Continue on this for over 0.5 miles (800m), until you reach the remains of Saltway Barn.

6. Go through a gateway and fork left, then into a field and walk to the right, along its upper right-hand margin. Walk on for just under 0.75 miles (1.2km), passing hedge and woodland and, at a crossroads of tracks, turn right through a gate, waymarked public bridleway, into a field. Keep the wall on your right.

7. Walk on and pass to the left of Hale Barn after a gate. Enter a track, with the large buildings of Bibury Farm away to your left, and keep on the same line through gates where they arise. When you eventually reach some cottages, descend to a drive which will, in turn, bring you to a road in Bibury. Cross the road to walk down the street with the row of cottages beyond the telephone box on your right. At the end, near the church and school, turn right. Walk along the pavement into the village, passing Arlington Row and the river on your left, back to your starting point.

Extending the walk You can extend the walk up the Coln Valley to Winson and Coln Rogers by leaving the main route at Point 3 to continue on Potlickers Lane. Shortly after Potlickers Lane becomes a road, turn left down a path into the woodland. When you reach the road, turn left (you will see the sign for Coln Rogers village on your right). Walk down the road, following the signs for Bibury and then another sign for Winson village only, always keeping left. About 150yds (137m) after the telephone box on your left, look for a small recreational ground. Walk down the right of this and go through the gate at the bottom on your right. Cross the squeeze stile and footbridge, head straight on and, when you come to a gate, take the path on the right in front of the trees. Go diagonally left uphill over the field until a path brings you back to Point 3, where you can continue the main walk.

Where to eat and drink
The Catherine Wheel is a pleasant pub on the Cirencester road, just beyond the mill. The Swan Hotel has a good restaurant and also serves teas. Snacks are also available at Bibury Trout Farm.

What to see
Ablington Manor is to your right (behind high stone walls) as you cross the bridge in the village. Look out, too, not just for the 18th-century barns, but also for Ablington House, guarded by a pair of lions that once stood at the Houses of Parliament.

AROUND COLN ST ALDWYNS

DISTANCE/TIME	3 miles (4.8km) / 1hr 30 min
ASCENT/GRADIENT	195ft (60m) / ▲
PATHS	Road walking, paths and tracks
LANDSCAPE	Undulating parkland, farmland and meadow in the Coln valley
SUGGESTED MAP	OS Explorer OL45 The Cotswolds
START/FINISH	Grid reference: SP145053
DOG FRIENDLINESS	Lead required in Coln St Aldwyns
PARKING	Roadside parking in Coln St Aldwyns
PUBLIC TOILETS	None on route

Through text and photographs, the Church of St John the Baptist at Coln St Aldwyns illustrates just how much the traditional English village has changed over the years – particularly during the 20th century. The effects of great social change, in this village and countless other rural communities, are recorded in this great place of worship, and the evidence can be witnessed in the surrounding streets.

Before the days of motorised transport, social life in villages such as Coln St Aldwyns was mostly limited to the community itself – a far cry from today when greater mobility enables people to travel easily and much further. In this particular village, the church, the hall, the pub, and the shop and post office were at the heart of village activity and formed its lifeline.

A local reading room was established here in 1884, with whist drives organised later. The reading room was an outstanding success and all manner of activities took place here. Ping-pong was introduced in 1902, a magic lantern was acquired in 1907 and a billiard table in 1911. An ever-widening range of pursuits led to the forming of a rifle club, launched in the village in 1903, with women joining for the first time in 1921.

The village school opened in 1856, and one day the headmistress surprised pupils and parents by introducing a lamb as one of her charges. The children adopted the lamb and eagerly monitored its growth. They wrote reports and essays on his character and development while the lamb happily slept through it all at the back of the classroom. The school closed in 1971 – like countless other village schools around the country, another victim of increasing social upheaval.

The school may have gone, but the pub remains at Coln St Aldwyns – and it was a different story a quarter of a century ago. In 1988, The New Inn was purchased by property developers, who wanted to convert the pub into weekend apartments. There was an immediate outcry in the village. The Coln St Aldwyns Society was set up to raise funds to prevent the unthinkable from becoming a reality.

With the help of several well-known residents, including the novelist Joanna Trollope, the fight began and £100,000 was eventually raised through a series of public events. The battle to rescue The New Inn became a national news story, with journalists and television crews descending on the village. Thankfully, the pub was saved, re-opening to the public in 1991 – and the people of Coln St Aldwyns proved themselves to be a spirited bunch.

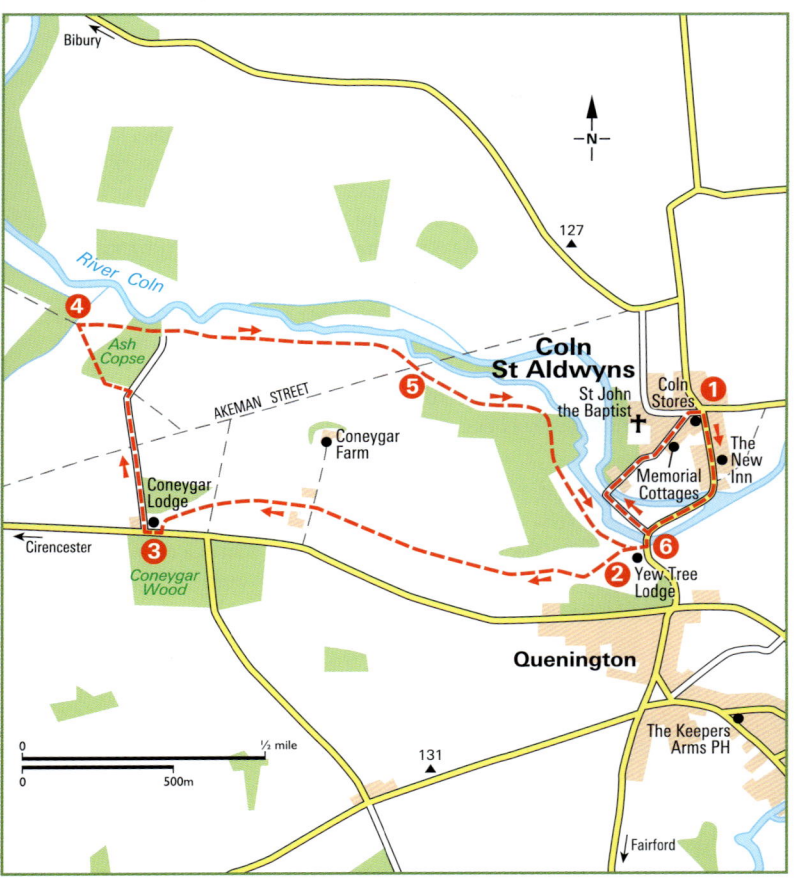

1. From the centre of Coln St Aldwyns, take the road south towards the river. Descend the hill, pass The New Inn and follow the road as it bears right. Head out of the village and along a straight stretch of road. Cross the stone bridge and bear right by Yew Tree Lodge to a meeting point of a footpath and a bridleway.

2. Take the bridleway and follow it ahead, passing a copper beech tree. Begin a steady climb and walk between ash and beech trees. Cross farmland, following a stone wall on the left, and make for a gate ahead in the field corner. Keep ahead on the bridleway, continue through the next boundary and on towards a pair of stone-built houses. Draw level with the houses and on the left is a

converted barn. Go across the next two fields, with trees on the right in the second pasture. Make for a house, and pass through a wooden gate just to the left of it.

3. Exit to the road and turn right. Follow the road for about 40yds (37m) and then turn right by Coneygar Lodge to join a track. Follow it between fields, crossing Akeman Street, a Roman road (no evidence of the route survives on the ground). The track bends right towards Ash Copse, and after 50yds (46m) reaches a junction. Bear left on a woodland path and follow it as it gradually descends to a gate beyond which is a meadow. Drop down to a footbridge, but do not cross it.

4. Instead turn sharp right, almost going back on yourself, and make for a gate in the trees and a footpath sign. Follow a stony track with Ash Copse on your right, go through a galvanized gate and cross meadows, with the River Coln meandering through the countryside to your left. Pass through another gate and at the end of the next field bear right away from the river, following the obvious path.

5. Walk beside extensive woodland, with the tower of the Church of St John the Baptist peeping between the trees. Follow the path into woodland, make for a gate on the far side of the trees and enter a meadow. The houses and cottages of Coln St Aldwyns can be seen across on the opposite bank. Keep woodland over to the right as you continue ahead on the path and return to Yew Tree Lodge.

6. At the road swing left, cross the bridge again and then turn immediately left along a drive. Follow it to the entrance to Upper Mill and turn right, across a bridge over the mill-race. Follow the path uphill and continue on a lane, passing the entrance to the church. At the next junction keep right and return to the centre of the village.

Where to eat and drink
Tea and coffee are served at Coln Community Stores in Coln St Aldwyns, while the nearby New Inn offers a range of traditional pub food, restaurant meals, a sun terrace and garden.

What to see
Near the Church of St John the Baptist is a row of dwellings known as Memorial Cottages. They were built in 1946 by Michael John Aldwyn, the 2nd Earl St Aldwyn, in memory of his grandmother, Lady Lucy, using materials from the demolished Soane wing of Williamstrip Park. Before World War II the field where the cottages were built was used to graze a Shetland pony that pulled one of the small carriages Lady Lucy used to ride in.

While you're there
Nearby Cirencester is the most historic of Cotswold market towns. It is also one of the most beautiful towns in the region, with a wonderful church and lines of town houses dating from the 15th century.

AROUND HAZLETON AND SALPERTON PARK

DISTANCE/TIME	4.5 miles (7.2km) / 2hrs 15min
ASCENT/GRADIENT	360ft (110m) / ▲
PATHS	Fields (muddy after ploughing), tracks and lanes
LANDSCAPE	Open wold, small valley, broad views and villages
SUGGESTED MAP	OS Explorer OL45 The Cotswolds
START/FINISH	Grid reference: SP080179
DOG FRIENDLINESS	Off leads over long, empty stretches of land unless requested otherwise by signs
PARKING	Roadside parking in Hazleton
PUBLIC TOILETS	None on route

Hazleton has a strictly rural feel to it. This little village lies on the wool-trading trail linking Chipping Campden, to the north, with the southern Cotswolds. More significantly, it is situated on the route of the ancient Salt Way, which linked the salt workings in Droitwich with the most convenient, navigable point of the Thames at Lechlade, from where the salt could be transported to London.

Much of the Cotswolds is linked to clichéd images of impossibly pretty cottages with roses around the door, sleepy pubs and lazy cricket matches, and while that picture is not entirely fanciful, it tends to miss the fact that the area is also characterised by gently undulating hills, or 'wolds' – a Saxon word for open downland. The fields crossed on this walk are exceptionally stony, even by Cotswolds standards. Studying them at close quarters, you can understand why medieval farmers favoured rearing sheep to the cultivation of crops. It is easy now to see the nature of wold country: small, sleek hills that five centuries ago would have been grazed by sheep producing wool that was the most highly prized in Europe.

Hazleton's St Andrew's Church, near the start of the walk, is well worth a look, with its Norman doorway and 13th-century font. The church was substantially restored by James Medland between 1864 and 1866. The church tower, dating back to about 1721, contains one of 5,000 bells made at the nearby Gloucester foundry.

The walk's next church, All Saints in Salperton Park, is deep in Cotswold Hunt country, is also worthy of inspection. It has a number of striking features. The most unusual of these, seen to the right as you enter, is a wall-painting of a dancing skeleton wielding a scythe. There are also interesting monuments to the Browne family. The church is set in the 2,000-acre (810ha) estate of Salperton Park, a 17th-century manor house designed by Richard Pace. The parkland is noted for its partridge shooting, a reputation helped by the quality of its beautiful combes, steep banks and secluded valleys.

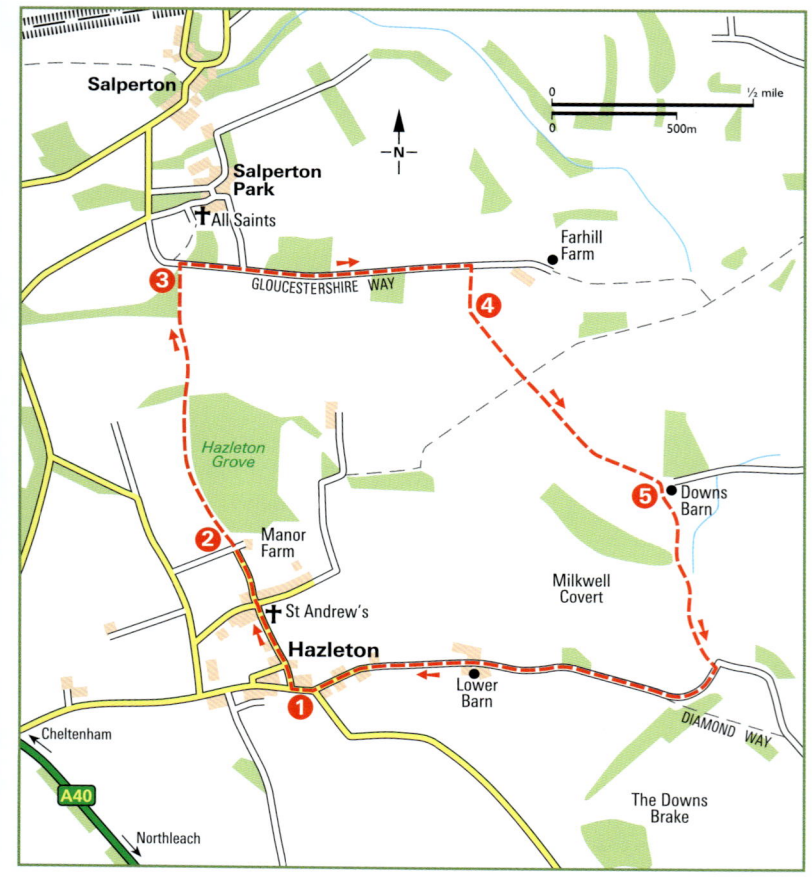

1. The walk begins in the southern part of Hazleton, near the barn conversions at Priors Range, formerly Priory Farm (the part you will reach first if approaching from the A40). Look for a signpost to St Andrew's Church and take the lane, down then up, which passes to the left of the church. Leave the village and church behind by continuing on the lane, to reach a junction. Cross this to join an obvious track opposite.

2. Remain on the track to pass to the left of a Manor Farm, crossing a drive and then finding yourself in fields with woodland to your right. Keep going in the same direction, and beyond the trees the route strides out across remote, open farmland to a gate carved with 'Salperton.' Go through and along a broad, walled track to a lane.

3. The walk continues along the lane to the right, but to visit Salperton's church, turn left over a cattle grid, then take the gated driveway immediately to the right. The church stands just a few paces from Salperton Park. The main route turns eastwards along the lane for 0.75 miles (1.2km). Where the hedge on your right comes to an end, about 200yds (183m) before a barn, turn right into a field and walk straight across it to a gap in the boundary.

4. Go through this and bear half left to another gap leading into the neighbouring field. The right of way runs diagonally across it, but crops may necessitate you skirting the field by keeping to the right-hand perimeter. In the corner turn left and follow the boundary to the point where a marked bridleway crosses your route. Several paces beyond it pass through a gap in the wall on the right and follow the obvious path through the crops to the next perimeter wall. Turn left to walk along the edge of the field, with the wall on your right-hand side. At the bottom turn right by some trees onto a track and walk to the right of Downs Barn.

5. Continue to a gate and down a track. At the point where fields rise up to the right, bear left to a gate. Go through into the field and follow its right margin, with a stream running beside you, for about 0.25 miles (400m) to reach a junction of paths and tracks. Pass through a gate and go through the first gate on the right, following a bridleway. Stay on the track, eventually passing through the farmyard of Lower Barn. Continue on the rough farm lane, following it uphill and back into Hazleton. St Andrew's Church can be glimpsed over on the right as you reach the village.

Where to eat and drink
Neither village has a pub, but there are choices near by. Across the A40 and visit Northleach, where there are two pubs, the Wheatsheaf Inn and the Sherborne Arms and a decent café in The Old Prison.

What to see
The Gloucestershire Way, met near Salperton and followed for part of the walk, stretches for 100 miles (161km) from Chepstow in Wales, eastwards to Stow-on-the-Wold, then northwest to Tewkesbury. It takes its theme from F W Harvey's poem, *A Song of Gloucestershire*.

While you're there
Northeast of Salperton, close to the A436, is Notgrove Long Barrow. Much of it has been removed over the centuries, but enough survives for you to gain an impression of its original size and appearance.

21 EXPLORING THE AMPNEYS

DISTANCE/TIME	10 miles (16.1km) / 4hrs
ASCENT/GRADIENT	320ft (97m) / ▲
PATHS	Fields, lanes, tracks; plenty of stiles
LANDSCAPE	Generally level fields and villages in all directions
SUGGESTED MAP	OS Explorer 169 Cirencester & Swindon
START/FINISH	Grid reference: SU099965
DOG FRIENDLINESS	Lead required near livestock, but plenty of stretches without, be careful on roads
PARKING	Down Ampney village
PUBLIC TOILETS	None on route

Ralph Vaughan Williams is considered by many to be England's greatest composer. He was born in 1872 in Down Ampney, where his father was vicar, spending the first three years of his life in the Old Vicarage. He studied music in London at the Royal College of Music with Parry, Stanford and Wood – the leading British musicians of the day – before studying in Berlin with Bruch and later in Paris with Ravel. This experience gave him the confidence to tackle large-scale works, many of which were based on English folk songs, which he had begun to collect in 1903. But Vaughan Williams was also interested in early English liturgical music, the result of which was his 'Fantasia on a Theme' by Thomas Tallis (1910) for strings, which combines the English lyrical, pastoral tradition with the stricter demands of early formal composition. Vaughan Williams went on to compose several symphonies, as well as a ballet based on the ideas of William Blake, and an opera based on *The Pilgrim's Progress* by John Bunyan. There were several sacred works, too, including a Mass and the Revelation oratorio. He also composed the atmospheric score for the film *Scott of the Antarctic* (1948). One of his best-known hymn tunes is 'Down Ampney' (1906), named in tribute to his birthplace. For many, however, Vaughan Williams is associated with two pieces in particular. The first is his version of 'Greensleeves' (1928), the song said to have been originally composed by Henry VIII; and the second is 'The Lark Ascending' (1914), the soaring work for violin and orchestra. He died in London in 1958.

There are four Ampneys altogether. Down Ampney church is the finest, and definitely worth a visit. It's crowned by a 14th-century spire and contains several interesting effigies. Next to the church is Down Ampney House, a 15th-century manor house that was remodelled by Sir John Soane. Next is Ampney St Mary, which is interesting because its original site was abandoned, leaving the little church you see today. The prettiest of the villages is Ampney Crucis, which takes its name from the 14th-century cross in the churchyard. The head of the cross was only rediscovered in 1854, having been secreted in the church, probably to protect it from Puritan zealots in the 16th or 17th century.

Your route visits the fourth Ampney, Ampney St Peter, whose church also has some interesting features, including a Sheela-na-gig (a carving of a naked female that is a relic of pagan folk customs) and a yawning figure under the eaves above a blocked doorway.

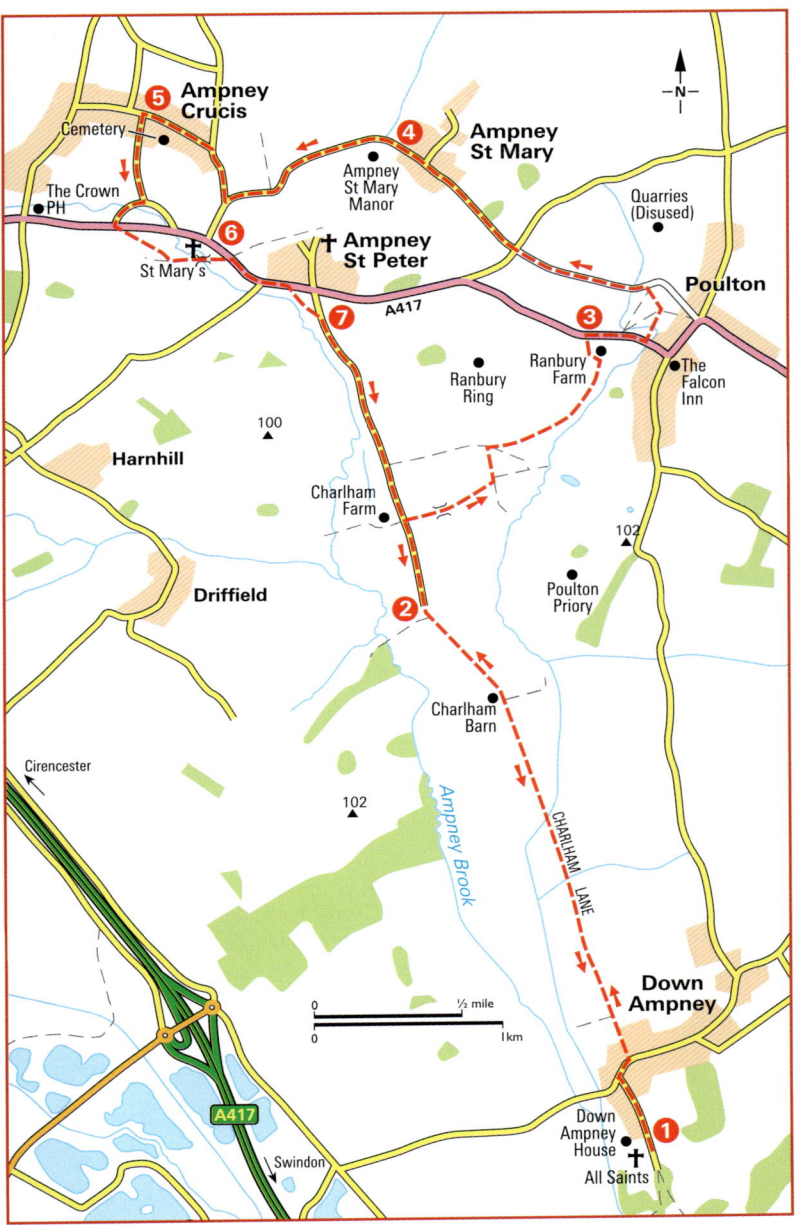

1. From the church, walk to the centre of the village. At the main road turn right and, after 130yds (119m), turn left along Charlham Lane. Pass through a gate onto a public bridleway and continue along the edge of three fields and across a fourth.

2. Join a grassy track to Charlham Farm House, passing outbuildings and barns on your left and going through a gate to a wooded area ahead. When you eventually arrive at Charlham Farm House, turn right into a field, and on the far side cross a ditch on the left into another field. Cross diagonally left to a gap and turn left onto a track. At a corner, turn right to join a bridleway. Go past houses to a road.

3. Cross over to the pavement and turn right. After 320yds (293m), turn sharp left along a grassy track, then in 30yds (27m) turn right by a Thames Water facility. Enter a field and walk diagonally across it, veering left down the slope when you come to the bushes at the top, to a stone stile in hedgerow to the right of the gate. Turn left along a track to a junction. Follow the lane opposite through Ampney St Mary.

4. Go through the village and and pass Ampney St Mary Manor on your left. Continue along the lane for approximately 0.75 miles (1.2km) to a junction. Go right and then next left into Ampney Crucis.

5. About 75yds (69m) after the cemetery on the left, turn left down a lane. At the bottom turn right to a main road. Cross to a stile. Enter a field and go round the edge of the field on the left for about 400yds (366m) until you see the river on your left. Shortly after this, look for the gap in the trees with a path leading to a bridge and the churchyard of Ampney St Mary. Walk round the right-hand edge of the churchyard and meet the road.

6. Cross over to the pavement and turn right, pass a lane, then carefully cross over once more for a bridleway that heads diagonally left across a small open field beside the road. Aim just to the left of a house on the far side and join a lane.

7. Turn right and stay on this lane as it becomes a track. From this point you retrace your steps to Down Ampney and your starting point.

Where to eat and drink
There are two pubs near the route, The Crown in Ampney Crucis, and The Falcon Inn, just off the route when you get to Poulton. Continue along the road at Point 3 and turn right.

AROUND CUTSDEAN AND FORD

DISTANCE/TIME	6 miles (9.7km) / 2hrs 30min
ASCENT/GRADIENT	516ft (157m) / ▲
PATHS	Tracks, fields and lane, several stiles
LANDSCAPE	Open wold, farmland, village
SUGGESTED MAP	OS Explorer OL45 The Cotswolds
START/FINISH	Grid reference: SP088302
DOG FRIENDLINESS	Best on leads – lots of livestock, as well as horses
PARKING	On street in Cutsdean village centre
PUBLIC TOILETS	None on route

One theory about the origin of the name 'cotswold' names Cutsdean as the source. Today, it is a small and pretty village on the high wolds above the beginnings of the River Windrush. However, it may once have been the seat of an Anglo-Saxon chief by the name of 'Cod'. His domain would have been his 'dene', and the hilly region in which his domain lay, his 'wolds'.

This is plausible, even if there is no verifiable record of a King Cod. Another explanation concerns the sheep that still graze many hillsides in the Cotswolds, a 'cot' referring to a sheep pen and 'wolds' being the hills that support them. (In Old English a 'cot' is also a small dwelling or cottage.)

Whatever the truth of the matter, the sheep remain, even if the species that in the Middle Ages produced the finest wool in Europe dwindled to the point of extinction. The ancestors of the so-called Cotswold Lion probably arrived with the Romans, who valued the sheep for their milk and their long, dense wool. The nature of the Cotswolds was perfect for these sheep – the limestone soil produces a calcium-rich diet, good for strong bone growth, and the open, wind-blasted wolds suited this heavy-fleeced breed, able to graze all year long on herbs and grasses. The hills teemed with Cotswold sheep; at one point the Cotswold wool trade accounted for half of England's income. It is believed that the medieval Cotswold sheep differed a little from its modern counterpart. Its coat was undoubtedly long and lustrous, but it may have been slightly shorter than that of its descendants.

Why, then, did the fortunes of this miraculous animal plummet? To some extent this is a misconception, since serious decline occurred only with the move to arable farming in the Cotswolds in the mid-20th century. Demand for the wool was still strong in the 18th and 19th centuries and the Cotswold was also prized for its meat and its cross-breeding potential. However, the market for long-stapled wool began to decline in favour of finer wool, and crop growing became more attractive to local farmers. Incredibly, by the 1960s, there remained only some 200 animals. It was suddenly clear that a living piece of English history was on the verge of extinction. The Cotswold Breed Society was reconvened and steps taken to ensure the sheep's survival.

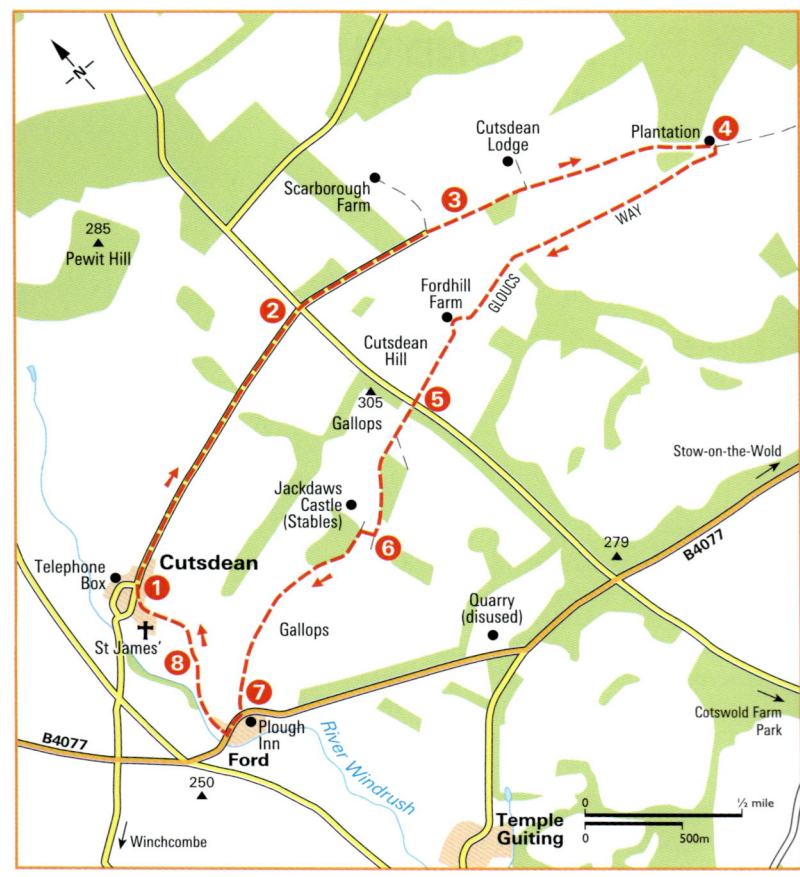

1. Walk up either of the two streets in the village centre. The church is partly hidden behind houses back to your right, and on the left is a telephone box. After the roads converge, go on past Stoneley. Continue uphill on this straight country road for just over a mile (1.6km), until you come to a T-junction with another road.

2. Cross this to enter another lane past a 'No Through Road' sign, at the margin of woodland. Beyond a second wood, where the track veers left towards a house, go straight on along a stony track.

3. Continue along the track, passing through a gate, until you reach woodland to the right. Shortly after the woods, go through a gate, ignoring a footpath to the left at the brow of the hill. Instead, follow the path along a stone wall to your left, and keep to the path. Then, halfway across a large field (look for the marker post on the left) the path goes diagonally right over the brow of a slope to head for a plantation.

4. Emerging beyond the plantation, turn immediately right at a track junction and right again, the plantation is now on your right. Follow this track for 1.5 miles (2.4km), passing through Fordhill Farm, all the way to a road.

5. Across the road, go through a gate signed 'Jackdaws Castle', and follow a tarmac lane that runs to the left of gallops used for training racehorses. Keep straight on where the track forks left into a neighbouring field.

6. Soon after passing the stables of Jackdaws Castle on your right, turn sharp right at a footpath sign across the gallops area (watch out for horses) to join a tarmac track, where you turn left. The track descends gently for 0.75 miles (1.2km), with the gallops and greensward to your left. Keep descending until you reach the bottom, via a stile, and arrive at the village of Ford. The welcoming Plough Inn is directly in front of you.

7. Turn right, along the road and at a bend in the road turn right again to cross a driveway, to a stile. Cross the stile and walk along a grassy path, with a post and rail fence to your right, and a stream in a valley to your left. Pass through a gate and follow the path ahead as it leaves the fence and then descends through the copse to a kissing gate.

8. Go through the gate into a field, and then go slightly right across it. Go down a bank, across a boggy area via a raised boardwalk, and up the bank on the other side to a kissing gate. Cross into a field and turn left along the side of the field towards Cutsdean. Pass to the right of the church, which sits back across a wall to your left. At the edge of the village come to a kissing gate. Go through this to join a path. This emerges onto the main street through the village, and your starting point.

Where to eat and drink
The route passes the old and attractive Plough Inn in Ford. It serves Donnington's, the local beer brewed in a lakeside brewery near Stow-on-the-Wold. The nearest towns with a greater choice of eateries are Winchcombe and Stow.

What to see
The countryside is covered in gallops, earthy tracks where racehorses can be exercised in safety. You'll also notice a large number of jumps, like the hurdles at a proper racecourse.

While you're there
The Cotswold Farm Park is a short drive to the south. It is one of the few places in Britain where you can still see native breeds of domestic animals and birds, many of which have been brought close to extinction by developments in farming practice. There is a café and a shop.

STANTON AND STANWAY FROM SNOWSHILL

DISTANCE/TIME	7 miles (11.3km) / 2hrs 45min
ASCENT/GRADIENT	1,252ft (381m) / ▲▲▲
PATHS	Tracks, estate grassland and pavements, several stiles
LANDSCAPE	High grassland, open wold, wide-ranging views and villages
SUGGESTED MAP	OS Explorer OL45 The Cotswolds
START/FINISH	Grid reference: SP096341
DOG FRIENDLINESS	On lead – livestock on most parts of walk, but more freedom in enclosed lanes and woodland
PARKING	Pipers Grove car park just north of Snowshill village
PUBLIC TOILETS	None on route

Villages in the Cotswolds have not always been prosperous. Many, like Stanton and Snowshill, were owned by great abbeys, and passed to private landlords after the Dissolution. Subsistence farmers were edged out by short leases and enclosure of fields. Villagers who had farmed their own strips of land became labourers. The number of small farmers decreased dramatically and, with the onset of the Industrial Revolution, so too did the demand for labour. Cheaper food flooded in from overseas and catastrophic harvests compounded the problem. People left the countryside in droves to work in Britain's industrial towns and cities. Cotswold villages, once at the core of the woollen industry in medieval Europe, gradually became impoverished backwaters, but the villages themselves resisted decay. Unlike villages in many other parts of Britain, their buildings were made of stone. Landlords who cherished their innate beauty turned them into restoration projects.

The three villages encountered on this walk are living reminders of this process. Snowshill, together with Stanton, was once owned by Winchcombe Abbey. In 1539, it became the property of Henry VIII's sixth wife, Catherine Parr. The manor house was transformed into the estate's administrative centre and remained in the Parr family until 1919. The estate was then bought by Charles Wade, who restored the house and amassed an extraordinary collection of art and artefacts, which he subsequently bequeathed to the National Trust. Now forming the basis of a museum, his collection – from Japanese armour to farm machinery – is of enormous appeal.

Next on this walk comes Stanway, a small hamlet at the centre of a large estate owned by the Earl of Wemyss. The most striking feature here is the magnificent gatehouse to the Jacobean Stanway House, a gem of Cotswold architecture built around 1630. The village of Stanton comes last on this walk. It was rescued from decay in 1906 by architect Sir Philip Stott, who bought and restored Stanton Court and much of the 16th-century village.

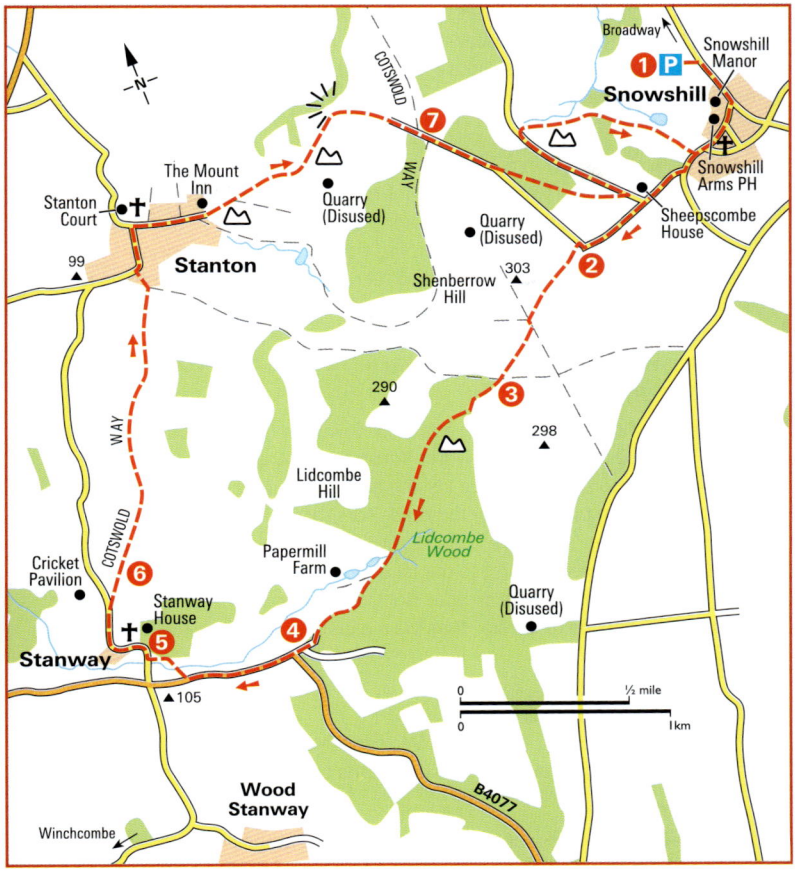

1. From the car park walk into Snowshill village, descending to the right at a Y-junction past Snowshill Manor on your right, and the church on your left. After a 0.25-mile (400m) climb, turn right down a lane signed 'Sheepscombe House'. After another 0.25 miles (400m), at a right-hand bend on the crest of the hill, turn left up to a gate and a field.

2. Go slightly right beside a fence up to a wall gap. In the next field go slightly right to the far corner and left along a track. Take the second track on the right through a gate into a field and walk slightly left to another gate. Cross straight ahead through the field to another gate, onto a track.

3. Ignoring the footpath to your right, walk down a stony track with a wood on your right. After 275yds (251m), fork right onto a stony track, veering right just before a stone barn. The track descends steeply through Lidcombe Wood. After 0.5 miles (800m), where it flattens out, a farm comes into view across fields to the right, after which the track bears left uphill. Continue straight along the track, which becomes a narrow footpath, to a road.

4. Walk along the pavement, and after 500yds (457m) turn right through a gate into a small orchard. Walk slightly left across this, bearing slightly right, to arrive at a kissing gate. Go through this and walk with a high wall to your right to reach a road.

5. Turn right and pass the impressive entrance to Stanway House and Stanway Church, both on your right. Follow the road as it bends right. Shortly after another entrance to Stanway House, turn right through a gate opposite a thatched cricket pavilion. Go slightly left to another gate, and in the next large field go slightly right.

6. Now walk all the way into Stanton, following the regular and clear waymarkers of the Cotswold Way. After 1 mile (1.6km), you will arrive at a gate at the edge of Stanton. Turn left along a lane to a junction. Turn right here and walk through the village, turning right at the war memorial. Walk straight on, passing the stone cross and then another footpath. Climb up to pass to the right of The Mount Inn. Beyond it, walk up a steep, shaded path to a gate. Then walk straight up the hill on a stony track (ignoring a path to the right after a few paces). Climb all the way to the top to meet a lane, passing through two gates.

7. Ignore the 'Cotswold Way' sign and walk down the lane for 250yds (229m), then turn left by a sign for Littleworth Wood. Follow the main path through the trees. At the bottom go through a kissing gate, continuing across the field to a kissing gate in the far corner by the road. Pass through, turn left and walk for 600yds (549m). Approaching a cottage, turn right through a gate into a scrubby field. Descend via steps at first to the far side and turn right through a gate into trees. Continue to a stile on your right, cross it and turn left. Follow the bottom of the hillside to a track, then via a gate back into Snowshill.

Where to eat and drink
The Snowshill Arms pub is next to Snowshill Manor and serves food daily, as does The Mount Inn at Stanton before the climb back to the start.

What to see
The thatched pavilion was presented to Stanway at the beginning of the 20th century by J M Barrie, creator of *Peter Pan*. The famous writer was a keen cricketer and a regular visitor to Stanway House.

While you're there
The museum at Snowshill Manor (National Trust) is more like a fantastical toy shop. The entrance is on the Broadway road. Stanway House (privately owned) has restricted opening hours, but is similarly worth a visit.

STANTON, LAVERTON AND BUCKLAND

DISTANCE/TIME	3.75 miles (6km) / 1hr 30min
ASCENT/GRADIENT	295ft (90m) / ▲
PATHS	Track, grassland, pavement, several stiles
LANDSCAPE	Grassland, wold, wide-ranging views, villages
SUGGESTED MAP	OS Explorer OL45 The Cotswolds
START/FINISH	Grid reference: SP067343
DOG FRIENDLINESS	Livestock throughout, especially horses, so dogs should be on leads
PARKING	Car park in front of Stanton village club
PUBLIC TOILETS	None on route

Stanton was rescued from oblivion in 1906 by the architect Sir Philip Stott, who bought and restored Stanton Court, as well as many of the village's 16th-century houses. The church, on a lane leading from the market cross, has two pulpits – one dating from the 14th century, the other Jacobean – and a west gallery added by the Victorian restorer Sir Ninian Comper. John Wesley, the founder of Methodism, preached his message here in 1733. Stanton has regularly been used as a location in period dramas for television and cinema.

Laverton is a large hamlet with many fine examples of Cotswold vernacular stone architecture. Buckland, though smaller, is a village with two particularly interesting buildings. The 15th-century rectory is the oldest medieval parsonage in Gloucestershire still in use. Although it can be admired only from the street, it has some fine stained glass and a timbered great hall, and was often used as a base by John Wesley. Handsome Buckland Manor is now a hotel, while the neighbouring church contains medieval glass restored by William Morris, and a painted panel originally in Hailes Abbey, 5 miles (8km) to the south.

Methodism, the largest of the Protestant free churches of Britain, originated among a group of devout 18th-century Oxford students under the influence of two brothers, John and Charles Wesley. As the name suggests, it is a radical and earnest creed, which arose out of dissatisfaction with the inadequacies of the established Church. The disillusionment of John Wesley, in particular, was fostered by a missionary voyage to the American colonies in 1738.

From then on he believed that he was destined to spread his beliefs – based on the idea of self-regeneration through faith, prayer and doing good works – across Britain. He travelled about the country preaching first in churches, then, as bishops and churchmen became uneasy and banned him from the pulpit, at large, outdoor gatherings. His direct and 'methodical' approach clearly met with the approval of many a despairing congregation, and in 1795 the movement, popular especially among the marginalised, lower ranks of society, was strong enough to secede from the Church of England.

This was not enough for some, and the Methodist movement fragmented into splinters of varying degrees of moderation or severity. By 1932, however, most branches had rejoined the fold, and as recorded in 2020, the modern Methodist Church had 164,000 active members in Britain. In some ways this modest number does not reflect the level of shock and concern that the movement engendered among the Establishment of 18th-century Britain.

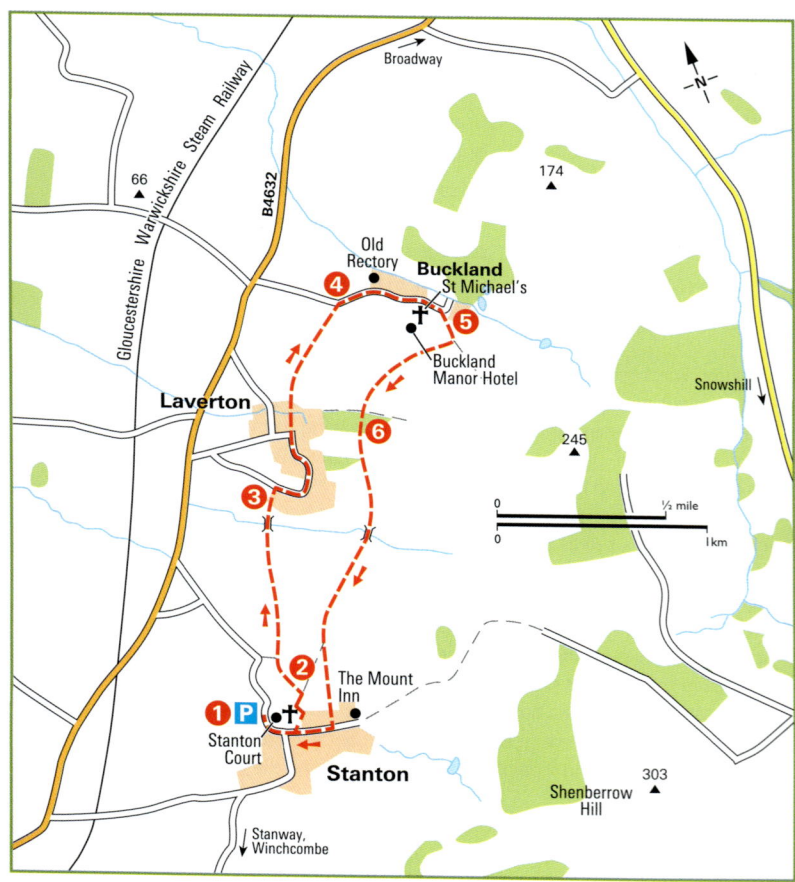

1. From the car park, turn right and then left into the village by the war memorial plaque. Turn left at Stanton village cross and head for the churchyard. Go through a gate into the churchyard, pass to the right of the church, and in the corner turn right along an alley.

2. At the end, turn left just before a double gate, and follow an enclosed path to a kissing gate. Follow the left-hand margin of the field, heading towards a kissing gate in a hedge gap. Go through and turn slightly right to pass stables to your left. Go through another gate, and at the next corner go through a gate, over a footbridge and through successive gates to walk to a stile. Cross the stile and walk ahead to another, just to the left of the field corner and continue, crossing a third stile, towards Laverton.

3. Go over a stile and at the road turn right. Follow the road through Laverton as it goes left, left again and then right. At a junction beside a tree with a seat, cross over to enter a firm bridleway and follow this all the way to the main street of Buckland.

4. Bear right and walk through the village, passing the Old Rectory on your left-hand side (shortly after a telephone box and a public footpath sign) and then the church to the right. At the top, where the road curves left, go straight on to come to a kissing gate (to the right of a field gate).

5. Go through to a field and turn right. Pass Buckland Manor on the right and go through another two kissing gates.

6. Continue along the contour path to go through a gate and continue straight on. Pass through some trees to a kissing gate. Continue on the same line, passing through successive gates and over a footbridge between kissing gates. Continue roughly along the contour through a large field on the flank of the hill. Follow the prominent waymarkers and, after 0.25 miles (400m), cross a stile beside a gate and go straight ahead for another 0.25 miles (400m), partly through trees, to another stile. Cross this and go straight on, ignoring the path descending slightly right towards the church, until you come to a stile at the edge of Stanton. Cross over this third stile and bear right onto a drive that becomes a lane into Stanton village. Turn right through the village to return to the village hall car park.

Where to eat and drink
There is one pub on the route – The Mount Inn in Stanton, which serves local beer and good food. Otherwise, the nearest centres are either Winchcombe or Broadway.

What to see
In Stanton, look for the dates and initials carved on the walls of some cottages, indicating the time of their construction and the name of the stonemason. Look too for Stanton Court, a Jacobean house that was owned and lived in by the saviour of the village, Sir Philip Stott.

While you're there
Snowshill Manor (National Trust), in the neighbouring village of Snowshill, is filled with Japanese armour, musical instruments, farm implements, clocks and toys, and is definitely worth a visit. Stanway House (privately owned but with limited summer opening) in the nearby village of Stanway, is the centre of a large estate owned by the Earl of Wemyss. The most striking feature of Stanway is the magnificent gatehouse to Stanway House, a gem of Cotswold architecture built c.1630 by Timothy Strong of Barrington. Stanway House itself is an outstanding example of a Jacobean manor house.

AROUND CHEDWORTH ROMAN VILLA

DISTANCE/TIME	4.5 miles (7.2km) / 2hrs
ASCENT/GRADIENT	310ft (94m) / ▲
PATHS	Tracks, lanes, fields and woodland; several stiles
LANDSCAPE	Meadows, streams, woods and shallow valleys
SUGGESTED MAP	OS Explorer OL45 The Cotswolds
START/FINISH	Grid reference: SP052121
DOG FRIENDLINESS	Plenty of quiet lanes and tracks
PARKING	Parking area in front of Chedworth Church (restricted to congregation during services)
PUBLIC TOILETS	None on route

The subject of this walk, Chedworth Roman Villa, sits in a secluded wooded stretch of the Coln Valley, protected from the elements and with a good supply of water – the spring later fed a temple to a water goddess. Despite our usual perception of a historically densely wooded Britain, the villa would have stood in open countryside. Originally, Chedworth was one of about 50 villas in the Cotswold region, and one of nine in a 5-mile (8km) radius; it was only discovered in 1864.

The Romans invaded Britain in AD 43 and appeared to have brought the area that is now Gloucestershire under their power within four years. The area west of the Fosse Way remained under military alert for another decade, but by AD 60 the Romans were established as rulers.

The process of colonisation was a long one, but by the early part of the 2nd century AD the Romans and their subjects, known as the 'Romano-British', felt sufficiently at ease to begin the construction of small, timber-framed villas in the valleys of the Cotswold escarpment. Later villas would be built of stone.

The Roman villa at Chedworth dates from about AD 120 and is open daily from mid-February to the end of November. Although it was eventually the home of a well-to-do family – probably native people who had thrown in their lot with the new rulers – in its earliest days it functioned primarily as a farmhouse. The surrounding land was used for cultivating crops and raising animals.

Two hundred years later Chedworth was transformed to reflect the wealth and status of a rich family. Steam baths were added and the common rooms were enlarged. Its beautiful mosaic floors were laid down in the last part of the 4th century AD, made by craftsmen from Cirencester. They include one in the villa's west wing where figures illustrating the four seasons are seen in each corner.

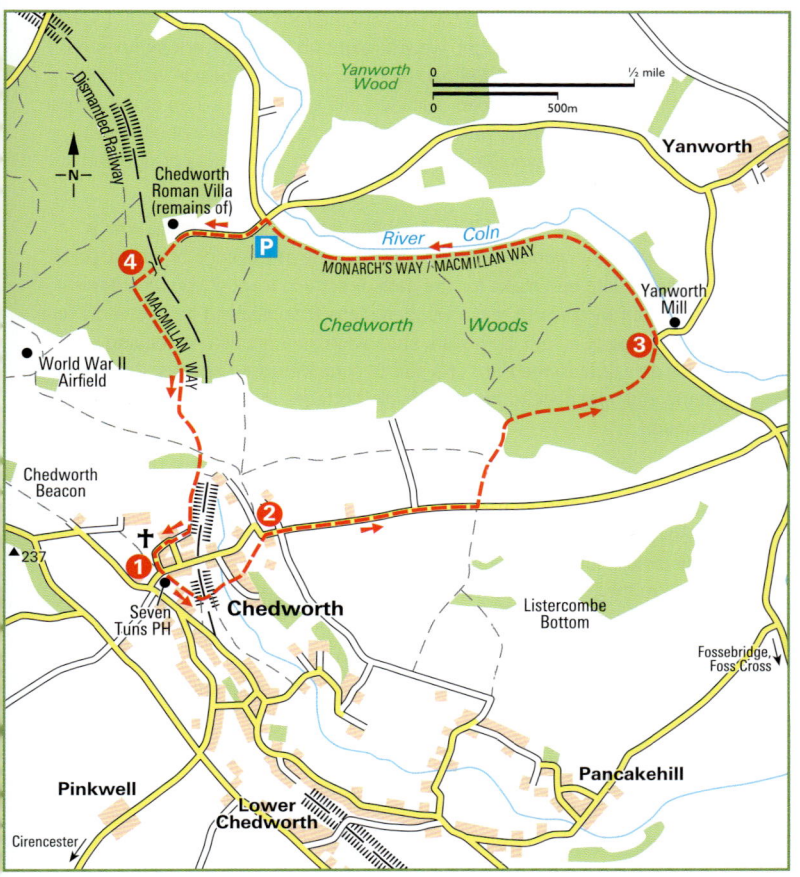

1. From Chedworth Church, surrounded by steep valleys and glorious Cotswold folds, drop down on to the path opposite the parking area and go through a gate to the right of the Seven Tuns pub. Beyond the stables behind the pub, enter a field via a stile and head for a second stile in the far corner. Just a dozen or so paces further, another stile takes you left, through trees and over the line of the long-dismantled railway. On the other side of it, bear left to reach a stile on your right. Go over it into a field and walk down this to cross another stile. Cross a stream via stone slabs, then bear left up to a lane. Cross it and then, keeping left of the cottages, go up to a gate. Go on up the field to another gate and walk along a path ahead, passing through two more gates to arrive at a lane.

2. Turn right here and walk along the lane for 0.5 miles (800m), passing barns on the left. When you reach a point where there are footpaths to the left and right, turn left into a field and walk dead ahead, passing just left of a tree and avoiding a left-hand path. Continue to the edge of woodland and follow a track through the woods for 550yds (503m). Then, at a wooden footpath sign, go diagonally left up to a track and keep right. After 40yds (36m) bear left on a path that will soon bring you down to a road.

3. Turn left here and, at a sharp corner, with the former Yanworth Mill (now Woodside Cottages) to your right, walk straight on along a track signposted 'Roman villa – footpath only'. Follow the track, much of it beside woodland, until it comes to an end at a road. Turn left and walk on to arrive at the Roman villa. Carry on past the villa, with its main entrance and nearby buildings clearly seen, and enter woodland. Pass beneath an old railway bridge and within 150yds (137m) reach a crossroads of tracks.

4. Turn left here (on the Macmillan Way) and follow the main track until it takes you out of the woods, bringing you to a gate at the edge of a field. Go to the top of this field and make for the gate directly in front of you. Avoid the stile on the left by trees to reach wooden steps that descend quite steeply to a stile at the edge of a field. Now walk ahead across this pasture, making your way towards a stile to the right of a pair of semi-detached houses. Cross this and follow the lane back to the church and cottages in Chedworth where the walk began.

Where to eat and drink
The Seven Tuns in Chedworth (closed on Mondays) is a delightful and highly picturesque pub, facing a bubbling stream in the shadow of the church. At the Roman villa there's a National Trust shop and café selling snacks and drinks. You'll also find pubs at Fossebridge and Foss Cross.

What to see
Early in the walk you will cross a clearly artificial embankment; later, in the woods beyond the Roman villa, you will pass under a bridge arch. Both are relics from the old Cheltenham–Swindon railway line which operated from 1891 until its closure in 1961.

While you're there
Extend the walk after visiting the Roman villa by walking through Chedworth Woods to have a look at the remains of an old disused airfield beyond the trees. This was a Fighter Command base operational from 1942, and from June 1944 was used by the US Air Force.

SOUTH CERNEY AND THE COTSWOLD WATER PARK

DISTANCE/TIME	5 miles (8km) / 2hrs 30min
ASCENT/GRADIENT	145ft (44m) / Negligible
PATHS	Track, towpath and lanes; several stiles
LANDSCAPE	Very flat – lakes, light woodland, canal and village
SUGGESTED MAP	OS Explorer 169 Cirencester & Swindon
START/FINISH	Grid reference: SU048974
DOG FRIENDLINESS	Good, but be aware of waterfowl around the lakes
PARKING	Silver Street, South Cerney
PUBLIC TOILETS	None on route

By their very nature, ancient landscapes and historic architecture evolve very slowly, changing little from one century to the next. In the Cotswolds, this is especially true. Here, building restrictions are strict – even sometimes draconian. The result is a significant area of largely unspoilt English countryside. Sometimes, however, thoughtful development has enhanced the skyline. The Cotswold Water Park, located in and around old gravel pits, is an example of this.

Gravel has been worked in the upper Thames Valley, where the water table is close to the surface, since the 1920s. The removal of gravel leads to the creation of lakes; in the areas around South Cerney and between Fairford and Lechlade there are now some 4,000 acres (1,620ha) of water, in 133 lakes. They provide an important wetland habitat for a variety of wildlife. Most of these lakes have been turned over to recreational use of one sort or another, and are a perfect place for game and coarse fishing, board sailing, walking, boating of various kinds, riding and sundry other leisure activities.

The landscaping has not just been a case of letting nature take over where the gravel excavators left off. The crane-grabs that were used for excavation in the 1960s, for example, left the gravel pits with vertical sides and therefore with deep water right up to the shoreline. Some forms of aquatic life flourish under these conditions, but in other lakes the shoreline has been graded to create a gentler slope, to harmonise better with the flat landscape in this part of the Cotswolds and to suit the needs of swimmers and children. In the same way, trees have been planted and hills have been constructed to offer shelter and visual relief. Old brick railway bridges have been preserved. Finally, a style of waterside architecture has been developed to attract people to live here.

The walk begins in South Cerney, by the River Churn, only 4 miles (6.4km) from the source of the Thames. Look inside the Norman church for the carving on the 12th-century rood. Later, the walk takes you through Cerney Wick, a small village on the other side of the gravel workings. The highlight here is an 18th-century roundhouse, used once by canal workers.

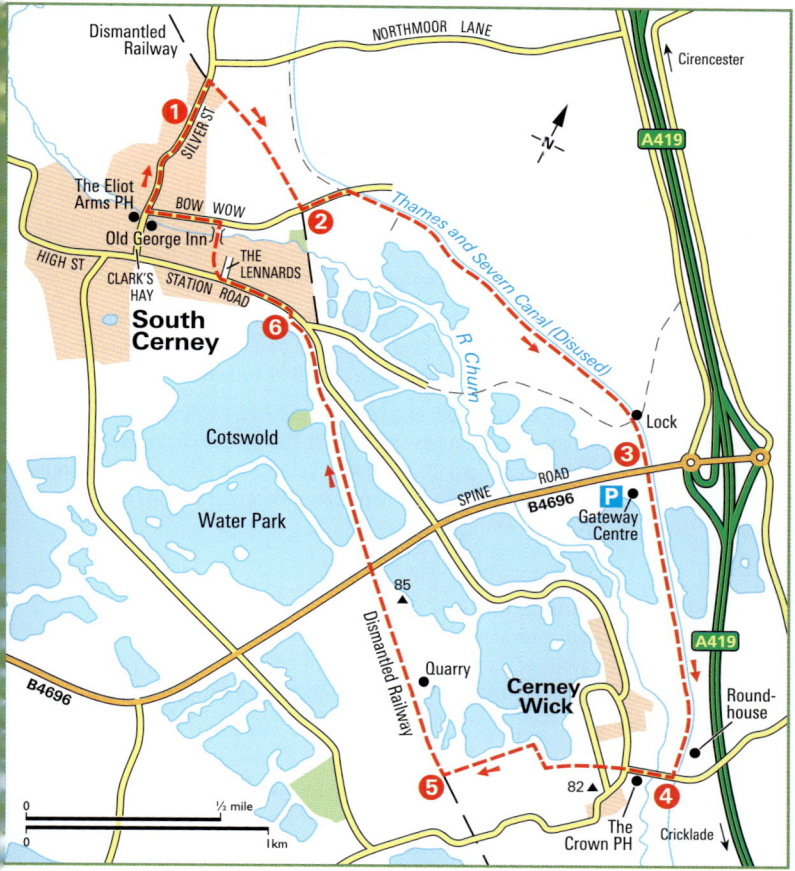

1. From Silver Street walk north out of the village. Just before the turning to Driffield and Cricklade, turn right onto National Cycle Route 45. Stay on this obvious path for 800yds (732m) to reach a brick bridge across the path. Turn right here up a flight of steps to reach a narrow road.

2. Turn left and walk along this for 200yds (183m) until you come to footpaths to the right and left. Turn right along a farm track, following a signpost for Cerney Wick. Almost immediately the shallow, overgrown remains of the Thames and Severn Canal appear to your left. When the track veers right into a farm, walk straight ahead over a stile to follow a path beneath the trees – this is the old canal towpath. Keep going straight ahead through kissing gates as you pass the partly restored Wildmoorway Lower Lock, just before the Spine Road bridge.

3. Continue under the bridge and past the café (with toilets) at the Gateway Centre until the path forks at an information panel. Here you have two choices: either continue on the towpath or take the path that skirts the lakes. If you take the lakeside path, you will eventually be able to rejoin the towpath by going left and over a bridge after 600yds (549m). Continue until, after just under 0.5 miles (800m), you pass an old canal roundhouse across the canal to the left and, soon afterwards, reach a lane at Cerney Wick.

4. Turn right here and walk to the junction at the end of the road, beside The Crown pub. Cross to a stile and enter a field. Walk straight ahead, come to another stile and cross it, aiming to the left of a cottage. Cross the lane, go through a kissing gate and enter a field. Walk ahead and follow the path as it guides you through a kissing gate and across a stile onto the grass by a lake. Walk around the lake, going right and then left. In the corner in front of you, go down steps and cross a footbridge into a field, then walk ahead past a quarry towards trees and go through a kissing gate to a track.

5. Turn right, rejoining the old railway line, and follow it all the way to Spine Road. Cross with care, and continue along National Cycle Route 45. Stay on this all the way to another road and follow a path that runs to its left.

6. Where the path ends at the beginning of South Cerney, continue along Station Road for 400yds (366m). A few paces past The Lennards on your right, turn right up the signposted footpath that takes you across a bridge and brings you to a lane called Bow Wow. Turn left here between streams and return to Silver Street and the start of the route.

Where to eat and drink
The walk passes the attractive waterside Gateway Café near the Spine Road bridge, as well as The Crown pub in Cerney Wick. There are also several pubs in South Cerney, including The Eliot Arms and Old George Inn in Clark's Hay.

What to see
Disused transport systems feature greatly in this walk. For much of it you will be beside or close to the old Thames and Severn Canal, or following the route of the old Andoversford railway line. The line linked Cheltenham and Swindon between 1891 and 1961. The roundhouse seen on the far side of the old canal as you approach Cerney Wick was used by lock-keepers and maintenance engineers. This design was a distinctive feature of the Thames and Severn Canal, and even the windows were rounded to afford the occupants maximum visibility of their stretch of canal. The downstairs would have been used as a stable, the middle storey as a living area and the upstairs held sleeping accommodation. The flat roof was also put to use collecting rainwater for the house's water supply.

THOMAS CROMWELL AND HAILES ABBEY

DISTANCE/TIME	5 miles (8km) / 2hrs 15min
ASCENT/GRADIENT	662ft (202m) / ▲
PATHS	Fields, tracks, farmyard and lanes, several stiles
LANDSCAPE	Wide views, rolling wolds and villages
SUGGESTED MAP	OS Explorer OL45 The Cotswolds
START/FINISH	Grid reference: SP050301
DOG FRIENDLINESS	Mostly on lead as livestock in fields
PARKING	Park at Hailes Church or Abbey only if you are planning to visit them, otherwise park by the road in Didbrook
PUBLIC TOILETS	None on route

In the decade from 1536 to 1547 just about every English religious institution that was not a parish church was either closed or destroyed. This was the Dissolution, Henry VIII's draconian policy to force the Church to give up its wealth. The smaller monasteries went first, then the larger ones and finally the colleges and chantries. All their lands and tithes became Crown property. Many of them were sold off, usually to local landowners. The Church as a parish institution was strengthened as a result of the Dissolution, but at the expense of wider religious life. The suppression of the chantries and guilds meant many people were deprived of a local place of worship.

This abbey was one of the most powerful Cistercian monasteries in the country, owning 13,000 acres (5,265ha) and 8,000 sheep. In 1270, Edmund, Earl of Cornwall, the son of its founder, had given the monastery a phial supposed to contain the blood of Christ. Thomas Cromwell was the King's Commissioner responsible for overseeing the closure of the monasteries. He is reputed to have surveyed the destruction of the monastery from a vantage point near Beckbury Camp. There is still a fine view of the abbey from here, as you should find at Point 5 on the map. According to Hugh Latimer of Worcester, who had been working with him, Cromwell also spent an afternoon in 1539 examining the so-called blood. Cromwell concluded that it was nothing more than an 'unctuous gum and compound of many things'.

The monastery lands were confiscated by the Crown, and then sold to a speculator who sold the land on in lots. In about 1600, the site of the abbey was bought by Sir John Tracy, the builder of Stanway House. The monks were dispersed: a few managed to secure positions as part of the parish clergy, while others took up posts with the cathedrals at Bristol and Gloucester.

Hailes Church is all that remains of the village of Hailes. It predates the abbey and survived the Dissolution, perhaps because it was a parish church and not directly linked to the neighbouring monastery. It has real charm, often overlooked by the many visitors to the monastery's ruins. It has a panelled chancel – floored with tiles from the monastery – and a nave with

14th-century wall paintings. Didbrook Church also survived the upheavals. Built in Perpendicular style, it was rebuilt in 1475 by the Abbot of Hailes, following damage caused by Lancastrian soldiers after the Battle of Tewkesbury.

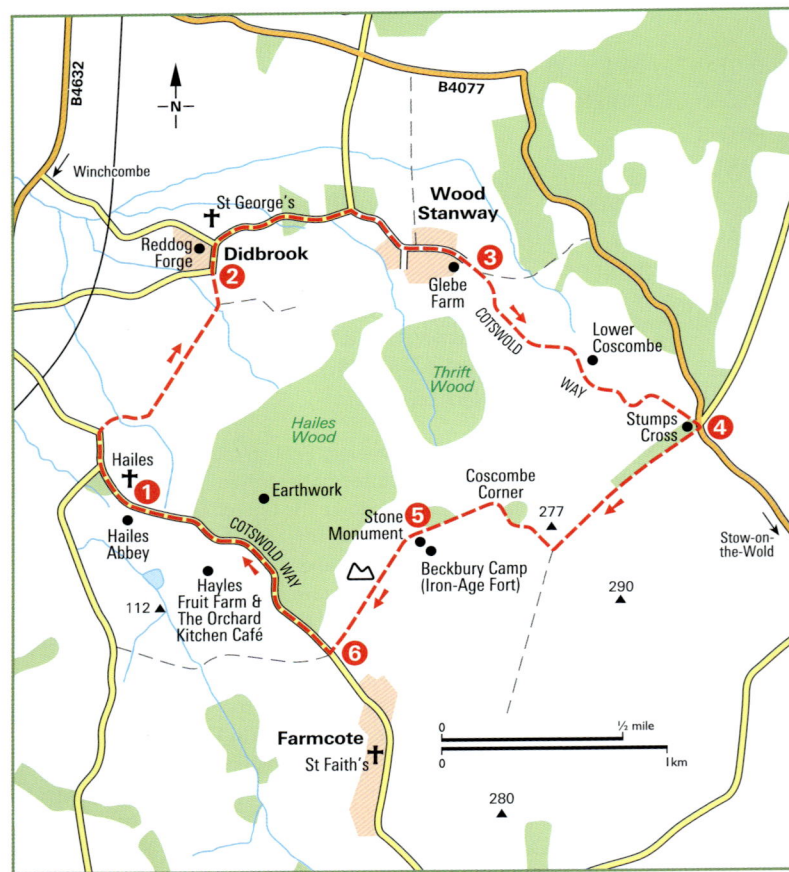

1. From Hailes Church turn right and follow the lane to a left-hand bend 200yds (183m) after a road on the left. Leave the lane through a gate on the right to join a footpath. Walk across an area of concrete and follow a track as it goes right and left, turning at an old oak tree, eventually becoming a grassy path beside a field. At the end go through a kissing gate, and in a few paces turn left over a stile amid bushes, ignoring a gate leading straight on. Cross the corner of the field to reach a gate at a road.

2. Turn right and follow the road as it meanders through the pretty village of Didbrook, and onto a stretch of countryside. At a junction, turn right for Wood Stanway. Walk through this village, bearing left at a cherry tree on a grass island, to reach the yard and barns of Glebe Farm.

3. Ignore a bridleway sign and gate on the left, and at another gate, go onto a track on the left of a field and walk ahead, aiming for a gate on the left. You are now on the Cotswold Way, well marked by posts with black acorn symbols. Cross into a field and go slightly right, keeping to the left of some electricity poles, to a gate in a hedge. Bear slightly left across the next field, heading towards farm buildings. Through a gate turn sharp right, up the slope (guide posts) to a gate on your right. Once through this, turn immediately left up the field to a guide post. Go through a gate. Follow the footpath as it wends its way gently up the slope. At the top, walk along the crest, with a dry stone wall to your right, to reach a gate at a road.

4. Turn right and right again through a gate to a track. Follow this for 0.5 miles (800m), passing through a gate, until at the top (just before some trees) you turn right to follow another track for 50yds (46m). Turn left through a gate into a field and turn sharp right to follow the perimeter of the field as it goes left and passes through a gate beside the ramparts of an Iron Age fort, Beckbury Camp. Continue ahead to pass through another gate, which leads to a stone monument with a niche. According to local lore, it was from here that Thomas Cromwell watched the destruction of Hailes Abbey in 1539.

5. Turn right to follow a steep path down through the trees. At the bottom go slightly left and across down the field to a gate. Pass through, continue down to go through another gate and head down to a gate beside a signpost.

6. Turn right and follow the lane (Cotswold Way). Pass a sign for Hayles Fruit Farm with its café to the left. Continue ahead along the road to return to Hailes Abbey and the start point by the church.

Where to eat and drink
Just near the end of the route is Hayles Fruit Farm. You can pick your own fruit, buy a variety of produce from the shop, or you can have a light meal in the Orchard Kitchen café. Winchcombe is the nearest town, offering many possibilities.

What to see
As you walk through the village of Didbrook, see if the blacksmith at the Reddog Forge is open. In Wood Stanway, the wall of one of the first houses you pass to your left is covered in vines, producing a very healthy looking crop of red grapes in the autumn, even though the English climate tends to favour white grapes.

While you're there
Hailes Abbey is worth a visit and the entrance fee includes an audio guide that explains the layout of the ruins. St Faith's church in Farmcote is another gem, little more than a chapel, but ancient and uplifting. Overlooking Hailes, it's located high up in a silent, tranquil corner of the wolds.

WINCHCOMBE AND SUDELEY CASTLE

28

DISTANCE/TIME	4 miles (6.4km) / 1hr 45min
ASCENT/GRADIENT	657ft (173m) / ▲▲
PATHS	Fields and lanes, many stiles
LANDSCAPE	Woodland, hills and town
SUGGESTED MAP	OS Explorer OL45 The Cotswolds
START/FINISH	Grid reference: SP024282
DOG FRIENDLINESS	On lead throughout due to livestock
PARKING	Back Lane pay-and-display car park
PUBLIC TOILETS	At car park

At the end of a long drive just outside Winchcombe is a largely 16th-century mansion called Sudeley Castle. The first castle was built here in 1140, and fragments dating from its earlier days are still much in evidence. Originally little more than a fortified manor house, by the mid-15th century it had acquired a keep and several courtyards. It became a royal castle after the Wars of the Roses, and was later given to Thomas Seymour, Edward VI's Lord High Admiral. Seymour lived at Sudeley with his wife, Catherine Parr – he became her fourth husband. Seymour was executed for treason in 1549. Consequently, the castle passed to Catherine's brother, William, but he was stripped of the title and lands after becoming involved in the plot to put Lady Jane Grey on the throne. Sudeley Castle was a Royalist stronghold during the Civil War. It was disarmed by the Parliamentarians, and left to decay until its purchase by the wealthy Dent brothers in 1863.

Henry VIII's sixth wife, Catherine Parr, is buried in Sudeley's chapel. She was born in 1512 into an influential northern family and educated in Henry's court. She was first married at the age of nine, but widowed six years later. When her second husband, Lord Latimer, died in 1543, Catherine was left one of the wealthiest and best-connected women in England, and an obvious choice of wife for Henry. After the king's death in 1547, Catherine quickly married Seymour and moved to Sudeley, where the future Queen Elizabeth was often her companion. Catherine died following childbirth in 1548.

In Anglo-Saxon times Winchcombe was a seat of the Mercian kings and the capital of Winchcombshire, until the shire's incorporation into Gloucestershire in the 11th century. It became a place of pilgrimage due to the presence of an abbey established in AD 798 and dedicated to St Kenelm, son of its founder, King Kenulf. The abbey was razed in the Dissolution, but the town's parish church survived and is a fine example of a 'wool church', financed from the medieval wool trade. The amusing gargoyles that decorate its exterior are particularly interesting, and are said to be modelled on real local people.

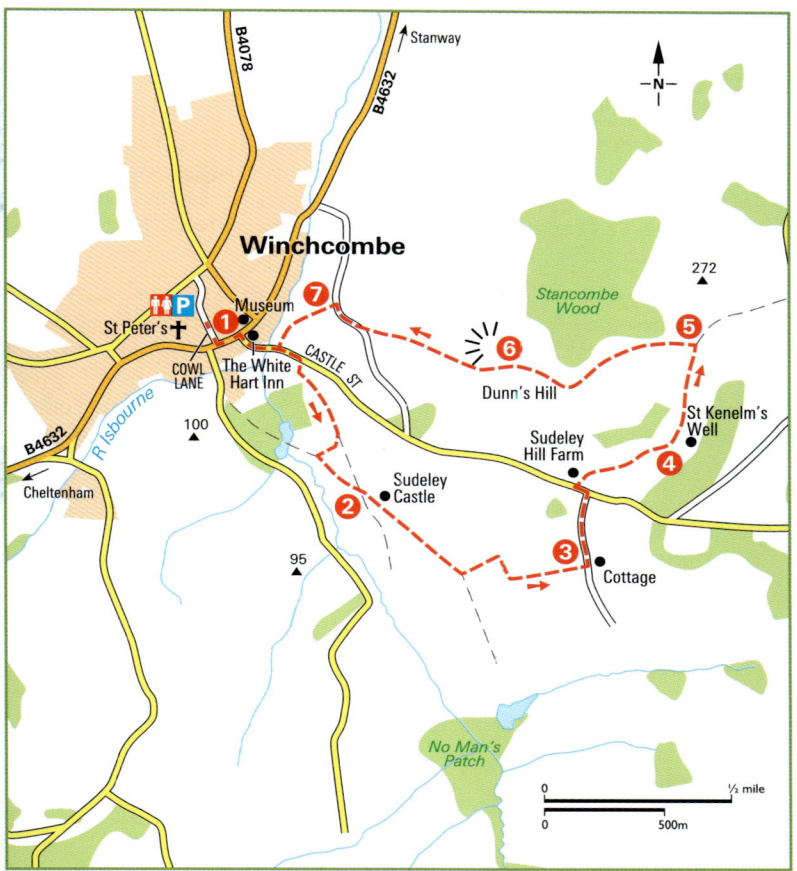

1. From the corner of the car park follow the town centre sign along Cowl Lane. At the end turn left, then right before The White Hart Inn, down Castle Street. Where it levels out, cross a river bridge, and after about 50yds (46m) bear right to leave the road near Sudeley Castle Country Cottages and ascend to a kissing gate. Follow the path through the middle of a long field to another kissing gate. At a track, with the castle visitor centre ahead, turn right for 50 paces, then left through a gate.

2. Walk between fences, under a bridge of a children's play fort, to a kissing gate. Follow the left fence past Sudeley Castle, then follow guide posts across its parkland. Go through a kissing gate in the very far corner, turn left, and after 25 paces go through another gate and walk alongside the left-hand field boundary, then right at the corner alongside a fence. In 100yds (91m), go left through a gate and walk uphill beside hedging towards a cottage.

3. Through a gate turn left onto a lane and follow this to a junction. Turn left and, after about 50 paces, just before Sudeley Hill Farm, turn right and go through a gate. Head slightly left uphill and through a kissing gate. Cross the middle of the next field, then bear to the left of a cottage to another gate.

4. Beyond this you will see a small church-like building in a fenced enclosure, which houses St Kenelm's Well. Pass to the left of this along a track. Cross a stream and go through a gate, and climb slightly right towards a gate at the right end of woodland.

5. At a woodland fence corner turn left through a kissing gate, just short of the field gate, and go alongside a small fenced field. Beyond this the path drops fairly close to the woods on your right, and then curves left near the end to two kissing gates. Continue alongside the wood, then a line of trees, to a gate in the far corner.

6. Descend slightly right towards Winchcombe, heading to the furthest corner. Via a gate descend, with a fence on your right. At the fence corner continue slightly right across the field. Walk through the hedge into the next field and continue slightly left towards a gate. Cross the field corner to a stile and a footbridge. Go slightly left in the next field, heading for the gate to the right of a cottage. Through the gate turn right onto a lane, passing a heavily buttressed kitchen garden wall on your left.

7. After about 100yds (91m), turn left through a kissing gate and head across the field towards Winchcombe church tower. Then veer left before the river valley bottom to a kissing gate by a stone cottage. Follow this path to Castle Street and turn right over the river bridge and back into the town centre.

Where to eat and drink
Winchcombe has a large number of possibilities, from pubs to tea rooms and restaurants, as well as a bakery. If you visit Sudeley Castle, the Castle Kitchen Pantry serves light meals and snacks (admission ticket is not required).

What to see
In the church at Winchcombe, note the embroidery behind a screen, said to be the work of Catherine of Aragon, Henry VIII's first wife. Behind Sudeley Hill Farm, look out for St Kenelm's Well, largely rebuilt in the 19th century, a holy well connected with the 9th-century martyred Mercian boy-king Kenelm, patron saint of the vanished Winchcombe Abbey.

While you're there
There is enough to detain you for a day in Winchcombe itself. Not only can you visit Sudeley Castle, which has gardens, a plant centre and exhibitions, but you will also find the fascinating Winchcombe Museum in the Victorian Town Hall building in the town centre. The Police Collection includes uniforms and equipment from a variety of police forces around the world, while the Folk Collection concentrates on the history of Winchcombe and its people.

WINCHCOMBE TO BELAS KNAP LONG BARROW

DISTANCE/TIME	5.5 miles (8.8km) / 2hrs 30min
ASCENT/GRADIENT	790ft (241m) / ▲▲
PATHS	Fields and lanes, several stiles
LANDSCAPE	Wooded escarpment and village
SUGGESTED MAP	OS Explorer OL45 The Cotswolds
START/FINISH	Grid reference: SP024282
DOG FRIENDLINESS	Lead required around livestock
PARKING	Back Lane pay-and-display car park
PUBLIC TOILETS	At car park

The Cotswolds are riddled with settlement remains from all eras, including early tombs. Belas Knap (medieval for 'beacon hill'), a huge green mound in a field overlooking Winchcombe, is one of the most evocative.

Barrows (often known in Scotland and Wales as cairns) are widespread throughout the country, especially in the south and west of England. The earliest types, neolithic long barrows, were built over a vast time span, between 4000 and 1800 BC. Usually constructed of earth or chalk, they are normally between 98ft and 295ft (30m/90m) long and between 30ft and 98ft (9m/30m) wide. They were used, it is thought, as the burial places of tribal chiefs and their families. Utensils – food vessels for example – were often buried with them in mortuary chambers of wood or stone, which were then, over time, covered with earth.

Round barrows were a feature of the Bronze Age (1800–550 BC). They are much more variable in size and form, but in general they are shaped like bowls, bells or discs and are up to about 20ft (6m) in height and between 12ft and 99ft (4m/30m) in diameter. Barrows were not a purely prehistoric phenomenon and they continued to be built – if irregularly – by both the Romans and the Saxons until about AD 750. Once the parish system took hold, and the rites of the Christian Church became established, the idea of communal earthen burial chambers fell away to be replaced by permanent buildings dedicated to public worship.

The long barrow at Belas Knap, dating to approximately 2500 BC, has a false portal (apparently to warn off intruders) of breathtakingly precise dry-stone work. The real entrances to the burial chambers are at the sides. It is unknown exactly who is buried here, but it is surmised that the mound was opened many times over the centuries to admit further generations of worthy souls. No doubt the whole community worked at its construction over many months, and maintained it devotedly. Thirty-eight skeletons have been found inside the tomb, which is constructed of slabs of limestone, covered in turf.

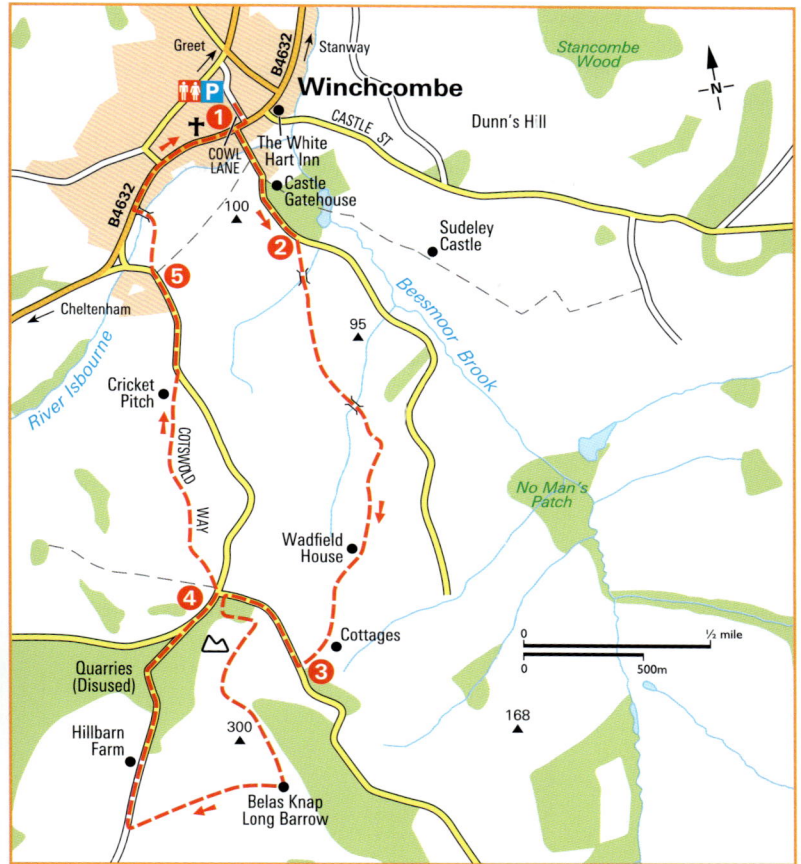

1. From the car park, walk down Cowl Lane to the town centre. At the end turn right, then turn left down Vineyard Street towards Sudeley Castle. Walk down the street flanked by pretty cottages, cross a bridge and come to the entrance to the castle, near a lodge. Stay on the road as it bears right and, after 300yds (274m), go through a kissing gate on the right.

2. Bear left to a stile and cross two further fields via a stile and footbridge on the same line. In the far corner of the third field, cross a footbridge to a field and follow its right-hand margin to a stile on the right. Go over the stile, turn left and follow the field margin as it rises. Cross a stile, pass Wadfield House, and walk on a track that goes past a pair of cottages, to a road.

3. Turn right. After 400yds (366m), turn left at a kissing gate onto a steep path among trees. Go through a field kissing gate and turn left to follow the field's north and east margin to the top. Go through a kissing gate and turn left. Eventually go through another kissing gate to arrive at Belas Knap over a stone stile. Leave the burial site via another stone stile on the opposite side and walk ahead until you come to a track. Turn right and descend for 0.5 miles (800m) to a road junction at a hairpin bend.

4. Go left through a gate into a field and descend towards a cricket pitch to a kissing gate at the bottom. Turn right along a track. When you reach the gate at the road, turn left. Then, after 500yds (457m), go right through a kissing gate into a field.

5. Go slightly left towards some willow trees, a kissing gate and footbridge. Continue up a path to the road. Turn right and make your way back to the town centre where your walk began.

Where to eat and drink
Winchcombe has a good choice of eateries, ranging from pubs to tea rooms and restaurants. If you are planning a picnic then pay a visit to the bakery and small supermarket. Sudeley Castle has a good café.

What to see
Visit the church at Winchcombe and look for the embroidery behind a screen, said to be the work of Catherine of Aragon, first wife of Henry VIII. Of particular interest are the gargoyles that decorate the exterior, believed to be modelled on local people.

While you're there
Just outside Winchcombe, on the road to Stanway, is Toddington Station, and the Gloucestershire Warwickshire Steam Railway. Run by dedicated volunteers, it operates on a restored stretch of line between Broadway and Cheltenham Racecourse Station, a round trip of 28 miles (45km) via Gotherington, Winchcombe and Toddington.

BROCKHAMPTON, WHITTINGHAM AND SEVENHAMPTON

DISTANCE/TIME	7.75 miles (12.5km) / 3hrs 30min
ASCENT/GRADIENT	280ft (85m) / ▲▲
PATHS	Fields and tracks; many stiles
LANDSCAPE	Woodland, wolds, villages and distant views
SUGGESTED MAP	OS Explorer OL45 The Cotswolds
START/FINISH	Grid reference: SP010236
DOG FRIENDLINESS	Lead required around livestock
PARKING	West Down Car Park, 2 miles (3.2km) northwest of Brockhampton
PUBLIC TOILETS	None on route

One of the key architectural and historic landmarks on this walk is Whittington Court. The house is mainly Tudor, but there has been a manor house on this site since well before the Normans – a moated version is mentioned in the Domesday Book. Earlier stonework is still visible at the base of the walls.

In the fields opposite Whittington Court some grassy bumps serve as a permanent reminder of Old Whittington. Although the Black Death of the 14th century devastated more towns than rural areas, a good quarter of Gloucestershire's population died. Many villages were abandoned and then resettled close by, and Whittington is an example of this.

The Church of St Bartholomew stands next to the house and is well worth a visit. Inside, you'll find the handsome brasses of Richard Coton – who built the present house – and his wife Margaret, as well as three Cotswold-stone effigies. It is said that the oak panelling in the chancel was made from the pews of neighbouring Sevenhampton Church. Look in the porch for a quote, reproduced in longhand, by historian Arthur Mee from his book *Gloucestershire – the Glory of the Cotswolds*, published in 1938. He fondly describes Whittington as 'an old world village under a wooded hill.'

A military camp was set up near the manor in Whittington during World War II, and in the 1950s the buildings helped solve a housing shortage in this area. The Whittington Press, established in 1971, is an authentic surviving cottage industry, with its original letterpress machines in a former gardener's cottage on the estate.

The next village encountered on the walk is Sevenhampton. This settlement was originally called Sennington and was located on the opposite hill, until the coming of the plague. Although the building is small, the parish church's flying buttresses and impressive vaulting aspire to something greater. Sevenhampton Manor dates from 1550, and was partially demolished in the 1950s.

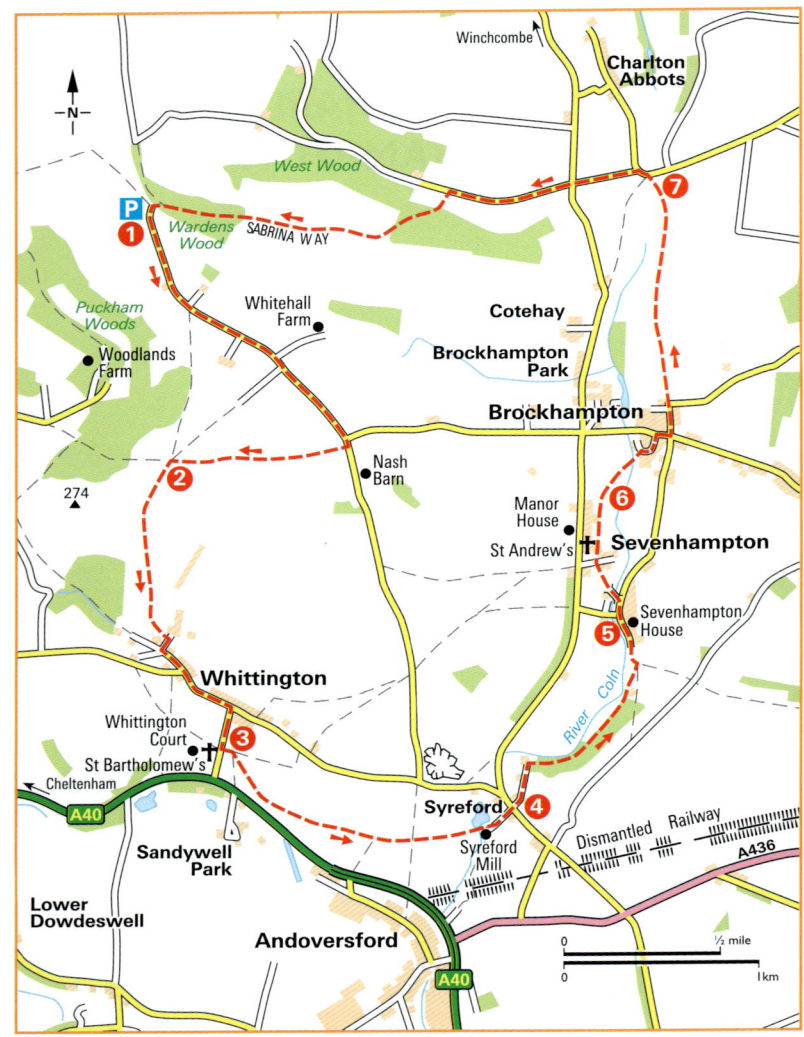

1. From the parking area, walk along the lane for 1.25 miles (2km) to a road junction. Avoid the left turn for Brockhampton and continue for about 20yds (18m), to turn right onto a footpath beside a pasture. Cross several fields as the path descends through undergrowth. Cross a field at the bottom to a stile, and enter a large field. Go forward, taking a rising path to a plantation and fence on the left. Follow the fence and, at the point where telegraph poles on the right converge with the path, reach a stile on the left.

2. Go over this onto a track. Follow it until you emerge in a large field with fine views ahead. Cross this field on the obvious track, descending steeply to a gate. Go through, follow the track to the bottom and bear right to a lane. Turn left, keep ahead at the first junction and at the next, almost opposite the Old School House, now residential, turn right (signposted 'Cheltenham') for 200yds (183m) to a gate on the left, opposite the entrance to Whittington Court.

3. Take the middle waymarked path, aiming just to the left of tall and broken trees, continuing on the same line over grassy bumps to a stile on the far side. Now keep ahead on a lengthy stretch of field path, initially across open fields, then beside the perimeter and ultimately across open farmland again. The path then descends into a thicket beside a lake. Keep right of this, then follow a clear path left of Syreford Mill to a track. Continue to a lane and cross over to a track (signposted 'Brockhampton').

4. Follow this as it passes houses and curves right (now a path) into woodland. Walk through the woods to emerge at the edge of a field. Go ahead for 440yds (402m), across fields and through a succession of gates. Approaching Sevenhampton, follow the good track beside houses, noting Sevenhampton House on the right just before the road junction.

5. Turn left for a few paces. Just before the ford at the River Coln turn right onto a grassy path (signposted 'Brockhampton via St Andrew's Church'). Follow this to a bridge and stile. The path then climbs up a bank to a gate. Cross a field to a road and then enter St Andrew's churchyard. Walk to the right of the church and turn right into a newer burial area. Turn left to pass through two kissing gates into another field. Continue down beside a wall and then enter the next field.

6. Now go half right across the field to a gate and follow a grassy path up into Brockhampton. Turn right, then left at the telephone box. Where the road turns right, go straight ahead. Walk for 0.75 miles (1.2km) on an obvious path beside or between fields to a road.

7. Turn left, pass a turning to Charlton Abbots and go straight over at the next junction. Follow the 'no through road' to a bridleway on the left (Sabrina Way) and climb steadily through woodland. Keep ahead at the Wardens Wood sign, and fork left to return to the start.

Where to eat and drink
There is nothing in Brockhampton, one of the nearest pubs is the Royal Oak in Andoversford, just the other side of the A40. It serves good pub food and has a range of beers; food served Thursday to Sunday only.

What to see
Cropping up on this walk is the waymarked Sabrina Way, a long distance footpath and bridleway intended primarily for horses and their riders. The trail runs for 203 miles (327km) between the Cotswolds and the Derbyshire Peak District, and links the Ridgeway and the Pennine Way national trails.

PRESTBURY AND SOUTHAM

DISTANCE/TIME	3.25 miles (5.1km) / 1hr 30min
ASCENT/GRADIENT	236ft (72m) / ▲
PATHS	Fields (could be muddy in places) and pavement, several stiles
LANDSCAPE	Woodland, hills and villages
SUGGESTED MAP	OS Explorer 179 Gloucester, Cheltenham & Stroud
START/FINISH	Grid reference: SO972239
DOG FRIENDLINESS	Lead necessary around livestock; some stiles have dog slots
PARKING	Car park near war memorial on Idsall Drive (2 hours maximum)
PUBLIC TOILETS	None on route

The village of Prestbury, on the northeast fringe of Cheltenham, is reputedly the second most haunted village in England, with The Burgage its oldest and most haunted street. The largest building along it is Prestbury House. During the Civil War it was occupied by Parliamentary troops. Expecting Royalists camped on Cleeve Hill to send a messenger to Gloucester, they laid a trap: a rope was stretched across The Burgage. When the Cavalier rode through the village, he snagged on the rope and was catapulted from his mount. No doubt relieved of his despatches and interrogated, the unfortunate rider was then executed. A skeleton discovered near by in the 19th century is thought to be his. It is said that the sound of hooves can often be heard here, as well as a horse's snorting and stamping.

More paranormal activity has been experienced in Prestbury House grounds, where they meet Mill Street. There have been sightings here of rowdy people in Regency dress. On this site, it turns out, there was once a fashionable meeting place called the Grotto, where the local gentry would take their ease. By the time of its closure in 1859, it had become known as a place of ill-repute.

Spectral abbots are regularly seen in Prestbury. The Black Abbot used to walk the aisle of St Mary's Church but, since his exorcism, he prefers the churchyard – a vicar came across him here, seated on a tombstone. The Abbot has also been spotted near The Plough Inn on Mill Street. In fact, there have been sightings of the Black Abbot almost everywhere in the village.

There are several other haunted places in the village. At Sundial Cottage, in The Burgage, a lovelorn girl plays the spinet; the Three Queens house in Deep Street had to be exorcised; two of three cottages next to Three Queens house are also haunted, one by soldiers from the Civil War, and another by the Black Abbot. Another abbot (or perhaps the same one) with 'an unpleasant leer' is said to haunt Morningside House, next to the car park.

There is more to the village than ghosts, however. The manor of Prestbury was established by AD 899. Remains of the moated hall can still be found on Spring Lane, close to Cheltenham racecourse. The village is associated with the jockey Fred Archer (1857–1886), as a plaque on the Kings Arms testifies, while the England cricketer Charlie Parker (1882–1959), was also born here.

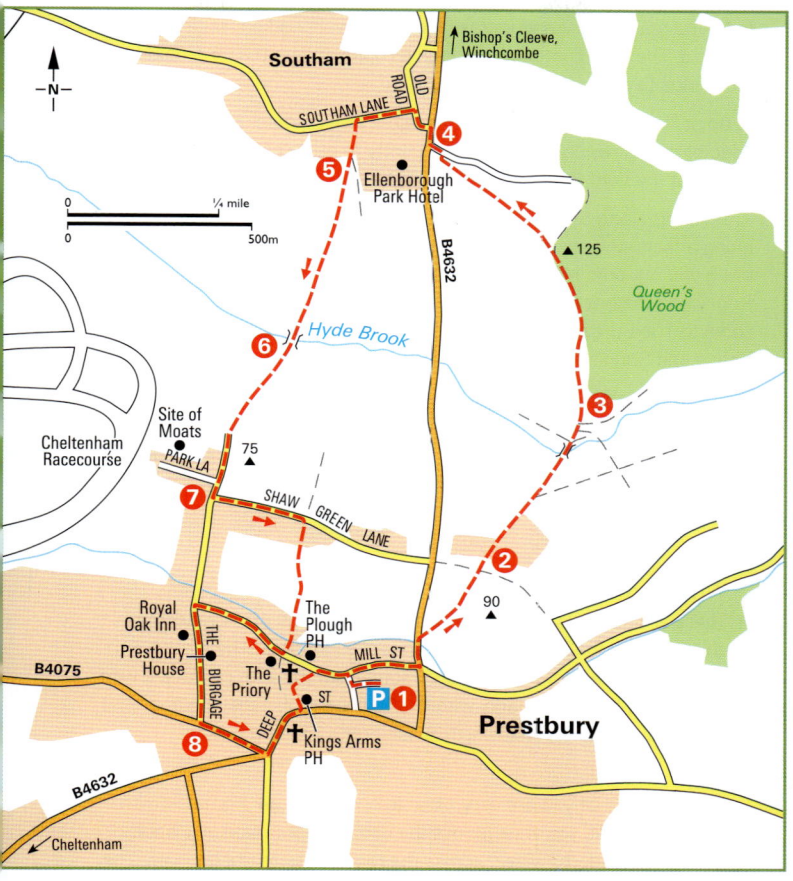

1. Leave the car park, turn left then turn right into The Bank and right again into Mill Street. At the main road turn left. After 100yds (91m), cross the road to a gate. Go into a field and head diagonally left to another gate.

2. Go through this and follow the track that is ahead of you and slightly to your left. Where it goes right, cross a stile in front of you. Cross a field heading slightly to the right, to another stile. Cross this, go over a small footbridge and continue heading up towards Queen's Wood.

3. Stay to the left of the woods. Eventually cross a track via two stiles and enter another field. Where the woods sweep uphill, continue straight on and drop down and through a field with old oak trees to a stile in the corner that takes you onto the main road.

4. Ahead of you are the medieval buildings of the Ellenborough Park Hotel. Cross the road and turn right. Follow the pavement as it bears left into Old Road, then Southam Lane. After 200yds (183m), turn left along a track to a gate. Go through this into a field.

5. Head across, bearing slightly right towards the corner of a line of trees and bushes, with the Ellenborough Park Hotel on your left. Cross over (but don't follow) a gravel track and instead look for a well-walked route to the far end of the field. The path continues through a copse and on the far side crosses a footbridge to emerge into more fields.

6. Go across the next field, then through a kissing gate, and keep to the right edge of the following field. Descend gently to go through a kissing gate at the corner of the field to a track and follow this to a road.

7. Turn left along Shaw Green Lane. After about 400yds (366m), turn right along a footpath passing between houses, just past No. 34. Eventually this will bring you out onto Mill Street, opposite the church. Turn right to walk past The Priory and the brick wall that marks the site of the haunted Grotto, until you come to The Burgage. Turn left here, passing the Royal Oak Inn, Prestbury House and Sundial Cottage.

8. At the junction with Tatchley Lane turn left and then left again at mini-roundabouts into Deep Street. Just before the Kings Arms turn left on a footpath leading to the church. Turn right just before the church and pass through the churchyard to return to Mill Street, opposite The Plough pub. Turn right and then right again and return to the car park.

Where to eat and drink
There are several pubs to choose from. The Kings Arms welcomes children, and the Royal Oak Inn also serves lunches. The Plough, on Mill Street, is a very fine old pub. Dating from the 17th century, it was originally a bakehouse and, with its thatched roof, flagstone floor and delightful garden, is well worth a visit at the end of the walk.

What to see
Don't forget that you are very close to one of Europe's greatest racecourses. As you walk across the fields towards Queen's Wood, there are wonderful views across the racecourse to Cheltenham. The Ellenborough Park Hotel is a striking Elizabethan mansion that was once home to Lord Ellenborough, a former Governor-General of India.

While you're there
Cheltenham, of which Prestbury is really a suburb, is definitely worth a visit. It has fine Regency and Georgian architecture, as well as two excellent small museums, one is the birthplace of composer Gustav Holst (1874–1934), the other has features devoted to the Antarctic explorer Edward Wilson, and to the Arts and Crafts Movement.

BRIMPSFIELD, SYDE AND CAUDLE GREEN

DISTANCE/TIME	4 miles (6.4km) / 2hrs
ASCENT/GRADIENT	536ft (163m) / ▲
PATHS	Fields, tracks and pavement, many stiles
LANDSCAPE	Woodland, steep narrow valleys and villages
SUGGESTED MAP	OS Explorer 179 Gloucester, Cheltenham & Stroud
START/FINISH	Grid reference: SO938127
DOG FRIENDLINESS	Some good long stretches free of livestock
PARKING	Brimpsfield Village Hall car park (in northwest of village)
PUBLIC TOILETS	None on route

There is something rather poignant about a vanished castle. The manor of Brimpsfield was given by William the Conqueror to the Giffard family. (In early Norman French a gifard was a person with fat cheeks and a double chin.)

The Giffards built two castles, the first of wood on another site, and its stone successor near Brimpsfield Church. In 1322, John Giffard fell foul of King Edward II, following a rebellion that was quelled at the Battle of Boroughbridge in Yorkshire. Giffard was hanged at Gloucester. Consequently the family castle was 'slighted' – that is to say, put beyond military use.

In such circumstances local people were never slow to appropriate building materials. Now almost nothing remains of the castle apart from the empty meadow just before the church and some earthworks to its right. Some of the castle masonry found its way into the fabric of the church: on the stone shed to the left of the church there are details that appear to be medieval and which perhaps originally decorated the castle.

Brimpsfield Church – rather lonely without its castle – distinguishes itself on two counts, one being the several medieval tombstones, thought to commemorate members of the Giffard family, that have been brought inside for their protection. The other is the huge base of the tower, which separates the nave from the chancel. It is surmised that this came about due to the addition of a bell turret in the 13th century, followed by a tower in the 15th century.

Syde overlooks the Frome valley. Its early Norman church, perched on the valley slope, has a saddleback tower and a rustic 15th-century roof. It's worth peering inside to search out the 15th-century octagonal font and the small round window featuring St James, dating from the same period. The box pews are from the 17th century. Don't miss the tithe barn just to the south of the church. Caudle Green is a typical example of a hamlet that has grown up around a single farm and expanded slightly over the centuries. It is dominated by an elegant 18th-century farmhouse overlooking the village green.

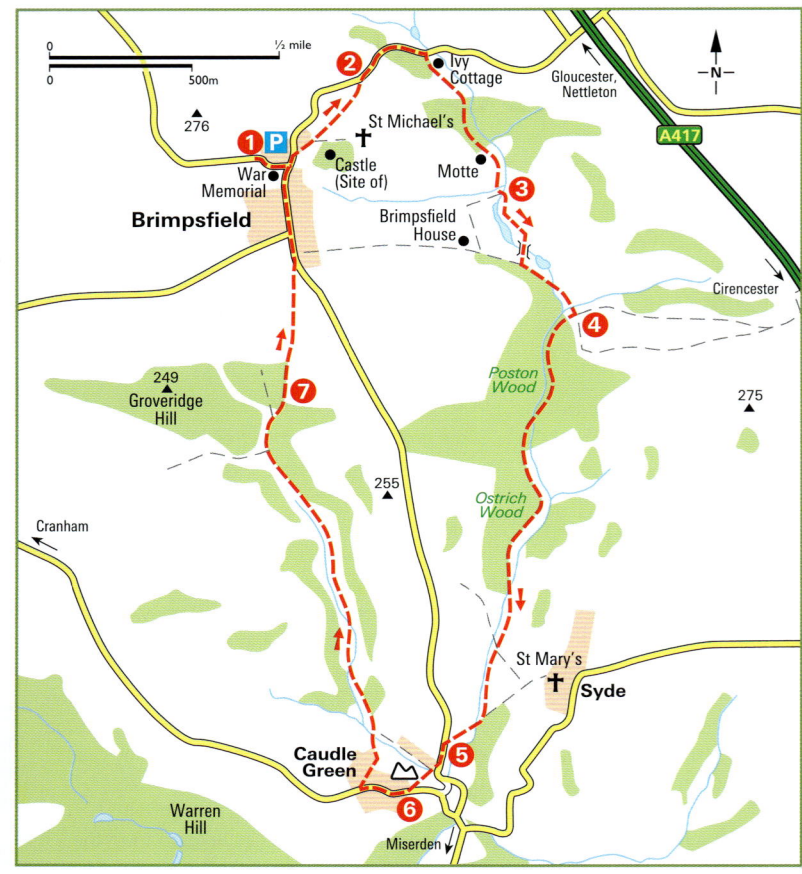

1. From the car park turn left and when the road bends right, by the war memorial, go left and up the path, signed 'church', opposite. Before you reach the church, leave the track by bearing left onto a worn path to a stile. In the next field, go slightly right to a corner and then go over a stile onto a road.

2. Turn right and follow the road down to just before Ivy Cottage near the bottom. Turn right onto a drive. After 35 paces drop down to the left onto a parallel path, which will bring you back onto the drive. Just before another cottage, turn left and go down into some woodland. Keeping a stream on your left, follow a path for 550yds (503m), joining a broader track, until you emerge on to a gravel track.

3. Turn left and follow the track as it rises to the right. After 100yds (91m), where the track bears left, go forward over a stile into a field with Brimpsfield House to your right. Go slightly right to another stile, pass a gate on your right, and bear right down to a stile in the bottom corner of the field (close to the pond) amid scrub. Follow the path to cross a bridge and bear left up to a track. Follow this for 250yds (229m), until you reach a waymarked track on the right, just past two gnarled old willows.

4. Follow the track along the bottom of a wooded valley for about 0.75 miles (1.2km). After crossing the stream on the right, bear left to continue on a grassy track via a gate, with the stream now on the left. Not far after re-crossing to the left-hand bank, you can go left up the slope to visit the church at Syde. Otherwise, remain on the valley floor and continue until you come to a gate. Go through it, then over a stile to pass to the left of a cottage. Follow a drive up to a road.

5. Turn left and follow the road downhill until it turns sharp left. At this point turn right over a stile to the left of a gate into a field and walk up a steep bank and over a stone stile to arrive on a road in Caudle Green.

6. Turn right and continue climbing to the village green. Keep ahead along a track towards a large Georgian house, shortly turning right at a sign for Brimpsfield. Follow a winding path in woodland down to the valley bottom and go through a kissing gate. Turn left through another and follow a path along the valley bottom for another 0.75 miles (1.2km). Eventually you will be funnelled between woods to a stile and gate leading into a field.

7. Continue along the left-hand field edge, then head across the field to a gate. In the next field, follow the left-hand edge ahead to a road and turn left. Re-enter Brimpsfield village, continuing past a telephone box. Turn left at the war memorial and retrace your steps to the village hall.

Where to eat and drink
Refreshments are not available on the route, unless you divert to the Golden Heart Inn at Nettleton Bottom. Otherwise, you can seek out The Carpenters Arms in Miserden to the south, or The Black Horse Inn in Cranham to the west.

What to see
The little stream encountered at certain points during the walk is the infant River Frome, which in its later, stronger stages to the south runs through the Golden Valley between Chalford and Stroud. As you ascend the valley slope into Syde, look out for the old sheep dip just below the village.

While you're there
In nearby Miserden stands Miserden Park, an Elizabethan mansion set in pretty gardens; they are open on certain days throughout the summer months. Sir Edward Lutyens designed the war memorial here. Further west is Whiteway, where a group of libertarians from Essex established a proto-anarchist community, based on the ideas of Leo Tolstoy, in 1898.

THE THAMES AND SEVERN CANAL AT SAPPERTON

DISTANCE/TIME	6 miles (9.7km) / 3hrs
ASCENT/GRADIENT	650ft (198m) / ▲
PATHS	Woodland paths and tracks, fields, lanes and canalside paths, many stiles
LANDSCAPE	Secluded valleys and villages
SUGGESTED MAP	OS Explorer 168 Stroud, Tetbury & Malmesbury
START/FINISH	Grid reference: SO948033
DOG FRIENDLINESS	Good – very little livestock
PARKING	In Sapperton village near church
PUBLIC TOILETS	None on route

Sapperton was at the centre of two conflicting movements during the late 18th and early 20th centuries – the Industrial Revolution and the Romantic Revival. In the first case, it was canal technology that came to Sapperton. Canal construction was widespread throughout England from the mid-18th century onwards. Investors poured their money into 18th-century joint stock companies, regardless of their profitability. Confidence was high and investors expected to reap the rewards of commercial success based on the need to ship goods swiftly across the country.

One key project was thought to be the canal that would link the River Severn and the River Thames. The main obstacle was the need for a tunnel through the Cotswolds, at unknown cost. But these were heady days, and investors' money was forthcoming to press ahead with the scheme in 1783. During the tunnel's construction, the diarist and traveller John Byng visited the workings. With obvious distaste he wrote, 'I was enveloped in thick smoke arising from the gunpowder of the miners, at whom, after passing by many labourers who work by small candles, I did at last arrive; they come from the Derbyshire and Cornish mines, are in eternal danger and frequently perish by falls of earth.'

The Thames and Severn Canal opened in 1789, linking the Thames at Lechlade with the Stroudwater Navigation at Stroud. The Sapperton Tunnel, at 3,400yds (3,109m) long, is still one of the longest transport tunnels in the country. Barges were propelled through the tunnel by means of 'leggers' – men who laid on their backs on boards sticking out from the barge and 'walked' the barge through the tunnel.

Yet the canal was not a success: either there was too much or too little water, and rockfalls and leakages required constant attention. The cost of maintaining the tunnel led to the closure of the canal in 1911.

It isn't just the great canal tunnel that is of interest in Sapperton. Some of the cottages here were built by disciples of designer William Morris (1834–96). He was the doyen of the Arts and Crafts Movement, which aspired to reintroduce to English life a simple yet decorative functionality, in part as a reaction to the growing mass-production methods engendered by the Industrial Revolution. Furniture makers and architects like Ernest Gimson (from Leicestershire), Sidney and Ernest Barnsley (from Birmingham) and Norman Jewson (from Norwich) all worked in Daneway, at Daneway House. Gimson and the Barnsley brothers are buried at Sapperton Church. And, in fact, you'll find the finest example of the Arts and Crafts vernacular-style architecture in Sapperton at Upper Dorval House. The entrance to the western end of the Sapperton Tunnel is in fact in the hamlet of Daneway, a short walk along the path from the Daneway Inn.

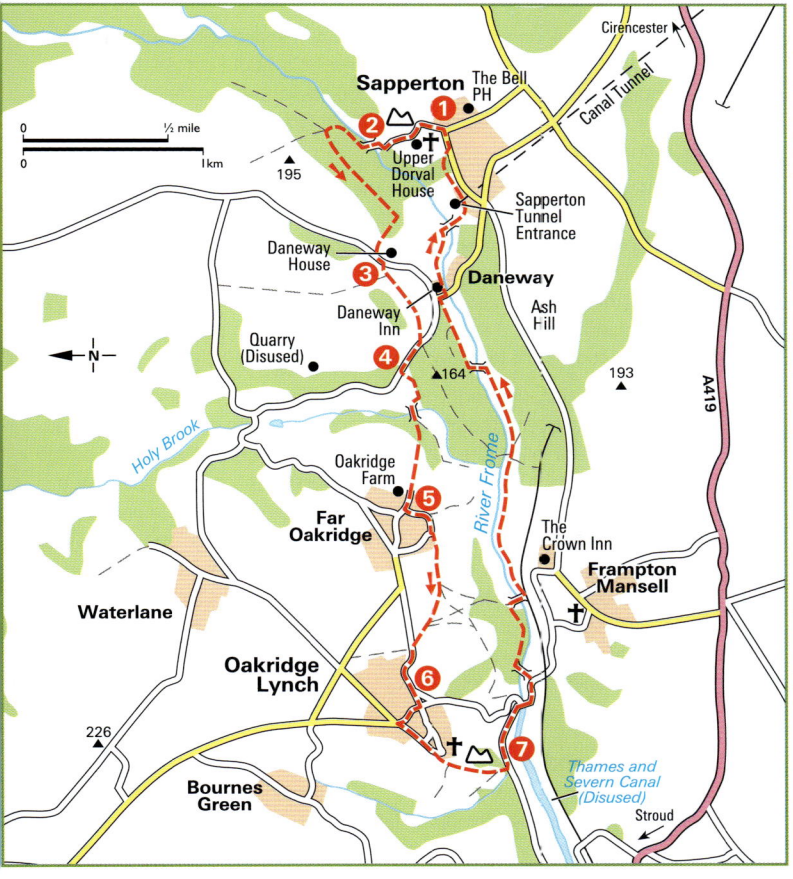

1. With the church to your left, walk along a 'No Through Road'. Descend rapidly to a house entrance at the bottom and turn left onto a footpath. Follow the path right and into woodland.

2. Cross a stream and continue left uphill into woodland. Take the main path and, where it forks, go left uphill. Climb to a junction of tracks. Turn left at the guide post and follow the track through woodland for around 0.5 miles (800m) to a gate at a lane.

3. Turn left and then immediately right over a stile opposite Daneway House. Walk through the lower part of Daneway Banks nature reserve along a wide grassy area with a fence to the right, to a kissing gate at a lane. Turn right for 250yds (229m), then left onto a drive.

4. Walk down the drive of a house called Spring Bank, ignoring the stile into woodland on the left. Go along a narrow path next to the fence on your right. Go over a stile, ahead to another and cross a stone slab bridge, then go through a field to a gate into woodland and follow the path to a stile into a field. Bear right to a gate and stile, then walk straight ahead towards farm buildings. Cross a stile to the left of the farm and walk ahead to a lane.

5. Turn left and pass a junction, signed 'Trillis'. At a sharp right corner go ahead into a field. Walk to a stile at the far end. Go straight across the next field and find a stile in the top right corner. Go straight ahead to follow the left margin of the next field to a stile at a road. Turn left along the road to descend through Oakridge Lynch.

6. At the bottom of the hill, bear left with the road, then take the right fork uphill. At a crossroads, turn right towards Bisley and climb steeply to a junction. Turn left. Walk to the end of the village green and bear right to a squeeze stile. Enter a field, keep close to a hedgerow on the left-hand side and cross three further stiles. Go across a field with a hedge close on your left to a stile into woodland. Descend steeply, then turn left over a stile and follow a footpath to a junction. Turn left downhill to reach a road.

7. Turn left to a junction, then right to cross a bridge. Bear left and, after 50 paces, turn left again over a footbridge with a stile at each end. Turn right onto the canal towpath and follow the canal for 600yds (549m). Cross a canal bridge on the right and continue along the canal for a further 1.5 miles (2.4km). At a split in the path, bear left over a modern footbridge and continue along the towpath to a road by the Daneway Inn. Turn right over a bridge and then left to continue by the canal, keeping to the left and above a grassy picnic area. At Sapperton Tunnel, fork right, then bear left above the tunnel's portico to a stile into a field. Bear slightly right up to a kissing gate, then left onto a path. Walk up to a lane, which leads back into Sapperton. Turn left and then right at the churchyard to return to the start.

Where to eat and drink

The Bell public house, near the church in Sapperton, is worth a visit, as is The Crown Inn at nearby Frampton Mansell. The Daneway Inn at Daneway is on the route and very handily placed for refreshments towards the end of the walk.

While you're there

Daneway House, the 14th-century house that was let to followers of William Morris by Earl Bathurst, is a short distance up the road from the Daneway Inn in Bisley-with-Lypiatt.

THE HAMLETS AROUND BISLEY VILLAGE

DISTANCE/TIME	5.5 miles (8.8km) / 2hrs 30min
ASCENT/GRADIENT	590ft (180m) / ▲▲
PATHS	Tracks, fields, lanes, many stiles
LANDSCAPE	Secluded valleys, villages, open wold
SUGGESTED MAP	OS Explorer 179 Gloucester, Cheltenham & Stroud
START/FINISH	Grid reference: SO903060
DOG FRIENDLINESS	Little livestock, but lots of stiles
PARKING	On-street parking near the Bear Inn in Bisley
PUBLIC TOILETS	None on route

There are many beautiful villages in the Cotswolds, and this walk takes you to one of the loveliest. Bisley is well known in the area for its well-dressing ceremony, which takes place on Ascension Day – a Thursday 40 days after Easter. This tradition, usually associated with the Peak District where wells have been dressed for centuries, was originally a pagan ceremony, but in the 14th century became a thanksgiving for wells that remained uncontaminated during the Black Death. In Bisley, the tradition dates from the restoration of the wells in Wells Street in 1863 by the Revd Thomas Keble. He was the vicar of Bisley at the time and the younger brother of John Keble (1792–1866), the poet, theologian and founder of Keble College in Oxford.

Before Ascension Day, moss and flowers are collected to cover the frames and hoops carried by 22 children from the local Bluecoat school in the procession to the wells. In the past, all of this was done in great secrecy, in the spirit of competition, while these days most of the decorative work is done in school. One problem is finding enough flowers at this time of year and keeping them fresh enough to use in the ceremony. On Ascension Day itself, a service is held in the parish church, then the children's procession forms; the oldest children carrying the largest floral stars at the front. The procession, preceded by the band and the vicar, marches through the village and down to the wells, where the vicar performs a short blessing. The flowers are arranged by the children to spell 'Ascension' and 'AD' and the current year, while garlands, floral hoops and Stars of David are laid about the wells.

Bisley is remarkable in a number of ways. In the churchyard is a 13th-century Poor Soul's Light, the only outdoor example in the country. It was used to light Mass candles on behalf of those who were too poor to buy their own. And then there is the Bisley Boy; legend says that the real Queen Elizabeth I is buried in Bisley churchyard. During a visit here as a girl, apparently, she fell ill and died. A local boy who resembled her took her place and went on to become queen.

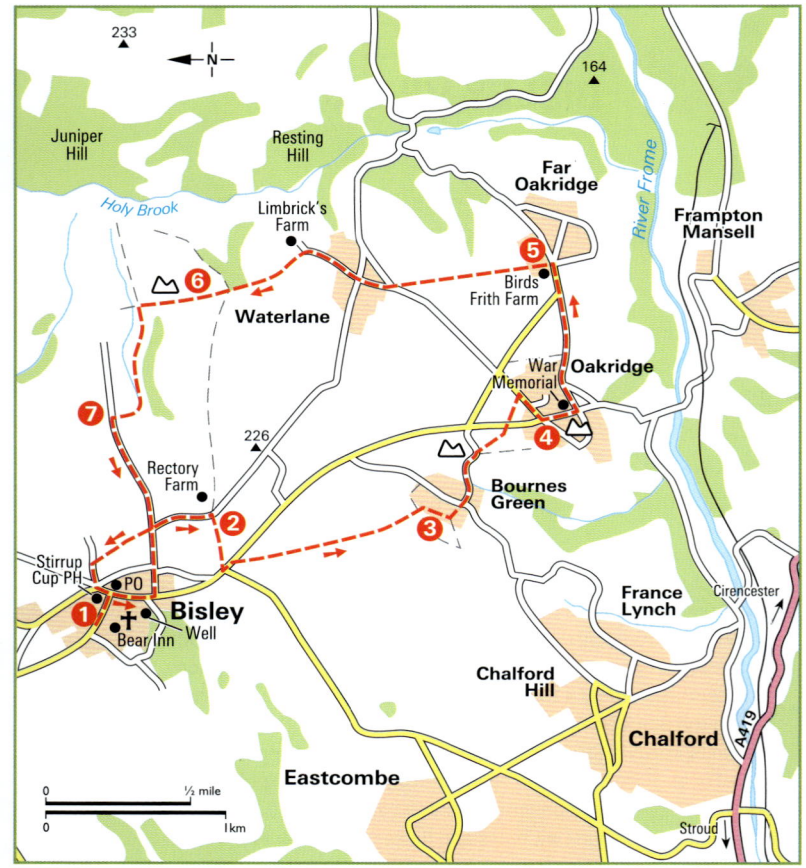

1. From your parking spot in Bisley village, walk down to the main street. At the T-junction opposite the post office, turn right and take the first turn left up a street to a junction. Go straight on, signposted 'Waterlane', then follow the road sharply right.

2. After 400yds (366m), turn right through a gate opposite Rectory Farm and walk through two fields. Go through a gate and drop to a road. Cross to a stile to the left of a stone stable, then go through a paddock to another stile. Go straight on across two further fields, then slightly right to a gap in the hedge and along the field margin to a hedge gap in the corner. Turn slightly left across the field to a stile in the corner and head for the stile at the trees' edge. Descend along a path through the trees to a small field. Go slightly right to cross a track and a stile. Cross to a path beside houses, bearing left soon after to descend to a track in Bournes Green.

3. Turn right to reach a junction and turn left. At the next junction, descend straight across to a lane via a grassy bank. Follow this lane steeply down across a stream and uphill to a hairpin bend. Turn right over a stile and go immediately left through a bank of trees to a double stile. Continue slightly right across the field to a stile onto a road. Cross the road to enter another field via a stile. Cross two fields to a road and turn right.

4. Take the second lane on the left (signed 'Frampton Mansell'), which descends steeply. Turn left just past the stone water pump and war memorial, following a sign for Far Oakridge. Stay with this lane as it bears right at Whitespring house and up and out of the village. At a junction with a wider road, keep ahead.

5. At a crossroads in Far Oakridge, turn left onto a track to the right of Birds Frith Farm. Continue to a junction with a road in Waterlane and take the leftmost of the two lanes to the right towards Bisley. Drop to a crossroads and take the dead-end lane straight ahead. At a farm, bear left onto a track, keeping ahead at a fork to a gate and stile.

6. Cross the stile and go straight on uphill to a stile at the crest of the field. Continue ahead to a stile into woodland and descend steeply into a field. Before reaching the bottom, turn left towards a stile and continue through fields alongside a stream and ponds. Cross one further stile then, approaching the end of the field, go right, across the stream via stone slabs. Follow the left edge of the field uphill to a stile and lane.

7. Turn left and walk all the way to a junction, then go right along a track and enter a field via a kissing gate. Go slightly left to the other side through a kissing gate and then left along a footpath to a road. Cross the road (watch out for traffic here as it can be busy) and descend some steps to central Bisley, and the starting point of the walk.

Where to eat and drink
There are two pubs in Bisley, both of which are good, comfortable locals. The Bear Inn on George Street has its origins in the 16th century and has been a pub since 1766. It serves traditional British food, and dogs and children are welcome. The Stirrup Cup also serves food along with Hook Norton and Wadworth's ales.

What to see
In Bisley, look for the impressive semi-circular structure on Wells Road, which houses the famous well.

While you're there
Nearby Cirencester is a town of great interest. Cirencester Park, partly designed by the poet Alexander Pope for the first Lord Bathurst, is a frequent venue for polo tournaments. The Corinium Museum is excellent, and on the main square is the largest parish church in England.

35 A CIRCUIT OF TEWKESBURY

DISTANCE/TIME	4 miles (6.4km) / 1hr 45min
ASCENT/GRADIENT	35ft (10m) / Negligible
PATHS	Fields, pavement and lanes
LANDSCAPE	River, distant hills and town
SUGGESTED MAP	OS Explorer 190 Malvern Hills & Bredon Hill
START/FINISH	Grid reference: SO891325
DOG FRIENDLINESS	Lead required along main roads
PARKING	Several car parks, most convenient on Howells Road
PUBLIC TOILETS	Gloucester Road car park near Abbey or Spring Gardens car park off Oldbury Road

The walk begins at Gander Lane, northeast of Tewkesbury Abbey. This spectacular Norman construction dominates the town, which is situated at the confluence of the rivers Severn and Avon. It was partly this geography which made Tewkesbury the site of one of the most important battles in English history.

The Vineyards, near the start of the walk, is where a Lancastrian army consisting of over 6,000 men stood on 4 May 1471, facing south. The conflict between the Houses of York and Lancaster had already been going on for 20 years. Edward IV was in exile and the Lancastrian Henry VI had been restored to the throne through the machinations of the Earl of Warwick. In April 1471 Edward returned to England, defeated Warwick and imprisoned Henry. Margaret of Anjou, Henry's consort, headed for Wales to drum up further support, but at Tewkesbury her army was intercepted by Edward.

The walk takes in several more key sites from the battle. Beyond The Vineyards lies Gupshill Manor, now a pub. This is where Queen Margaret is said to have stayed the night before the battle. In the field by a house called Crosslands stood the wing of the Yorkist army led by Edward's brother (later Richard III). It was in the vicinity of Lincoln Green Lane, that the first clash of the battle occurred.

Overpowered, the Lancastrians fled to the sanctuary of Tewkesbury Abbey. After two days they were given up, and were executed in the abbey grounds. Margaret's army had suffered a bloody defeat, and the Yorkist cause remained safe until the Battle of Bosworth in 1485.

A tour of the town reveals many splendid reminders of its ancient past. Chief among these, at the heart of a maze of medieval streets lined with quaint black-and-white buildings, is the famous abbey. Founded in 1087 and consecrated in 1121, it was eventually bought from Henry VIII by the townsfolk for the sum of £453. Its stone came from Normandy, and had been shipped across the English Channel and then conveyed to Tewkesbury by river. Beside the abbey graveyard is a striking terrace of houses – Abbey Lawn Cottages –

dating back to the late 15th century and built for the Benedictine monastery. The buildings were originally constructed as shops, with their shutters lowered to act as counters.

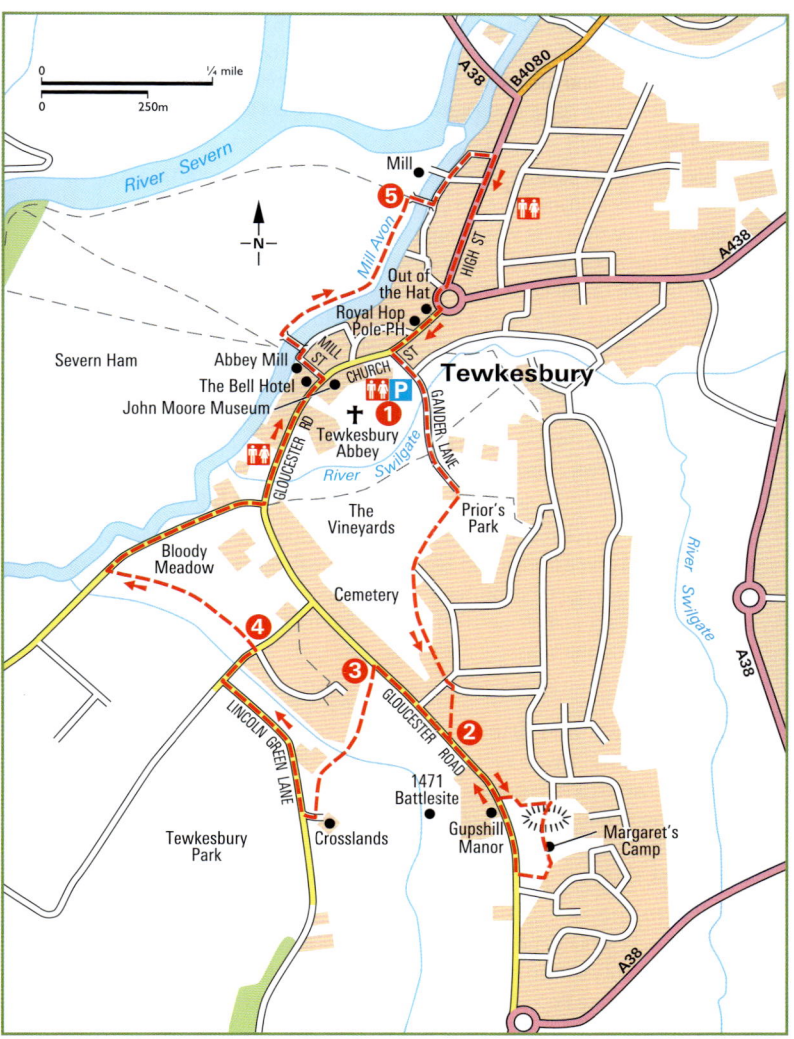

1. Walk away from Tewkesbury Abbey and the town centre. Cross the River Swilgate and continue to a pair of iron gates. Stay on the tarmac path as it traverses the area known as The Vineyards, where the monks of the abbey once cultivated grapes. It's now an open grassy area, home to several sports clubs. Notice a commemorative plinth on your right and keep to the left of the cemetery. Soon reach a road, cross into Conigree Lane, then turn immediately right, taking the path that runs to the left of houses. This will bring you to Gloucester Road, at a point where a wing of the Yorkist army stood.

2. Turn left along the pavement. Walk 100yds (91m) beyond a bus stop, then turn left along a path, towards houses. At the end swing right to follow another path, turning left at a corner. This brings you to a gate on your right into Margaret's Camp. The field, named after Margaret of Anjou, is believed to be where the Lancastrian army bivouacked before the battle. Keep ahead and cross the field to a gate on the far side. Turn right along a cycle path, return to Gloucester Road and turn right again, passing Gupshill Manor across the road. Continue along the road to the second bus stop, cross to the gate beside it and enter a field.

3. Walk across the pasture to the other side. Ignore the 'Battle Trail' sign to your right and go 50yds (46m) to cross a stile leading over a small brook. This is thought to be the point where King Edward stood. Continue ahead beside a fenced-off barn conversion and a house, Crosslands, to reach a lane. Turn right now on Lincoln Green Lane and right again at the next T-junction. After about 50yds (46m) turn left through a kissing gate into Bloody Meadow, where the remnants of the Lancastrian right wing were slain.

4. Follow the grassy path with trees and vegetation on the right and then onto a road. Turn right, pass a depot and meet Gloucester Road yet again. Opposite are The Vineyards. Turn left and follow the pavement to The Bell Hotel at the corner of Mill Street. Turn left here, down to the Abbey Mill. At this point cross over to The Ham. Turn right to follow the bank of the Mill Avon.

5. Just before a flour mill turn right over a footbridge. Turn left (Back of Avon) at traffic lights and a bridge and keep ahead into Red Lane, curving right to the High Street. Turn right, noting Tewkesbury's historic timber-framed buildings, then half right at the main junction along Church Street and left into Gander Lane to return to the start.

Where to eat and drink
Tewkesbury has a wide range of pubs and restaurants to choose from. Some have historical or literary associations. Gupshill Manor has connections with the Battle of Tewkesbury, while The Royal Hop Pole (now a Wetherspoons) is where Mr Pickwick feasted in Dickens' *The Pickwick Papers*.

What to see
As you walk around the town, look out for the narrow alleys that lead off Tewkesbury's main streets. They owe their existence to the tendency for the Severn to flood, forcing the population to make the best use of available space.

While you're there
On Church Street, and delighting in the name Out of the Hat Heritage Museum is the venue for 'living history' weekends, children's activities and much more. Near by is the John Moore Museum, which commemorates a local, early 20th-century author and conservationist.

PAINSWICK – THE QUEEN OF THE COTSWOLDS

DISTANCE/TIME	7.5 miles (12.1km) / 3hrs 30min
ASCENT/GRADIENT	1,080ft (329m) / ▲▲
PATHS	Fields, tracks, golf course and a green lane, many stiles
LANDSCAPE	Hills and valleys with villages, isolated farmhouses and extensive views
SUGGESTED MAP	OS Explorer 179 Gloucester, Cheltenham & Stroud
START/FINISH	Grid reference: SO865095
DOG FRIENDLINESS	May be off the lead along lengthy stretches, but lots of stiles
PARKING	Stamages Lane car park, just off A46
PUBLIC TOILETS	At car park

Local traditions continue to thrive in Painswick, the 'Queen of the Cotswolds'. These are centred around its well-known churchyard, where the Victorian poet Sydney Dobell is buried. The churchyard is famously filled not only with the 'table' tombs of 18th-century clothiers, but also with 99 beautifully manicured yew trees planted in 1792. The legend goes that only 99 will ever grow at any one time, as Old Nick (the Devil) will always kill off the hundredth. Should you be minded to do so, try to count them. You will almost certainly be thwarted, as many of them have grown together, creating arches and hedges.

This old tale has become confused with an ancient ceremony that still takes place here on the Sunday nearest to the Feast of the Nativity of St Mary, in mid-September. This is the 'Painswick Clypping', which has nothing to do with cutting bushes or trees, but derives from the old Saxon word clyppan, meaning 'embrace'. Traditionally, the children of the village join hands to form a circle around the church or churchyard, and advance and retreat to and from the church, singing the Clipping Hymn. Perhaps this ceremony is the distant descendant of a pagan ceremony involving a ritual dance around an altar bearing a sacrificed animal. The children wear flowers in their hair and are rewarded with a coin and a bun for their efforts. There was, and maybe still is, a special cake baked for the day, known as 'puppy dog pie', in which a small china dog was inserted.

There are yew trees in other gardens, many older than those in the churchyard, and one of which is said to have been planted by Elizabeth I. The other famous tradition that continues to be observed in the area takes place further along the escarpment, at Cooper's Hill. Here, on Spring Bank Holiday Monday, the cheese-rolling races take place. From a spot marked by a maypole, competitors hurtle down an absurdly steep slope in pursuit of wooden discs, each of which contains a double Gloucester cheese.

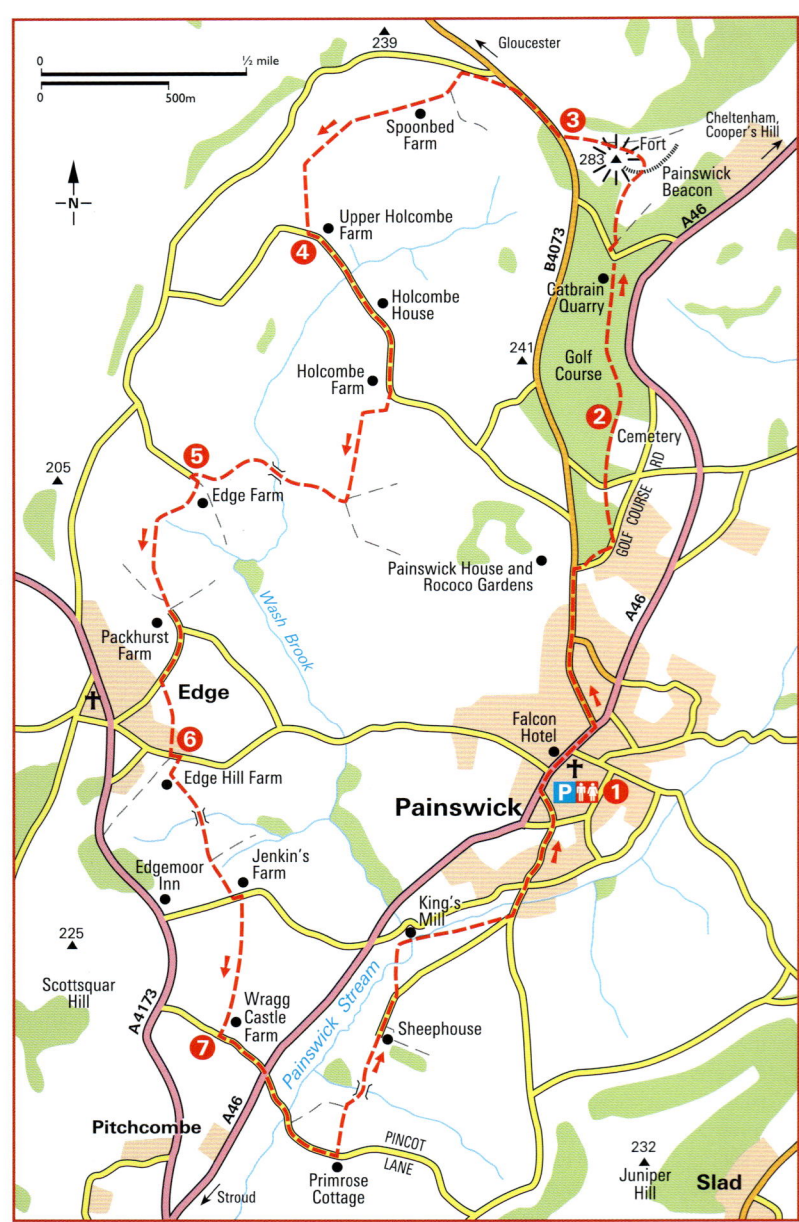

1. Turn right out of the car park and right along the main street. Turn left along Gloucester Street, join another road and continue uphill, then go right onto Golf Course Road. Bear left onto a track (signed 'Cotswold Way'), pass through the ramblers' car park and turn left into a lane. After about 50 paces follow the Cotswold Way left into woodland, then immediately right across a fairway (watch out for flying golf balls).

2. Keep to the left of a cemetery, then cross another fairway to a woodland path. Join a track past a quarry and continue to a road. After 50 paces turn right on the Cotswold Way, then after 60 paces bear left onto an unsigned path along the left edge of the golf course. Climb to a trig point for panoramic views and start descending on the other side. After a short while turn left, aiming for a track visible below. Turn left onto the track and continue to a road.

3. Turn right to reach a 50mph sign and cross to a path diverging from the road amid trees. At a junction with a lane, turn left down a track to Spoonbed Farm, bearing right at a track junction. Go straight through the farm into a field, and in a second field keep left of an ash tree to enter a new copse through a hedge gap. Cross a field in the direction of a distinctive three-storey house, then cross a stile on the left.

4. Turn left onto a lane and descend as far as a stream before Holcombe House. Climb to Holcombe Farm and continue straight on along a track, passing some gates at a bend on the left. Continue round a right-hand bend, then turn left across a stile into a field. Follow the left-hand field edge to a second field; continue across the field to a stile and turn right onto a green lane and descend to a footbridge with stiles. Cross over the stream and bear right; and follow the path uphill through trees to cross a stile. Follow the left-hand field edge curving up to a stile.

5. Walk ahead and up to a drive towards Edge Farm. Turn left along this drive, then fork right at farm buildings to a gate and stile. Continue on a grassy path beside a wooden fence to another gate and stile, then keep ahead along the right-hand edge of a field to a gate by a house. Follow a track onto a lane and shortly bear right at a Y-junction after Packhurst Farm. Opposite a house (behind a dense hedge) turn left over a stile, then bear right to another stile and onto a path between a hedge and a fence to enter Edge.

6. Turn left, then sharp right at the postbox and go past the village hall. Before the farmhouse, turn left over a stile, then another, and descend along the field margin to a footbridge. Ascend a field to a stile in the opposite hedge, then bear right across a field towards the far corner. Before the end of the field, turn right through a gate signposted 'Cotswold Way', then turn left along the field edge to a kissing gate onto a lane. Go left for 30 paces, then right, through a gate onto a track. Keep ahead along the right-hand edge of a field to a stile, then bear left to a field gate. Go through another and past a house to a road.

7. Turn left, descend to cross the A46 with care and walk along Pincot Lane. At Primrose Cottage turn left over a stile and then cross to another. Descend to cross a footbridge, then climb and cross the field to a gate, left of Sheephouse. Walk along the drive and where it forks go left down to King's Mill. Bear right through a gate and go over a weir. Cross a stile and follow the stream to a lane. Turn left to return to Painswick.

Where to eat and drink

There are several tea rooms in Painswick, as well as a couple of restaurants, shops and the Falcon Hotel. The Edgemoor Inn, to the south of Edge is a few minutes' walk off the route.

THE SLAD VALLEY AND CIDER WITH ROSIE

DISTANCE/TIME	3.75 miles (6km) / 2hrs
ASCENT/GRADIENT	700ft (213m) / ▲▲
PATHS	Track, fields and quiet lanes, many stiles
LANDSCAPE	Hills, valleys and woodland
SUGGESTED MAP	OS Explorer 179 Gloucester, Cheltenham & Stroud
START/FINISH	Grid reference: SO877087
DOG FRIENDLINESS	Lead required around livestock
PARKING	Lay-by at Bulls Cross
PUBLIC TOILETS	None on route

The Slad Valley is one of the least spoiled parts of the Cotswolds, and it has a long-standing association with the area's most important literary figure, the poet Laurie Lee (1914–97). And yet he is not instantly remembered for his poetry, but for his enchanting book, *Cider With Rosie*. This autobiographical account of a Cotswold childhood has, for thousands of students, been part of their English Literature syllabus.

For anyone visiting the area, *Cider With Rosie* is well worth reading, but it is especially pertinent here as it is largely set in Slad, where Lee was brought up and lived for much of his life. The book charts, in poetic language, the experiences of a child growing up in a world that is within living memory and yet has quite disappeared. Some of the episodes recounted in the book are said to have been products of Lee's imagination, but – as he said himself – it was the 'feeling' of his childhood that he was endeavouring to capture.

The story of his life is, anyway, an interesting one. Lee spent a considerable time in Spain, and became involved in the Spanish Civil War and the struggle against Franco. Afterwards he established a reputation as a poet, mixing with the literati of the day. He was never very prolific – much of his energy appears to have been poured into love affairs – but he wrote plays for radio and was involved in filmmaking during World War II. It was with the publication of *Cider With Rosie* in 1959 that Laurie Lee became a household name. Readers from all over the world identified with his magical evocation of rural English life, and the book has not been out of print since.

To some extent Lee became a prisoner of a *Cider With Rosie* industry. The picture of an avuncular figure living a bucolic idyll was not a strictly accurate one – much of the author's time was spent in London. He was susceptible to illness all his life, but in his later years he managed to complete his autobiographical trilogy. The second volume, *As I Walked Out One Midsummer Morning*, published in 1969, describes his journey from Gloucestershire to Spain as an itinerant fiddle player. The third, *A Moment of War* (1991), recounts his experiences there during the Civil War. Lee died in 1997 and is buried in

Slad churchyard. Many of the places in and around the village mentioned in *Cider With Rosie* are readily identifiable today, such as The Woolpack Inn and old schoolhouse opposite, and the valley remains as beautiful as it ever was.

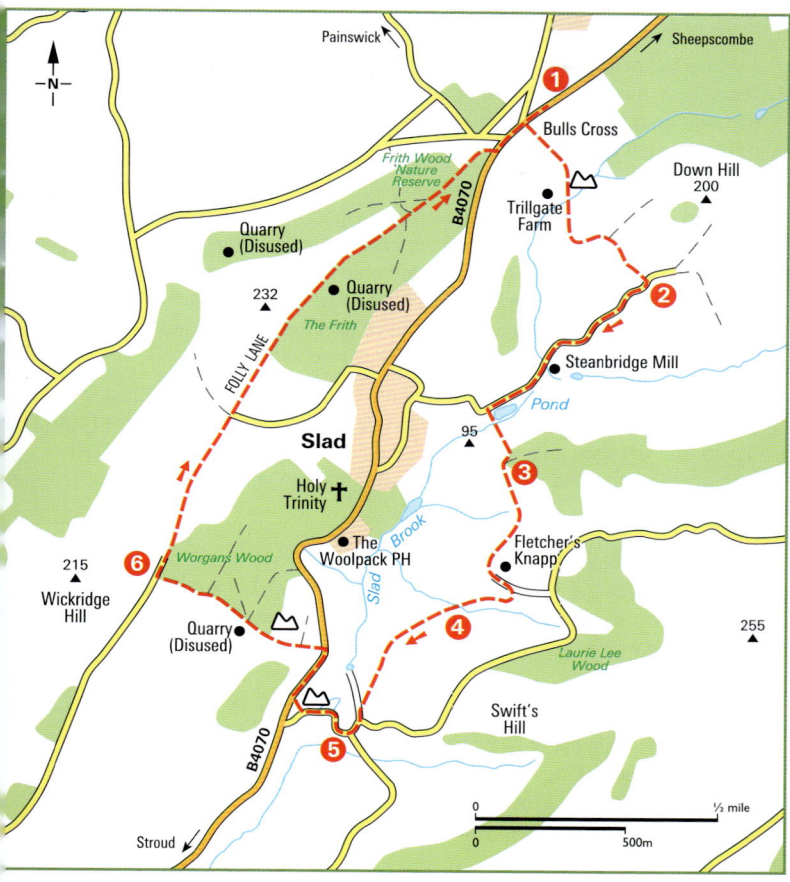

1. From Bulls Cross walk to the south end of the lay-by and turn left onto a tarmac-covered footpath, the Wysis Way. Follow it down and, immediately before Trillgate Farm, turn left over a stile into a field. Go slightly right down the field to a stile and gate, then continue up the next field to a gate at the top and turn left along a track. Where it joins another track, stay right and continue walking until you reach a lane.

2. Turn right and walk to the bottom of the valley. Pass Steanbridge Mill, ignoring a restricted byway soon after on the left. If you want to visit Slad, follow the lane into the village, otherwise turn left along a second restricted byway immediately after a large pond, and walk to a stile. Cross into a field, with a hedge on your right, and continue to a stile at the top.

3. Cross and follow a path along the right-hand woodland edge to another stile. Follow the left side of the next field and go over another stile, then continue along the path to a stile and gate. Keep ahead through a gate onto a track, staying to the right of Fletcher's Knapp and curving left. About 30yds (27m) after the curve, turn right onto a wooded path and after 130yds (118m) go right again over a stile into a field. Walk ahead, with the farm above you and to the right. Cross another stile and then keep to the right of a small pond.

4. At the top of the pond cross a stile into a field. Go straight across it to a gate and stile. In the next field head straight across its lower part. Where the field narrows, go down to cross a stile on the right by a gate and onto a surfaced track. Turn left to meet a lane.

5. Turn right and follow the lane to the valley bottom. Start to climb the other side and at a corner go over a stile on your right by The Vatch Cottage. Ascend steeply, skirting the garden, to another stile at the road. Turn right along the pavement. After 150yds (137m), bear left onto a public footpath and climb steeply. At a junction with a track, bear left and continue to a field. Follow the right margin of the field up to a stile, then follow the path as it weaves between a fence and dry-stone wall along the edge of woodland.

6. At the top go over a stile, turn right onto Folly Lane and continue to a junction. If you want to go into Slad, turn right, otherwise continue ahead onto a path that will soon take you through the Frith Wood Nature Reserve. Walk through the woods, finally emerging at your starting point at Bulls Cross.

Where to eat and drink
The Woolpack Inn in Slad features in *Cider With Rosie*. Laurie Lee was a regular there in his later years, and they have a small collection of his books, as well as serving real ales and food. In the neighbouring village of Sheepscombe, good food can be found at the Butchers Arms.

What to see
There are a number of landmarks on or near the walk that are readily associated with *Cider With Rosie*, including Steanbridge Mill. The church at Slad contains an evocative display about the life of Laurie Lee, as well as the author's last resting place in the churchyard.

While you're there
In its heyday Stroud was the centre of the 19th-century wool weaving industry. The small town centre offers a pleasant stroll featuring The Shambles, the Town Hall and the Subscription Rooms. The Museum in the Park has some excellent displays of local history. Also worth a visit is the Laurie Lee Wood, a beautiful 7-acre (3ha) ancient woodland set up by Laurie Lee's widow and daughter, which is full of native flora and fauna, including rare species such as white helleborine, with bluebells in spring. It is beside Swift's Hill nature reserve.

CHALFORD AND THE STROUD VALLEY

DISTANCE/TIME	6 miles (9.7km) / 3hrs
ASCENT/GRADIENT	1055ft (321m) / ▲▲▲
PATHS	Fields, lanes, canal path and tracks, several stiles
LANDSCAPE	Canal, road and railway, valley and steep slopes, villages
SUGGESTED MAP	OS Explorer 168 Stroud, Tetbury & Malmesbury
START/FINISH	Grid reference: SO892025
DOG FRIENDLINESS	Good, with few stiles and little livestock
PARKING	Lay-by east of Christ Church Chalford on A419
PUBLIC TOILETS	None on route

Wool has been associated with the Cotswolds for centuries. During the Middle Ages the fleece of the Cotswold Lion breed was the most prized in all of Europe. Merchants from many countries sent their agents to the fairs and markets of the wold towns in the northern part of the region – most famously Northleach, Cirencester and Chipping Campden. Woven cloth eventually became a more important export and so the industry moved to the southern Cotswolds, whose valleys and streams were suited to powering woollen mills.

The concentration of mills in the Stroud area was evident by the early 15th century. Its importance was such that when a 1557 Act of Parliament restricted cloth manufacture to towns, the villages of the Stroud area were exempted. By 1700, the lower Stroud Valley was producing about 4.5 million square metres of cloth every year. At this time the spinning and weaving was done in domestic dwellings or workhouses, the woven cloth then being returned to the mill for finishing. The Industrial Revolution was to bring rapid change with the introduction of mechanical spinning and shearing machines, followed, in 1795, by the development of the improved broadloom with its flying shuttle. The expectation was that weavers would be compelled to work in mills, and there would be mass unemployment. However, by the mid-19th century there were more than 1,000 looms at work in the Stroud Valley. The industry declined as steam replaced water power, and it migrated northwards to the Pennines. By 1901 only 3,000 people were still employed in the cloth industry, compared with 24,000 in the mid-17th century.

This walk begins in Chalford, an attractive village built on the steep sides of the Stroud Valley. Its streets are lined with 18th- and 19th-century clothiers' terraces and weavers' cottages. On the canalside the shells of woollen mills are plentiful. The 18th-century church contains fine examples of craftsmanship from the Arts and Crafts period. Nether Lypiatt Manor is a handsome manor house formerly owned by Prince and Princess Michael of Kent. It was built in 1702 for Judge Charles Coxe, with classical features and estate railings that are unusual in the Cotswolds.

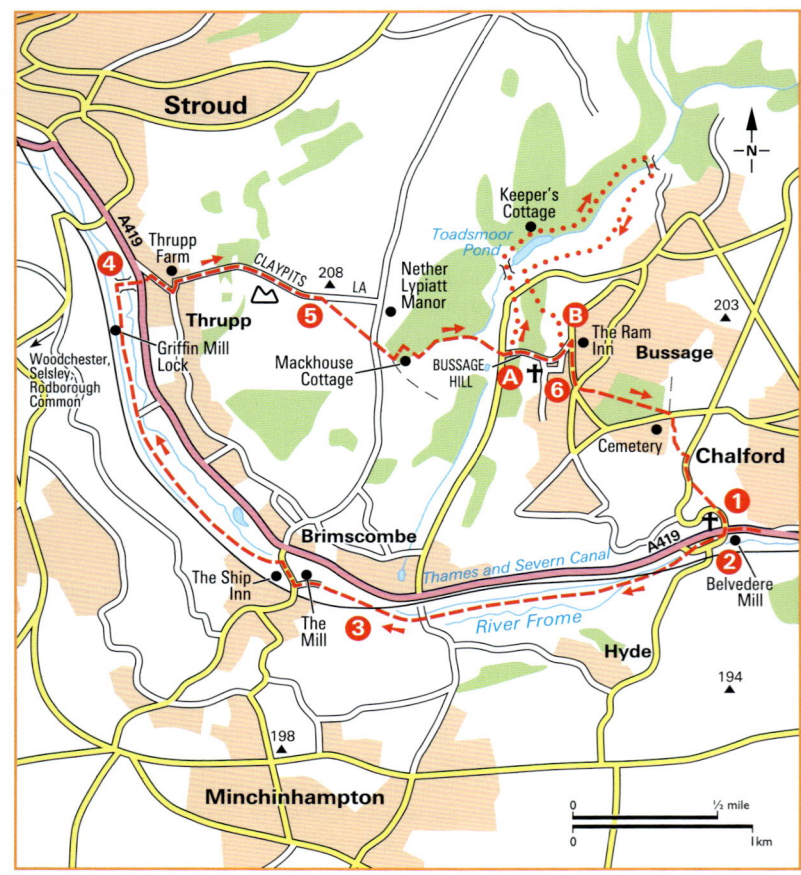

1. Walk towards Christ Church Chalford. Immediately before it, cross the road and locate a path going right, towards a canal roundhouse. Note the Belvedere Mill across to your left and follow the towpath alongside the Thames and Severn Canal on your right.

2. Cross a road at the junction with Belvedere Mews and descend steps. The path shortly passes under a railway line via a gloomy culvert so that the railway is now on your right, on the far side of the canal. Old mills and small factories, some being demolished, line the route, which continues for a further 2 miles (3.2km) to Brimscombe.

3. Shortly before arriving in Brimscombe, the towpath passes beneath the railway again and continues past a restored mill. Soon after, it becomes a road leading into an industrial estate. Opposite the old mill building in Brimscombe Port turn left to come to a junction. Cross the road and turn right. Immediately after The Ship Inn, turn left along a road among offices and workshops. Continue straight on along a path with factory walls to your right. The canal reappears on your left. As you walk on into the country, you will pass beneath two brick bridges and a metal footbridge.

4. Go past Griffin Mill Lock and at the next bridge, with a hamlet seen above the slopes on your left, turn right to follow a track via a bridge to a road. Cross this and turn left. After passing a bus shelter, turn right up a short path to meet Thrupp Lane. Turn right up to the first bend, then turn left. Just before Thrupp Farm, turn left then right into Claypits Lane and climb steeply.

5. After a long climb, as the road levels out you will see Nether Lypiatt Manor in front of you. Turn right beside a sycamore tree and go over a stile into a field. Go diagonally to the far corner. Cross a stone stile and follow a narrow path ahead beside trees to a road, then descend a lane opposite. Where it appears to fork, go straight on to Mackhouse, then hairpin left to descend past the house. Continue onto a narrow track into woodland, forking right near the bottom of the hill. Keep a pond on your left and cross a road to climb Bussage Hill. After 75yds (69m), pass a lane on the left and, at the top by a 30mph sign, turn left opposite the church lychgate onto a path that becomes a lane. Keep walking to a junction (The Ram Inn is a short distance down the road to the left) and turn right.

6. Where the road turns left to a junction, keep ahead to a telephone box and bus shelter. Turn left opposite the shelter to follow a path among houses into woodland. Go through a kissing gate and continue ahead until you meet a road. Turn left and immediately right down a path beside a cemetery. Keep left at a path junction. Descend to another road and turn right for 150yds (137m), walking with care on this short stretch of road. Bear left down a steep tarmac path among trees and continue on a lane descending into Chalford. Turn left at the bottom to return to the start of the walk.

Extending the walk Between points 5 and 6 you descend into the Toadsmoor Valley, one of the less accessible Cotswold valleys. You can make an interesting detour up the valley, which has fine woodland and a pond, from Point A, taking the first lane on the left off Bussage Hill. At a T-junction with a wider road, cross over onto a dead-end lane. Follow a track to the right, past a small lake to Keeper's Cottage, and continue up the valley along a woodland path. At a junction with a track turn right, across the stream, then immediately right again onto a track heading back down the valley. Cross a road to a path opposite, climbing steeply through woodland. Enter fields and follow a waymarked path up to a road a short distance from The Ram Inn at Point B.

Where to eat and drink
Try The Ship Inn at Brimscombe or The Ram Inn at Bussage. Alternatively, visit the Lavender Bakehouse and coffee shop in Chalford east of the church.

What to see
As you head west along the waterway, look out for moorhens, coots, voles, stoats and, if you're lucky, a heron or even the occasional adder.

While you're there
On the far side of the Stroud Valley, Woodchester has a well-preserved Roman mosaic and an unfinished 19th-century Gothic mansion, and Rodborough Common is the site of an 18th- and 19th-century fort that was originally built as a luxurious palace by a wealthy wool dyer.

ALONG THE RIVER SEVERN AT GLOUCESTER

DISTANCE/TIME	7 miles (11.3km) / 2hrs 45min
ASCENT/GRADIENT	30ft (9m) / ▲
PATHS	Canal and river tow path, busy streets; several stiles
LANDSCAPE	City centre and outskirts, rural approaches, river meanderings
SUGGESTED MAP	OS Explorer 179 Gloucester, Cheltenham & Stroud
START/FINISH	Grid reference: SO832188
DOG FRIENDLINESS	Quiet, rural stretches along Severn Way between Hempsted and Gloucester, but lead required in town
PARKING	Many car parks in the city. Nearest long stay option to the start is Westgate Street car park
PUBLIC TOILETS	Within Gloucester Quays shopping centre
NOTES	At Point 5, access to the Gloucester and Sharpness Canal through Llanthony Priory is restricted after dusk and at weekends – use Llanthony Road if necessary.

As with any large settlement of historic and architectural interest, the only way to discover and appreciate the fine city of Gloucester is on foot. At its heart, of course, is the Cathedral Church of St Peter and the Holy Trinity, one of the country's most beautiful Gothic buildings. It was here that William the Conqueror commissioned the writing of the Domesday Book, Henry III was crowned and Edward II buried.

The original church, founded around 680, began life as the Abbey of St Peter. It was rebuilt several times but by 1072 it had fallen into disrepair. It was then that King William appointed Serlo of Bayeux as its new Abbot. Serlo implemented an extensive programme of rebuilding work. His input and contribution were visionary, and the cathedral is his lasting legacy. Much of the work had been finished by 1121, but another period of rebuilding began more than 200 years later in 1331, paid for by the income from pilgrims visiting the tomb of Edward II. Later additions included the tower, which dates back to 1450.

Centuries after building work began, Gloucester Cathedral is now immortalised on the big screen. In recent years the splendid cathedral cloisters were chosen as a setting for Hogwarts school in the much-loved *Harry Potter* film series.

Only a stone's throw from the cathedral lies a tight maze of courtyards and winding streets which contain some of the city's loveliest buildings. A museum is housed in the building which inspired Beatrix Potter to write and illustrate *The Tailor of Gloucester* (1903).

Gloucester is Britain's furthest inland port, and close to the start and finish of the walk are the famous Gloucester Docks. These date back to 1794 and were enlarged and extended throughout the Victorian era. Dickens described them as 'extraordinary.' By the 1980s – barely a century later – they were virtually redundant and unused. Changes in the method of transport had rendered them surplus to requirements.

Thankfully, that wasn't the end of the story. Most of the former docks and warehouses have been imaginatively transformed into stylish restaurants, bars, designer outlets and museums. The dock basins themselves are now the preserve of leisure craft, cabin cruisers and the like.

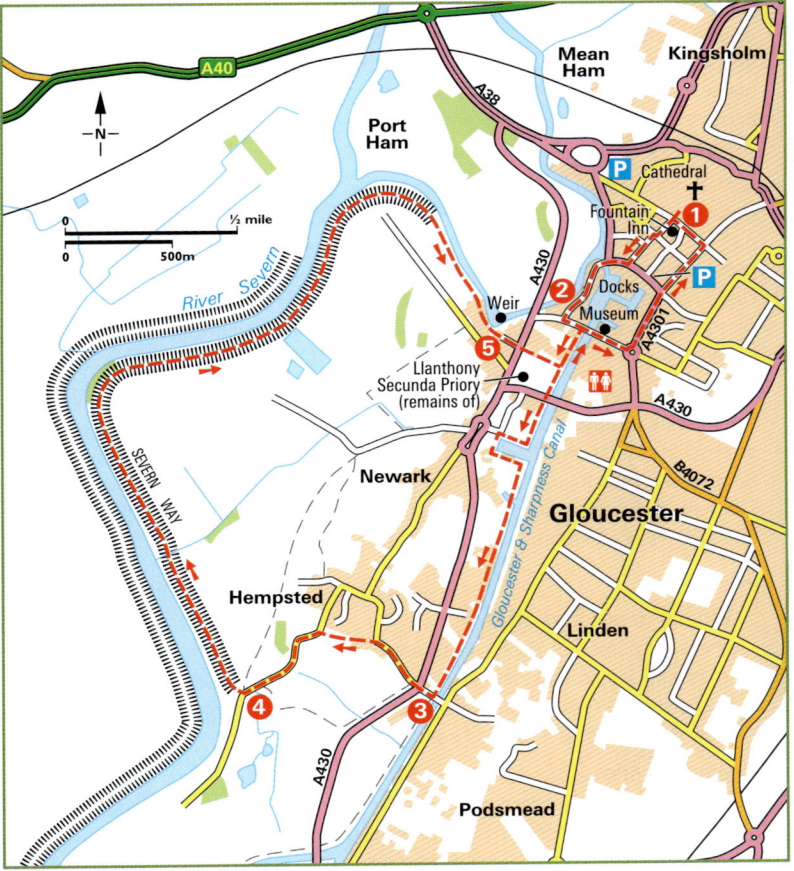

1. From the front of the cathedral, follow the signs for the Historic Docks and city centre. Pass King Edward's Gate on the right and follow College Street to Westgate Street. Cross into Berkeley Street, and on the left is the Fountain Inn. At the next junction go right, then immediately left into Barbican Road. Keep

ahead on a narrow stretch of road when Barbican Way runs off right. At the next junction, opposite the docks, turn right along Commercial Road. When it bends right, bear left into Severn Road.

2. Follow Severn Road to the next main junction with Llanthony Road. Turn left and walk along to the lift bridge spanning the Gloucester and Sharpness Canal. Turn right immediately before it to join the tow path. Along this stretch a variety of old buildings and warehouses line your route. Continue to Monk Meadow mooring basin, follow the tow path around it and return to the canal. Pass through woodland with the waterway over to the left; factories and a brick chimney are visible on the opposite bank. Follow the tow path beside canalside apartments and houses, and pass into further woodland to skirt a housing estate. Return to the canal bank and continue beside trees to the next bridge.

3. Turn right onto Hempsted Lane, and go straight across the A430. When the lane bends right continue ahead still on Hempsted Lane. Go forward between houses to join a grassy path leading to the road. Turn left and follow what becomes a leafy lane running to the Severn. As the road bends left before the river, go right over a footbridge to a kissing gate and left to a second gate.

4. Make for the obvious path and follow it, with the River Severn a short distance away on the left. Pass through two gates and stay on the riverside path as it coils between floodbanks towards Gloucester. Cross two stiles, pass beneath pylon cables and go through a gate, with the city's cathedral seen clearly ahead. Make for the next stile and keep the river close by on the left. On the right are a wall and fencing. A weir is now visible between the trees. Ahead is a gate by a row of houses.

5. Join a road and walk ahead to the next junction. Cross over to Llanthony Priory, walk through the grounds and rejoin the canal tow path. Turn left and on reaching Llanthony Road turn right. At the roundabout turn left into Southgate Street, following it through the city centre to Westgate Street. Turn left, then right into College Court, with its picturesque overhanging upper floor, and return to Gloucester Cathedral.

Where to eat and drink
There are numerous pubs, restaurants, cafés and coffee shops to be found in the city and around the restored docks area. Try the Fountain Inn, on the corner of Westgate Street and Berkeley Street, where hot and cold food and a choice of snacks are served.

What to see
Llanthony Priory is where Henry III held court, and Edward II is thought to have been imprisoned here before being taken away and murdered at nearby Berkeley Castle. Royalist forces occupied Llanthony Priory while besieging Gloucester during the Civil War.

While you're there
Gloucester's Historic Docks offer plenty to see and do. Shopping, eating and visiting museums are among the attractions, and there are even boat trips to enjoy. The Gloucester Waterways Museum is located in the Docks – it illustrates the history of Britain's canals and waterways.

AROUND TETBURY

DISTANCE/TIME	3.5 miles (5.7km) / 1hr 45min
ASCENT/GRADIENT	100ft (30m) / ▲
PATHS	Fields, lanes and tracks; several stiles
LANDSCAPE	Rolling hills, farmland and town
SUGGESTED MAP	OS Explorer 168 Stroud, Tetbury & Malmesbury
START/FINISH	Grid reference: ST890931
DOG FRIENDLINESS	Lead required in town and around livestock
PARKING	Long-stay car park at Railway Yard; other car parks in town centre
PUBLIC TOILETS	Old Brewery Lane or near The Snooty Fox

Tetbury's early prosperity was based on the wool trade, but in the 18th century industrial demand for fast-flowing water – which Tetbury was unable to provide – led to the town's decline. One happy consequence of this is that Tetbury has not been blighted by inappropriate development.

Today, Tetbury's most attractive aspect is its streets of stone houses reflecting all styles and all ages. The centre is built around the Market Place, which is dominated by the pillared Market House. Built in 1655, it was later enlarged to accommodate the town's fire engine and lock-up. The town's parish church stands in complete contrast to almost every other church in the Cotswolds. It is a striking example of late 18th-century Georgian Gothic architcture, completed by Francis Hiorne, with a tall spire and an interior that is delicate and simple. Inside, the church has a gallery supported on wooden columns, as well as box pews and several striking monuments from an earlier church.

One of Tetbury's most fascinating attractions is the Police Museum and Courthouse, located in the former police station in Long Street. You can view the old cells, and the museum includes an intriguing collection of relics of Cotswold law enforcement.

Near the start the walk passes Chipping Steps – *chipping* is an old English word for 'market'. The area close to the steps, lined with weavers' cottages, was for centuries the site of 'Mop Fairs', where unemployed labourers could offer their services for domestic and farming posts. Over the wall on the right at this point is a street called Gumstool Hill. The hill is used for the annual woolsack races and at one time there was a ducking-stool (or gum-stool) here, used for the punishment of scolding wives. Founded in 1972, the races demand that participants must carry a 60-pound (27kg) sack of wool up and down the hill. The popular event takes place annually on the last bank holiday Monday in May.

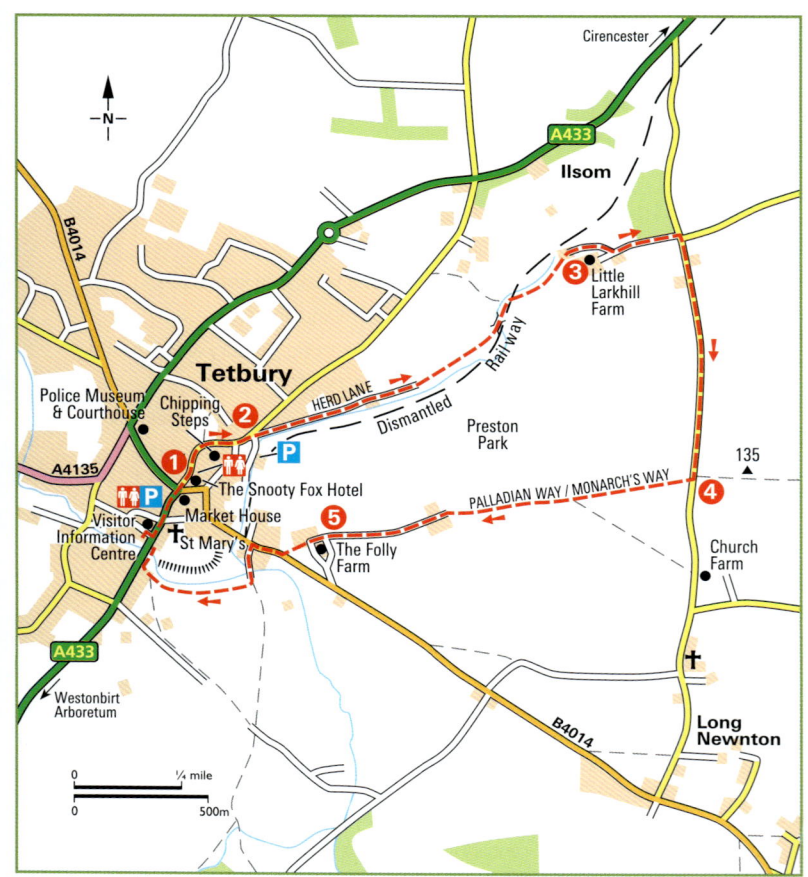

1. From the centre of the town pass the Market House on your right and then The Snooty Fox Hotel. Walk down Chipping Street, which becomes The Chipping, and descend to pass – the steep Chipping Steps on your right.

2. At a road junction just before The Royal Oak fork right, keeping to the left of the entrance to the Railway Yard car park. Follow the track beside allotments, pass to the left of a transformer station and continue to a kissing gate leading into Preston Park. Go through and walk straight ahead. There are conveniently placed seats at regular intervals. Make for the top of a knoll and then descend on the far side, keeping to the right of a fence to cross a stream via a stone bridge. Continue along the path to a gate. Go through and keep left, crossing the dismantled railway, then head up a bank to another gate.

3. Pass through it and keep ahead, following a path along a grassy area of shrubs. Follow the path around to the right, then pass between Little Larkhill Cottage and Little Larkhill Farm to join their shared track. Stay on this and follow it all the way to a crossroads of lanes, where you turn right. Stay on the road for 0.5 miles (1.2km) – look for the ruin of a brick-built gun emplacement – and then just beyond a waymarked track on the left, turn right over a stile into a field. This is part of the Palladian Way and the Monarch's Way.

4. Follow the field path ahead, keeping to the right-hand boundary of the pasture. Skirt a pond and carry on to find a stile in the corner. Cross the next field to a gate in the right-hand corner, keeping an eye out for the church in Tetbury ahead, and in the next field head for some farm outbuildings. Turn right just before them to a gate. Turn left to walk through the farmyard and continue on a concrete track. Just before the cottages complex of The Folly Farm, make for a stone stile and a metal kissing gate, both under a tree on the right.

5. Once through these take the fenced path to meet the main road beside the hospital. Turn right along the pavement to a minor road (restricted byway) on the left, just before a bridge. Follow this down to a stone bridge and turn right just beyond it, up to a kissing gate. After 10yds (9m) turn right, taking a path under trees then through a deciduous plantation to a stile. Cross this, continue across a field towards houses by the A433 and cross a stile. Turn sharp right and follow a descending track. Pass through the furthest arch of the bridge, then bear right up a path. Turn right towards the church, then left to return to the centre of Tetbury.

Where to eat and drink
The Snooty Fox Hotel, on the square, is a well-known former coaching inn. (It was called the White Hart from the late 16th century until the 1960s.) During the 19th century it also acted as the Assembly Rooms, in an attempt to attract the cream of society. There are many other pubs and cafés scattered about the town.

What to see
Note the cupola on the roof of the Market Hall, containing a bell and surmounted by a weathervane featuring a pair of dolphins. These have come to be adopted as an unofficial coat-of-arms for the town.

While you're there
Visit Westonbirt, The National Arboretum, just over 3 miles (4.8km) south of Tetbury. It has one of the most important collections of trees and shrubs in the world with over 15,000 specimens and over 2,500 species of tree.

ON THE SEVERN WAY AT DEERHURST

DISTANCE/TIME	3.25 miles (5.3km) / 1hr 30min
ASCENT/GRADIENT	115ft (35m) / ▲
PATHS	Fields, pavement and riverbank; many stiles
LANDSCAPE	Hills, villages and river
SUGGESTED MAP	OS Explorer 179 Gloucester, Cheltenham & Stroud
START/FINISH	Grid reference: SO868298
DOG FRIENDLINESS	Lead required around occasional livestock
PARKING	Car park outside Odda's Chapel
PUBLIC TOILETS	None on route

Deerhurst, a small, pretty village on the banks of Britain's longest river, the Severn, is endowed with a chapel and a church of particular, if not unique, significance. Both buildings hark back to that poignant period of English history immediately before the Norman Conquest. At the time of their arrival in the 5th and 6th centuries AD (after the withdrawal of the Romans), the Saxons were a pagan people. They were gradually converted to Christianity through the influence of St Augustine and the preaching of the British or Celtic Church. Deerhurst was in the Saxon kingdom of Hwicce, an area that was converted to Celtic Christianity by Welsh missionaries.

In AD 800 Aethelric, ruler of Hwicce, was inspired by a visit to Rome – on his return he set aside a large acreage of land at Deerhurst for the construction of a monastery. The monastery became the most important in Hwicce, and one of its monks, Alphege, would become Archbishop of Canterbury. The monastery was partially destroyed by the Danes in the 9th century, and finally levelled at the time of the Dissolution. However, the monastery church at Deerhurst, once as important as Gloucester and Tewkesbury, has survived as the finest Saxon church in England. It contains some 30 Anglo-Saxon doors and windows, as well as a 9th-century font. The Deerhurst Angel, located outside on the east wall, dates from the 10th century.

A short distance from the church is Odda's Chapel, one of only a handful of wholly Saxon buildings left in England. It takes its name from Earl Odda, a kinsman of Edward the Confessor. When his brother, Aelfric, died at Deerhurst in 1053, Odda had this chapel built, to be used as an oratory and to be served by the monastery monks. It owes its survival entirely to chance. The monastery and chapel eventually became the property of Westminster Abbey. The chapel was deconsecrated and subsumed into the adjoining abbot's house. After the monastery's dissolution in 1540, the abbot's house became a farmhouse, and the existence of the chapel was quite forgotten. It was only in 1885, during restoration work on the house, that the chapel was rediscovered and its significance understood. The building you see today is one of great simplicity

– a stone room with high walls and only two windows – but its antiquity, its location, and its almost pristine state are awe-inspiring.

Nearby, and also visited on this walk, is the scattered village of Apperley. Here you'll see some very fine timbered houses, one of which was once the post office. The Coalhouse Inn, on the river bank, was built in the 18th century to cater for bargees who were transporting coal from the Forest of Dean upriver to Gloucester and Tewkesbury.

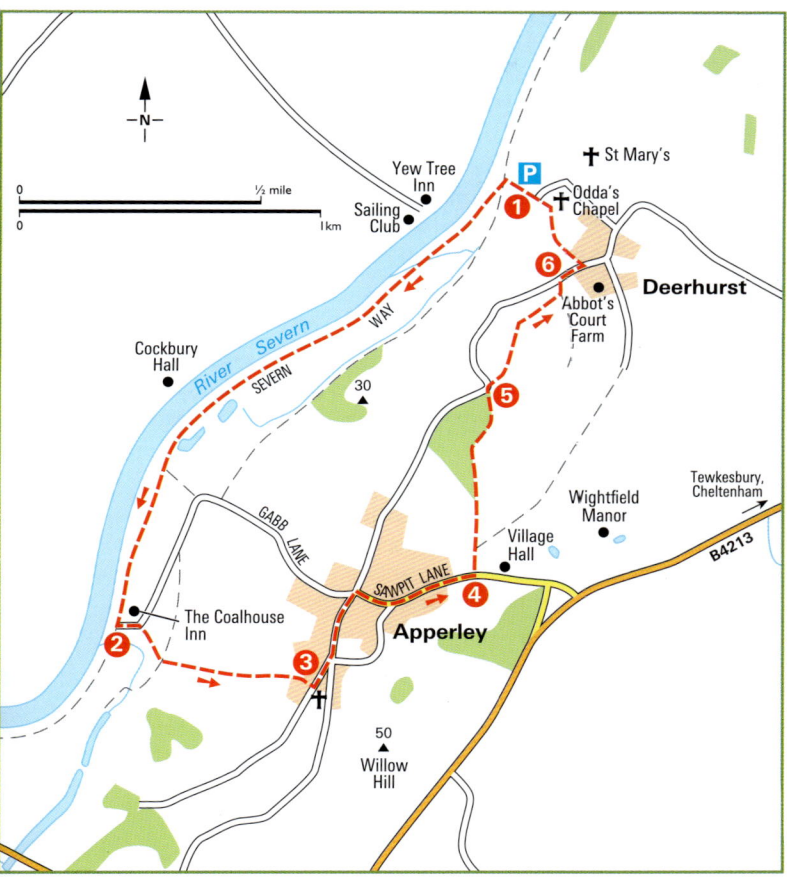

1. With Odda's Chapel behind you, turn left and then right through a gate to walk along a track as far as the river bank. Turn left to follow the Severn Way. Continue through a number of gates and over stiles, following an obvious path (sometimes a little overgrown), with the river always close by on the right. Eventually you reach The Coalhouse Inn, set back a little to the left.

2. Turn left after the pub to follow a road. Once behind the pub turn right on a track for a few paces. When it veers left, go straight ahead to a stile and cross into a field. Continue to another stile. In the following field go uphill to find another stile at the top, beside a gate. Go over and follow the right-hand margin of the field to another gate. Go through, and continue to the road in Apperley.

3. Turn left to walk through the village. At a four-way signpost turn right, heading along Sawpit Lane towards Tewkesbury.

4. Just before the village hall turn left and walk across the playing fields to a double stile. Cross and stay on the same line to the far side of the field. Follow the enclosed path through a tunnel of trees and beside fencing. This eventually brings you to a stile at a lane.

5. Go over to the lane and turn sharp right to a gate. Once in the field turn left to come swiftly to another stile. Cross this to enter another field and then walk down, crossing a dilapidated stile by a gate and a stile to the right of a house. Go ahead, then, after passing new barns on your right, find a kissing gate and fingerpost in the hedge to your left. (Odda's Chapel is visible beyond.) At the road turn right.

6. Continue to a flood gate. Turn left to walk atop further flood defences alongside a private garden. Go through a gate into a meadow and continue diagonally right, heading for a stile and gate beside Odda's Chapel and the timbered building next to it. This will bring you to a gate by your starting point.

Where to eat and drink
During the walk you will pass The Coalhouse Inn, prettily situated on the riverbank near Apperley. Otherwise, try The Swan Inn at Coombe Hill, towards Cheltenham. Here you'll find a bar and restaurant menu, with real ales.

What to see
This part of the River Severn is much used by river craft of all sorts – although commercial traffic has completely disappeared. Look out for boats from the sailing club on the far bank, rowing boats and beautifully painted narrowboats that have been rented by holidaymakers.

While you're there
At Twigworth, towards Gloucester, you will find Nature in Art, an art gallery and museum dedicated exclusively to nature-inspired art of all kinds. It has a café, too. In nearby Tewkesbury you can visit Tewkesbury Abbey, which has the largest Norman tower in Europe (see Walk 35).

ASHLEWORTH, HASFIELD AND THE HAW

DISTANCE/TIME	7.25 miles (11.7km) / 3hrs 15min
ASCENT/GRADIENT	65ft (20m) / Negligible
PATHS	Tracks, fields, lanes and riverbank; many stiles
LANDSCAPE	Flat: river, meadows, woods, farms, villages and distant hills
SUGGESTED MAP	OS Explorer 179 Gloucester, Cheltenham & Stroud
START/FINISH	Grid reference: SO818251
DOG FRIENDLINESS	Not much livestock, but lots of stiles to negotiate
PARKING	Grass verges in vicinity of tithe barn
PUBLIC TOILETS	None on route

Medieval tithe barns, such as the impressive example at Ashleworth, still survive around the country in surprisingly large numbers. In many cases they are still in use, even if the original purpose for which they were built has long been an irrelevance. They date back to the period before the 16th century when the great monasteries owned much of the land that was not held by the Crown. Around Ashleworth the land belonged to Bristol Abbey and the local people who worked the land were its tenants. There were different categories of tenant, and in return for working the land of their landlord they were permitted access to common land and also to work a certain amount of land for themselves.

Whatever category they belonged to, they all shared one special obligation and that was the payment of tithes – taxes – to the abbey. This was most often in the form of produce, which would be stored in the tithe barn, which usually stood close to the church and the abbot's residence. If the abbot was not in permanent residence then he would make regular visits with his entourage to ensure that the tithes were paid correctly and on time.

The presence of a huge tithe barn here, in what today is a comparatively remote village, has a geographical explanation. Ashleworth is situated at an easily fordable part of the river – an important consideration before the era of easy transportation. There had been a church at Ashleworth since before the compilation of the Domesday Book. A manor house certainly existed during the Norman period, and no doubt before. The barn, and Ashleworth Court next to it (which was used as an administrative centre), date from the late 15th century.

The vast limestone barn is 125ft (38m) long, consisting of 10 bays. If you look up to the stone slate roof you can only marvel at the deceptively simple timber braces that support it. In this barn 'queen post trusses' are used – that is, a trellis of posts standing vertically from the horizontal tie beams (as opposed to a 'king post truss', consisting of a single vertical post). The bays would have been used to store both tithes and also the normal produce of the farm. Had you wandered through the barn 500 years ago you would have seen different types of grain, honey, dairy produce and, of course, bales of Cotswold wool, all of which would have been subsequently shipped downriver.

Ashleworth Court, next door, is a fine example of a medieval stone building barely changed since the time of its construction. The black-and-white timbered Manor House, built as the abbot's residence, stands a short distance along the road.

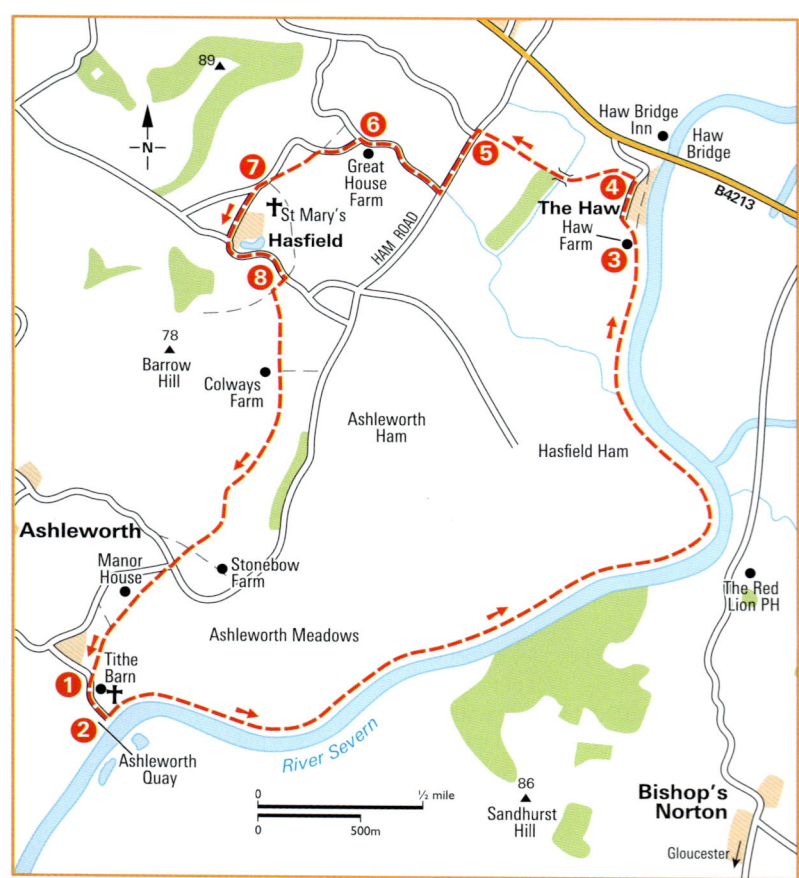

1. From the tithe barn walk along the road towards the River Severn.

2. At Ashleworth Quay turn left over a stile to walk along the riverbank. Follow it for a little over 2 miles (3.2km). In general the path is obvious, negotiating a series of gates and stiles close to the river. (You may find some gates locked or tied when livestock is around – there is usually an accompanying stile to be found in the undergrowth.) Sandhurst Hill will come and go across the river, followed by The Red Lion pub (sadly also out of reach across the river).

3. Eventually you will pass Haw Farm. Immediately after it bend left, away from the river, with the track graduating to a lane, passing a line of houses and cottages. The Haw Bridge will appear before you.

4. Just before the lane goes left, turn left over a stile into a field. Walk straight on and then, as the field opens up at a corner, bear half left to arrive at two gates either side of a drainage channel. Continue straight on across two fields to a lane.

5. Turn left, and within 400yds (366m) turn right along Great House Lane, passing Great House Farm.

6. Stay on the lane as it bears left. After passing two houses, cross left into a field. Head downhill, diagonally right, to a corner and rejoin the lane.

7. Turn left and continue into Hasfield, keeping left for Ashleworth. Turn left to visit the church and return to carry on through the village, still heading towards Ashleworth at the next junction.

8. Before a row of cottages on the right, turn right at a footpath sign. Follow a good farm track to Colways Farm. Pass beside outbuildings, keep left of a bungalow, and as the track veers left continue ahead to the end of the buildings. Keep the hedge to your left in the first field, then in the next pasture drift over to the right corner to cross two footbridges, then through gates and beside a pylon. At a lane go over a stile just left of the road opposite. Head across to a gap. Now follow the path on the right side of fields all the way back to a point just before the tithe barn.

Where to eat and drink
Just off the route on the B4213 at Haw Bridge is the Haw Bridge Inn. A little to the west are The Watersmeet Hartpury and The Royal Exchange, both in Hartpury and both on the A417.

What to see
The River Severn can flood quite badly and you will notice a number of damage limitation devices built in the vicinity of Ashleworth and elsewhere. In the past floods have reached as far as the church every two or three years. The level the water, in 1947, reached is recorded on the wall of the south aisle.

While you're there
Explore St Mary's church in Hasfield, which occupies a peaceful rural setting. Lift your head while in the churchyard and you'll glimpse the formidable gargoyles at the corners of the 14th-century tower. The church was probably founded by the lords of Hasfield Manor.

ULEY AND ITS MAGNIFICENT HILL-FORT

DISTANCE/TIME	3 miles (4.8km) / 1hr 30min
ASCENT/GRADIENT	345ft (105m) / ▲▲
PATHS	Tracks and fields
LANDSCAPE	Valley, meadows, woodland and open hilltop
SUGGESTED MAP	OS Explorer 168 Stroud, Tetbury & Malmesbury
START/FINISH	Grid reference: ST789984
DOG FRIENDLINESS	Lead required around livestock
PARKING	Main street in Uley
PUBLIC TOILETS	None on route

Uley is a pretty village, strung along a wide street at the foot of a high, steep hill. It is distinctive for several reasons: it has its own brewery, which produces some fine beers including Uley Bitter and Uley Old Spot; in the past, the village specialised in the production of 'Uley Blue' cloth, which was used in military uniforms; and then there is Uley Bury, dating back to the Iron Age and one of the finest hillforts in the Cotswolds.

There are many hundreds of Iron Age forts throughout England and Wales. They are concentrated in Cornwall, southwest Wales and the Welsh Marches, with secondary concentrations throughout the Cotswolds, North Wales and Wessex. Although the term 'hillfort' is generally used in connection with these settlements, the term can be misleading. There are many that were built on level ground and others that were not used purely for military purposes – often they were simply settlements located on easily defended sites.

Broadly speaking, there are five types, classified according to the nature of the site on which they were built, rather than their construction date. Contour forts were built more or less along the perimeter edge of a hilltop; promontory forts were built on a spur, surrounded by natural defences on two or more sides; valley and plateau forts (two types) depended heavily on artificial defences and were located, as their names suggest, in valleys or on flat land respectively; and multiple-enclosure forts were usually built in a poor strategic position on the slope of a hill and were perhaps used as stockades.

Uley Bury, covering about 38 acres (15.4ha), is classified as an inland promontory fort and was built in the 6th century BC. It falls away on three sides, and the fourth side, which faces away from the escarpment, is protected by specially constructed ramparts that would have been surmounted by a wooden palisade. The natural defences – that is, the Cotswold escarpment, facing west – were also strengthened by the construction of a deep, wide ditch, as well as two additional ramparts, an inner one and an outer one, between which the footpath largely threads its course. The three main entrances were at the northern, eastern and southern corners. These vulnerable parts of the fort would have been fortified with log barriers. Some tribespeople would have lived permanently in huts within the fort, but most would have lived outside.

In an emergency, therefore, there was space for those who lived outside the fort to take shelter within. Eventually the fort was taken over by the Dobunni tribe – Celtic interlopers from mainland Europe who arrived about 100 BC – and appears to have been occupied by them throughout the Roman era.

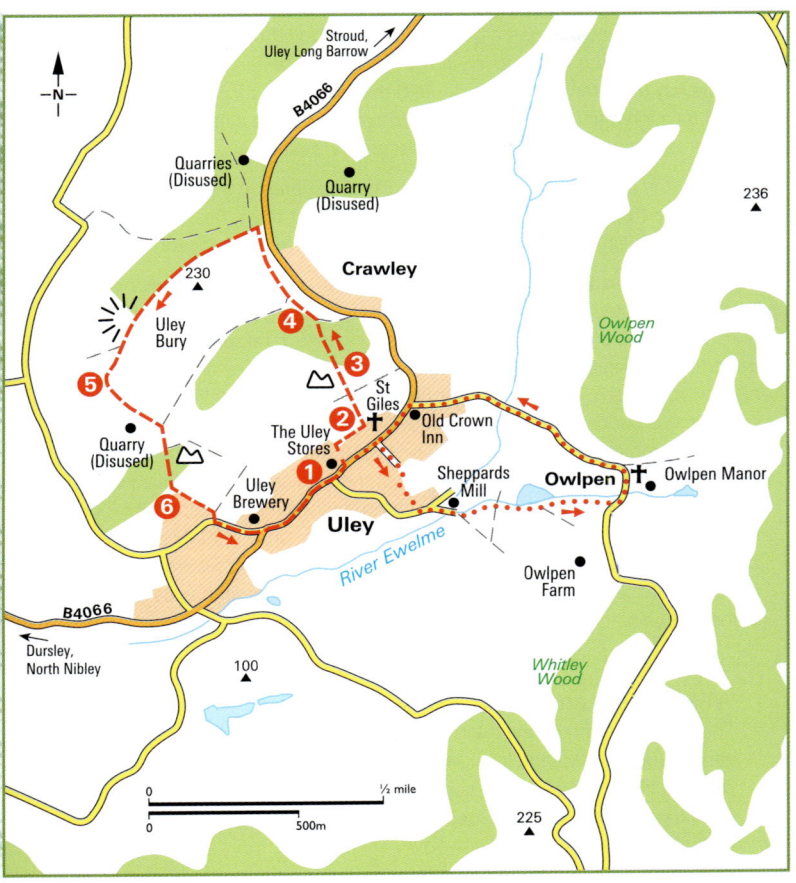

1. On the main street, locate The Uley Stores (the post office, on your left as you walk up the street), and take the narrow lane to their right. Pass between houses as the lane dwindles to a track. Some 13yds (12m) before a stile, turn right along a public footpath towards the church.

2. When you see the churchyard on the right, turn left up a narrow path beside a cottage. This rises fairly sharply and brings you to a kissing gate – pass through it into a meadow. Climb steeply up the grassland towards woodland.

3. At the treeline, keep left of the woods. In a corner on the far left, go through a gate and follow a winding woodland path ahead uphill. When you come to a fence stay on the path as it bears left. Pass through a gate and continue straight on uphill to exit the woods. In 40yds (37m), bear left as the path rises across grassland to a junction.

4. Turn right to follow the contour of the hill – the edge of the ancient fort. You are following the perimeter of the fort in an anticlockwise direction, with steep drops to your right. Pass through a gate to meet a junction of paths. Go left along the edge of the hill, with views to the west, disregarding a stile to your right that invites you to descend.

5. At the corner, go through a gate and continue to follow the edge of the fort. When you get to the next corner, at the fort's southeastern point, bear right on a bridleway (look for the waymark post) that descends through hillocks. Keep ahead through a gate and drop steeply through trees to a stile into a meadow and the access path to Whitecourt underground reservoir.

6. Follow the path down to a cottage and kissing gate. Go through this and pass beside the cottage to arrive at a lane. Turn left down this, passing the Uley Brewery. On reaching the main road, turn left to return to the start.

Extending the walk Owlpen Manor is well worth a visit. Walk down Woodstock Terrace, opposite the church, to South Street, and turn left. Go right by Sheppards Mill, and at the gate beyond the river turn left and walk through three fields to reach Owlpen Manor. You can return to Uley on the road or retrace your steps. The 15th-century manor house (with additions from later centuries) is bedded into a green hollow. In fact, the foundations of the house are far earlier, dating back to 1080. The house was restored in the 1920s by Norman Jewson, an influential member of the Arts and Crafts Movement in Sapperton and Daneway. The house's charming name is actually a corruption of 'de Olepennes', the family that owned the manor until 1490. The Victorian church has a colourful interior and a number of brasses commemorating members of the Daunt family, who succeeded the de Olepennes as lords of the manor, remaining until 1805.

Where to eat and drink
The Old Crown Inn on the main street opposite the church in Uley is a very picturesque village local, with lots of memorabilia on the walls, exposed beams and a small, sunny garden. Beers come from the local brewery and include Uley Bitter and Uley Old Spot, named after the Gloucestershire pigs.

What to see
Two sites are worth a closer look while you're in the area. Nearby is the little village of North Nibley, over which towers the 111ft (34m) Tyndale Monument. Built in 1866, this is a tribute to William Tyndale (c.1494–1536). He was born at Dursley near Gloucester, and was the first to translate the New Testament from Latin into English. It is possible to climb to near the top of the tower for magnificent views. Just to the north of Uley Bury, and still on the escarpment, is Uley Long Barrow – otherwise known as Hetty Pegler's Tump.

DYRHAM PARK

DISTANCE/TIME	6 miles (9.7km) / 3hrs
ASCENT/GRADIENT	660ft (200m) / ▲
PATHS	Cotswold Way, field tracks, farmland paths, mainly quiet roads; several stiles
LANDSCAPE	Pleasant mixture of established parkland and rolling farmland at the southern foot of the Cotswolds
SUGGESTED MAP	OS Explorer 155 Bristol & Bath
START/FINISH	Grid reference: ST749757
DOG FRIENDLINESS	Several sections of road, and busy crossing point on the A46; not permitted in Dyrham Park
PARKING	At Dyrham Park
PUBLIC TOILETS	In car park at start

Dyrham Park lies in 274 acres (111ha) of garden and undulating parkland and is one of the loveliest houses in the west of England. The baroque mansion dates back to between 1692 and 1705 and was built by William Blathwayt, civil servant and William III's Secretary of State. Blathwayt was also an accomplished linguist, traveller, art lover and MP for nearby Bath. He appreciated architecture and good books but was cautious with money. The house was designed by several eminent architects of the period. The Huguenot architect Samuel Hauduroy was commissioned to create the west front in 1692, while the Chatsworth architect, William Talman, designed the east front in 1704.

Much of Dyrham Park is accessible to the public, including the servants' quarters, complete with Victorian kitchen and larders. Also on view are exotic timbers and vibrant blue-and-white Delft tiles set against a backdrop of dark panelling and faded tapestries for maximum effect. Following an extensive programme of repairs, the house was given to the National Trust in 1961. The deer park was later purchased with a grant from the National Heritage Memorial Fund.

Most of the once-legendary gardens at Dyrham have disappeared over the years, but the statue of Neptune is a tangible reminder of the elaborate Dutch-style water garden that once decorated the grounds. Dyrham's landscaped 18th-century parkland now replaces it.

The first glimpse of the striking sandstone house looming into view in its own secluded valley may strike a chord. Observant moviegoers will recognize Dyrham Park as Darlington Hall in the film *The Remains of the Day*, made in 1993 and starring Anthony Hopkins, Emma Thompson and James Fox. The movie was based on Kazuo Ishiguro's prizewinning novel (1989). Typically, director James Ivory made clever use of real locations for the production, employing only the exterior of Dyrham Park. Other country houses in the region were used for interior shots. The film is a haunting evocation of a lost way of life during the middle years of the 20th century. At the heart of the story is a great English house where the daily routine is defined by class and culture.

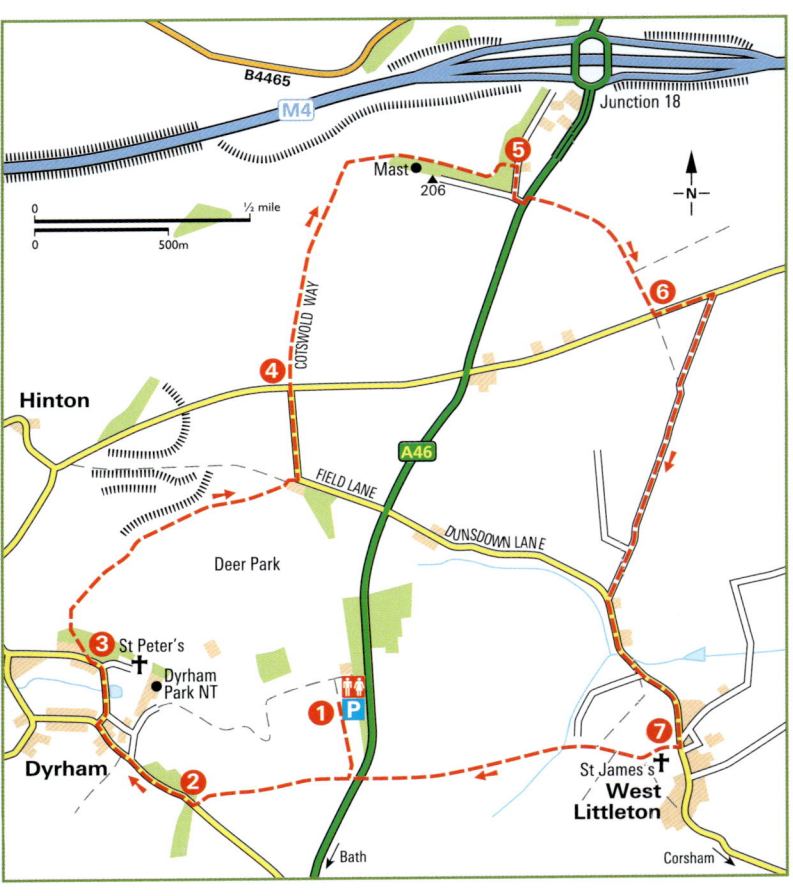

1. Leave the car park at its southern end and almost immediately turn right. Go through a kissing gate, cross the drive and continue with fencing on the right. Keep ahead, with views over the park and down to Dyrham Church's tower to the right through wire fencing. A wide sweep of countryside can be seen beyond. Pass through another gate and continue into woodland, before descending several steps to the road.

2. Turn right, pass a private drive to Dyrham Park on the right and follow the road. At a small traffic island bear right and pass an entrance to Dyrham Park. Follow a stone wall to a gateway where there is a magnificent view of Dyrham Park house and the church. Bear left on the road, pass the Garden House on the left, and turn right at the Cotswold Way sign.

3. Pass a seat among the trees and go ahead through two gates. After the second gate bear right and follow the field-edge. Pass through a series of gates, avoid a footpath on the left, and keep ahead to a lane. Turn left and head north to the next road junction.

4. Cross over, continue on the Cotswold Way and keep a hedge on your left. Pass under pylon cables until you reach an opening in the field corner. Turn right and follow the field-edge as it curves left in line with a curtain of woodland. Make for a gap on the right among the trees.

5. Turn right on a tarmac access road and left to meet the A46. Cross over and follow the Cotswold Way sign. Turn left for a few paces, then right to join an enclosed path signed 'Todmarton'. Emerging from the tree cover, continue along the field-edge; keep ahead when the Cotswold Way turns left, and go straight on to the field corner, exiting to a lane.

6. Turn left, then right (signposted Dyrham), following a bridleway track along the left edge of the field. At the top of the field continue ahead on the track between stone walls. Descend to the road, turn left and walk into West Littleton.

7. Turn right at the village green into the churchyard, make for the stone stile in the west wall, and pass alongside a riding school to a gate. Turn right in the paddock, then left to a gate. Cross a narrow meadow to a ladder stile, and descend the field to a farm track with stiles either side. Keep ahead to a dirt track and then enter the large field in front of you and go all the way across before entering another sizeable field to reach the A46. Cross it, look for a gap in the wall and go through a gate, turn left to the car park.

Where to eat and drink
During the season, there is a refreshment kiosk near the visitor centre at the entrance to Dyrham Park. Ice cream, crisps and hot drinks are available. If going into Dyrham Park there is a café in the Old Lodge. For something more substantial, there is a good choice of inns in the nearby towns and villages.

What to see
Dyrham Park (not the house) is open every day of the year, apart from Christmas Day. Dyrham's Church of St Peter, next to the house, dates from 1280. The tower was built about 1420 and the church was substantially enlarged and altered towards the end of the 15th century.

While you're there
Extend the film theme by visiting the nearby town of Corsham in Wiltshire. Corsham Court, an Elizabethan mansion dating back to 1582, was used for several interior shots in *The Remains of the Day*, and the house and gardens are open to the public. Corsham Court was acquired by Paul Methuen in 1745 to house his family's collection of Italian and Flemish paintings and statuary.

ON THE COTSWOLD WAY BY HORTON COURT

DISTANCE/TIME	3.75 miles (6km) / 1hr 45min
ASCENT/GRADIENT	245ft (75m) / ▲
PATHS	Tracks, fields, woodland and lanes; several stiles
LANDSCAPE	Meadows and open hilltop
SUGGESTED MAP	OS Explorer 167 Thornbury, Dursley & Yate
START/FINISH	Grid reference: ST759844
DOG FRIENDLINESS	Livestock in initial fields, thereafter reasonably good
PARKING	Roadside parking in Horton village
PUBLIC TOILETS	None on route

A route along the Cotswold edge was first mooted in the early 1950s, but only in 1968, when Gloucestershire County Council carried out a recreational survey, was the idea resurrected. In 1970, it was decided to create the Cotswold Way, based on existing roads and public rights of way. Amendments were made over the following years, with enthusiastic voluntary help from the Cotswold Warden Service. In 1983, the first official application for national status was made. However, it took another 15 years before the go-ahead was finally given, and, along with it, entitlement to grant aid for its creation and maintenance.

In this way, some 55 years elapsed between the birth of the notion of a continuous route through the Cotswolds and the 'official' opening of the Cotswold Way in 2007 between Chipping Campden in the north and Bath in the south. In total the route runs for just under 100 miles (161km), keeping close to the Cotswold escarpment.

Horton Court is just one of several historically important sites and landmarks encountered on the Cotswold Way. Founded in 1140, it is one of the oldest inhabited buildings in the Cotswolds, and probably the oldest rectory in England. The original limestone house was little more than a single great hall, which still survives, although the house was greatly embellished and extended under the ownership of William Knight in the 16th century. He was both Bishop of Bath and Wells and Chamberlain to King Henry VIII.

The house later belonged to Hilda Proctor Wills, a member of the Bristol-based Wills family, wealthy proprietors of the Imperial Tobacco Company. Miss Wills bequeathed Horton Court to the National Trust in memory of her nephew Sir George Wills of the Coldstream Guards, who was killed in action in Italy in 1945.

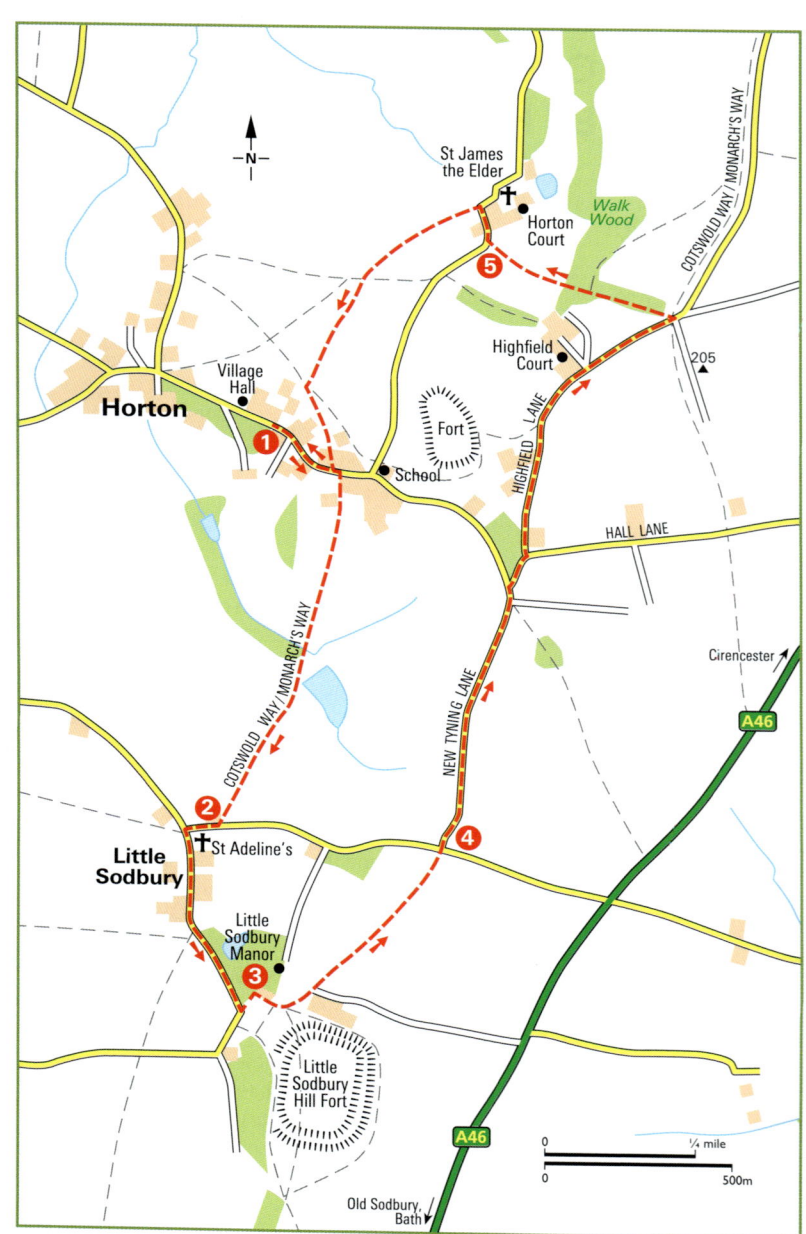

1. Walk up the hill out of Horton. About 50yds (46m) before a road junction turn right onto a track towards Little Sodbury. After 20yds (18m) keep left through a fence gap to a path. Continue to a stile, to follow the Cotswold Way and Monarch's Way between paddocks. Make for a stile on the far side and descend a steep bank. Ascend again, passing a small reservoir. Cross a stile and go ahead across pasture for 0.25 miles (400m), easing right towards a hedge and

158

passing under pylon cables. Cross a stile in the field corner and continue ahead across farmland to the next stile by a cottage. Cross onto a path and turn left to follow it to a lane in Little Sodbury.

2. Turn right, and at the next junction go left, still on the Cotswold Way. Pass Little Sodbury's Church of St Adeline on your left and continue along this lane for 550yds (503m), the last part uphill. At a junction at the top fork left by a Cotswold Way sign along what is really the drive to Little Sodbury Manor.

3. After a few paces turn right onto a path. Then, at a triangle of conifers, bear left as the path rises up the slope and brings you to the fortified-looking walls of a farmhouse. To visit Little Sodbury hillfort, turn right and then left through a kissing gate. The fort is considered to be one of the finest in the Cotswolds. Continue on the main path and at the end of the wall turn right through a gate. Turn left across gravel and then cross a paddock to a gate. Go through to a field and follow the clear path through crops to a ladder stile. Climb over to join New Tyning Lane, opposite.

4. Follow this for 700yds (640m) until you come to a junction. Turn right along Hall Lane. Follow the road for 80yds (73m) then, at a corner, turn left into Highfield Lane. Beyond woods pass the fort at Horton Camp, then some houses. About 300yds (274m) beyond Highfield Farm, at a left bend with a passing place, turn left before gates to join a path marked by a wooden post (Monarch's Way logo). Follow the path through woodland, keep right at a fork further down, and make for a gate into a field. Cross the field to another gate and exit to a lane.

5. Turn right and walk down to the entrance to Horton Court. At a sharp right corner turn hard left to a bridleway. Cross a field, then pass through a hedge to reach a gate. Continue to another gate and then keep left, following a hedge to a kissing gate. Pass through it into a field, bear right to another gate and briefly follow an enclosed path to a tarmac lane. Turn right and return to the centre of Horton.

Where to eat and drink

Just south of Little Sodbury is Old Sodbury, where you will find The Dog Inn, with stucco outside but traditional stone and beams within.

What to see

The Church of St Adeline at Little Sodbury is worth visiting because of its historical connection with William Tyndale, who translated the New Testament into English. He was chaplain and tutor at the nearby manor in 1522. The church is said to have been built from the stones of the manor chapel.

While you're there

In this southern part of Gloucestershire you are not far from the city of Bath, one of the most beautiful cities in Europe and now a UNESCO World Heritage Site. Above all it is a city of elegant Georgian architecture, but there are plenty of other attractions including the Roman Baths and new spa baths, the abbey and many museums and galleries.

ARLINGHAM AND THE SEVERN BORE

DISTANCE/TIME	7.5 miles (12.1km) / 3hrs 30min
ASCENT/GRADIENT	85ft (25m) / ▲
PATHS	Tracks, fields and lanes; many stiles
LANDSCAPE	River, meadows and distant hills
SUGGESTED MAP	OS Explorer OL14 Wye Valley & Forest of Dean
START/FINISH	Grid reference: SO708109
DOG FRIENDLINESS	Good, despite stiles, with some long, empty stretches; lead required on Severn bank
PARKING	Roadside parking in Arlingham village
PUBLIC TOILETS	None on route

The River Severn is at its most impressive around Arlingham, in its lower reaches before opening up to the Bristol Channel. Here Gloucestershire juts out into the river to form a large promontory, forcing the river into a huge sweeping loop, widening to well over half a mile (800m) at certain points. To the west it is overlooked by the Forest of Dean ridge, to the east by the Cotswold escarpment.

Shallow and placid though it might appear here, the River Severn has a capricious nature. The area has been devastated by floods in the past, most notably in the 16th century. Flooding is rarely a problem here now, as the flood control measures you see as you walk have succeeded in containing the river. It does, though, continue to create havoc every winter further upstream.

The Severn Bore, for which the river is justly famous, is a tidal wave that is formed a little way downstream, where the river narrows at Sharpness. The fundamental cause behind the bore is the combination of a large volume of tidal water, funnelled into a quickly narrowing channel, hastening onto rock rising from the riverbed. A wave is created, which is then free to roll on to the Severn's middle reaches. Significant sea tides at the river's wide mouth make the Severn Bore such a spectacle. In fortnightly cycles over the course of each month the tides reach their highest and lowest points. Near the Severn Bridge the second highest rise and fall of tide in the world has been recorded (the first is in Canada, on the Petitcodiac River). Once a month, for a few days, the spring tides occur, reaching a height of 31 feet (9.4m) at Sharpness. Whenever the tides reach 26ft (8m) or more, a bore will be unleashed.

Because of its tendency to extremes, the Severn can be dangerous. Nonetheless, there are those who love to ride the bore. Surfers and canoeists ride it for the thrill, and the waves will sometimes reach almost 10ft (3m) and travel at 12mph (19kph), finally losing impetus near Gloucester.

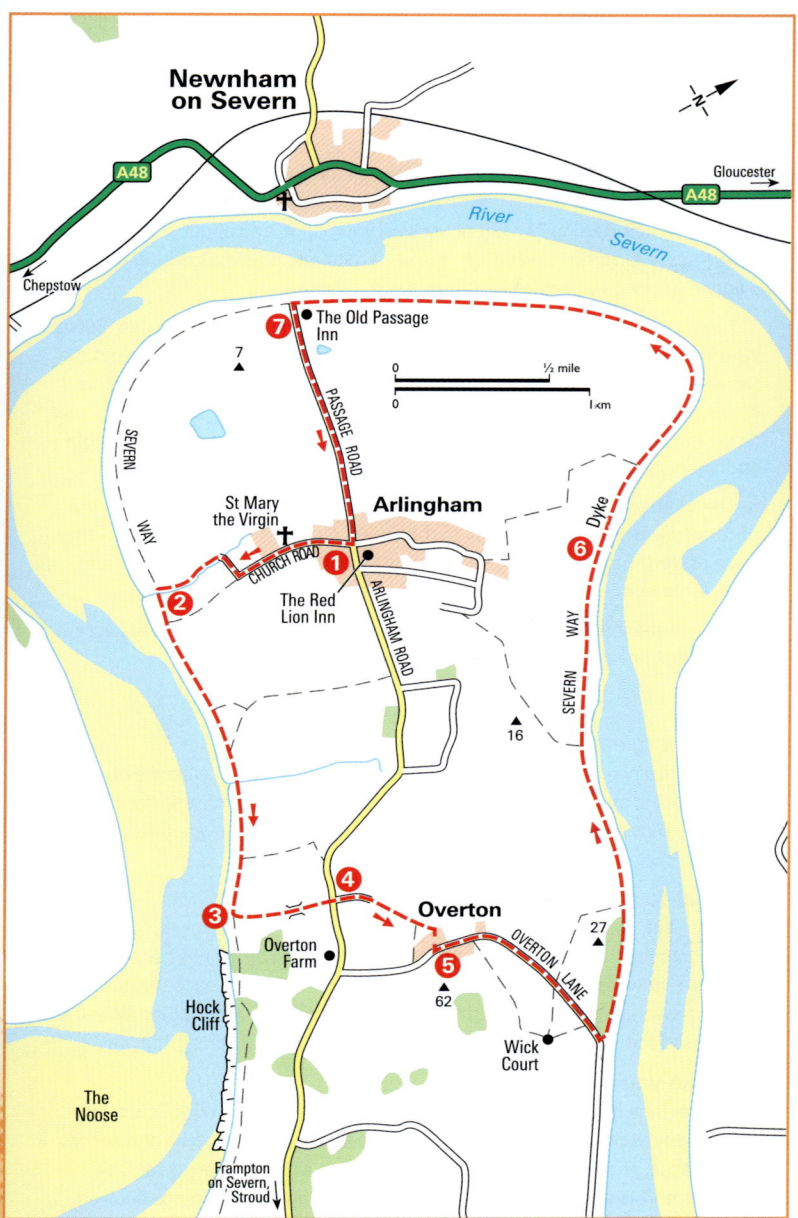

1. From the centre of the village, with The Red Lion Inn at your back, walk along a 'No Through Road'. Pass the church and continue along the road. It becomes a track which brings you to a kissing gate. Go to the top of the bank.

2. With the River Severn in front of you, turn left through a kissing gate. Continue along this route, passing through kissing gates where they arise, until you see Hock Cliff in front of you. Pass into the field that begins to slope up towards the cliff.

3. Turn sharp left to walk down the bank and along the left side of a field. Cross a bridge into the next field. When the field-edge swings right go ahead to two stiles with a farm track between them. Follow the path ahead between hedges.

4. Cross a road and enter the 'No Through Road' in front of you. Follow it towards some houses. Just before a gateway turn left through two kissing gates into a field. Follow its right-hand side to a stile and then continue on the same line. Just beyond two big houses on your right, and about 100yds (91m) before some farm buildings, turn right at a gate into a field. Crossing this diagonally brings you to a kissing gate and a lane.

5. Turn left and follow the lane through Overton for just over 0.5 miles (800m). Where the road goes sharply right beside a long house, turn left to rejoin the Severn Way. The path will lead away from the river briefly, among trees, to emerge at a stile beside a meadow. Continue walking ahead, maintaining your direction, passing through gates, always with the River Severn on your right and again ignoring any paths leading inland.

6. The footpath soon takes the form of a raised bank, or dyke. It reaches its northernmost point then swings to the south, just after passing a farm – the town of Newnham on Severn should now be clearly visible on the opposite bank. Continue to a pub, The Old Passage Inn, on your left.

7. Beyond the inn take the long, straight lane on your left, which leads across the flood plain, all the way back to Arlingham.

Where to eat and drink
There are two pubs on this route. The Red Lion Inn is in the centre of Arlingham, and The Old Passage Inn (which specialises in fresh fish) is on the riverbank to the west of Arlingham. The nearest towns offering a wider choice are Stroud or Gloucester.

What to see
Hock Cliff, composed of clay and limestone, is well known for its fossils, including the so-called Devil's toenails, ammonites, belemnites and many others. Towards the walk's end, approaching The Old Passage Inn, you will see Newnham on Severn across the river. Tradition has it that the Romans crossed the river here by elephant to attack fugitive Britons.

While you're there
On the lane between Overton and the river you will pass Wick Court. This moated medieval farm or manor house is surrounded by apple and perry orchards. The farm is now run by the children's charity, Farms for City Children. Here children learn about farm life among rare breeds such as Gloucestershire cattle, Gloucester Old Spots pigs and Cotswold sheep. Gloucester cheese is also made at the farm.

FROM KEMPLEY GREEN TO DYMOCK

DISTANCE/TIME	9.25 miles (14.9km) / 4hrs 15min
ASCENT/GRADIENT	100ft (30m) / ▲
PATHS	Fields and lanes; many stiles
LANDSCAPE	Woodland, hills, villages, rural farmland and streams
SUGGESTED MAP	OS Explorer OL14 Wye Valley & Forest of Dean and Explorers 189 Hereford & Ross-on-Wye and 190 Malvern Hills & Bredon Hill
START/FINISH	Grid reference: SO673292
DOG FRIENDLINESS	Stiles and some livestock, but plenty of off-lead potential
PARKING	Northern end of Kempley Green, beside telephone box and bus shelter
PUBLIC TOILETS	Just up from Beauchamp Arms PH

Dymock lies in a remote, frequently overlooked corner of the county, on the border with Herefordshire. In the years leading up to World War I this pretty, unspoilt area became the home and inspiration to a group now known as the Dymock Poets. Some went on to lasting fame, while others have been all but forgotten. The first to settle in Dymock, in 1911, was Lascelles Abercrombie. He was followed by Wilfrid Gibson and then by the American poet Robert Frost. Edward Thomas rented a cottage here in 1914 and all played host to John Drinkwater, Rupert Brooke and Eleanor Farjeon. Were it not for the war, they may well have continued living and working here, united as they were by a love for the English countryside and a respect for each other's abilities. As it was, their friendship was the catalyst to a considerable body of work, much of which can claim to have been inspired by experiences and friendships gained at Dymock.

Abercrombie lived at a cottage called Gallows, at Ryton, to the east of Dymock. Forgotten though he is, at the beginning of the 20th century he was hailed by the *Times Literary Supplement* as a great talent. His move to Dymock was emulated by Gibson, who settled at the Old Nail Shop in Greenway Cross. Gibson, too, is now unknown, but at the time he was the best-read poet in the country. His move to Dymock led to frequent visits by Brooke and Drinkwater. The four of them contributed to a quarterly called *New Numbers*, published from Ryton in 1914 and which contained some of Brooke's poems.

Robert Frost, who became involved through a review of his poetry by Abercrombie, rented a cottage called Little Iddens, while Edward Thomas (who immortalised the Cotswold village of Adlestrop in his most famous poem, see Walk 1) lived in a cottage near by, called Old Fields. It was Frost who persuaded Thomas to concentrate on his poetry rather than his prose.

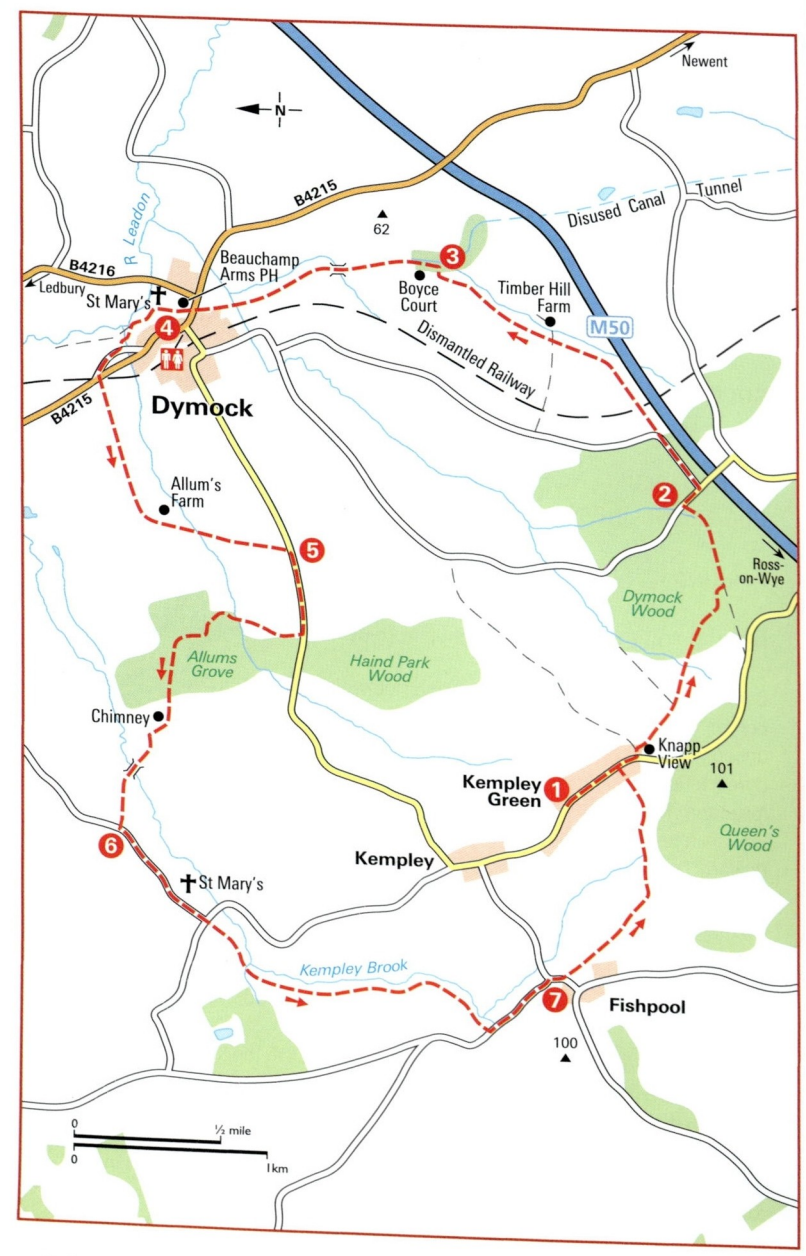

1. Walk through Kempley Green and turn left just before Knapp View. Take the right-hand of two paths (Daffodil Way). Go through gates, pass a barn and then enter an orchard. Enter Dymock Wood to follow a path and Daffodil Way signs for over 0.5 miles (800m) to a road.

2. Turn right and then left before a motorway bridge. Where this road bears left, proceed ahead through a gate into fields and follow the route down to a stream. Turn left before it. Cross a track, pass through gates and walk straight along a track for 600yds (549m) towards Boyce Court.

3. At a T-junction with a track, turn right, then left (Daffodil Way) to follow a derelict canal beside trees and then across farmland alongside a stream. At one point follow the path left round the field corner and then right at a gate. Continue to a stile and road at Dymock.

4. Go into the churchyard and out the other side, through a gate into a field. Turn half left and take the second bridge on the right. Then bear half left to a stile. Turn right along a disused road and cross the B4215. Follow a track, leaving it to keep to the right of Allum's Farm at a waymarker. Pass a barn and go half left across the field to a gate. Enter an orchard, turn right and follow its left margin and then that of a field, to a road.

5. Turn right. After 600yds (549m) turn right into a field alongside woodland. After 120yds (110m), at a stile go half right over a mound to soon enter the woods. Turn right and follow the boundary to a gate. Turn left, shortly re-entering woodland. Follow a path, keeping right at a junction, to a stile. Cross a field, keeping to the left of a chimney, and then right into a field. Look for a gate on your left, cross into the adjacent field and then turn right to find a bridge across the stream. Go half left across fields to a road.

6. Turn left past St Mary's Church. At the next T-junction go into the field ahead. Proceed into the next field and continue for over 0.75 miles (1.2km), with the stream on your left, across several fields to a lane. Turn left to a junction at Fishpool.

7. Turn right, and after 50yds (46m) turn left over a stile. Curve right and then pass a series of stiles to aim to the right of a cottage. Follow the path through gates by loose boxes, and then bear left over stiles so that a house is on your right. Go right into a field. Turn left and follow the same line, ascending gently, to Kempley Green. Turn left, back to the start.

Where to eat and drink
The route takes you right past the Beauchamp Arms in Dymock, an old pub with a good lunch menu. The pub was saved from closure in 1997 when it was bought by the parish council to be managed as a local amenity.

What to see
The isolated St Mary's Church, which was once the parish church of Kempley, contains some fine 14th-century mural fragments depicting a wheel of life and St Michael weighing souls. The chancel contains the most complete set of Romanesque wall-paintings in England. Completed between 1132 and 1140, they had been painted over and were not rediscovered until 1872.

While you're there
Newent has some very attractive medieval buildings and a museum of Victorian life. Near by is the Three Choirs Vineyard Estate, established in 1973 and now covering 75acres (30ha). Wine tasting, an accompanying lunch and a vineyard walk is available at the weekends, booking is advisable.

ON OFFA'S DYKE AT BROCKWEIR

DISTANCE/TIME	4.5 miles (7.2km) / 2hrs 15min
ASCENT/GRADIENT	740ft (226m) / ▲▲
PATHS	Tracks, fields, lanes, stony paths and river bank
LANDSCAPE	River, meadows, woodland, farmland and village
SUGGESTED MAP	OS Explorer OL14 Wye Valley & Forest of Dean
START/FINISH	Grid reference: SO540011
DOG FRIENDLINESS	Off lead for long stretches, but occasional livestock
PARKING	Lay-by near telephone box in Brockweir or The Old Station, Tintern, on other side of river
PUBLIC TOILETS	None on route

Offa's Dyke is a massive earthwork constructed by King Offa, the ruler of the Saxon kingdom of Mercia, in the 8th century AD. The dyke represented the western frontier of his kingdom and ran for about 170 miles (274km) from Chepstow in the south (near the confluence of the Wye and the Severn) to Prestatyn in the north. Its basic construction consisted of a bank of earth, 20ft (6.1m) high and 8ft (2.4m) wide, with a ditch at the foot of its western flank. Even today the frontier between Wales and England runs largely along the course of the dyke. (On this stretch of it the River Wye forms the precise modern boundary between Gloucestershire and Monmouthshire.)

The construction of the dyke was felt to be necessary at a time when, after the Romans decamped and the Angles and Saxons invaded, Britain was divided into a number of warring kingdoms. Among these Mercia finally became pre-eminent in England, but the Celtic Britons clung tenaciously to their western mountains. Under Offa, Mercia absorbed other kingdoms and its king became de facto ruler of the English in England.

It is not thought that the dyke was conceived as a fortification – it was rather a means of definitively marking the boundary between Mercia and its neighbouring kingdoms. Nor was it the first such structure of its kind. Other Saxon rulers had defined their kingdoms in a similar fashion, but none had done so on the scale undertaken by Offa. It is an impressive achievement for its time. The Offa's Dyke Path, opened in 1971, is more or less the same length as the dyke itself but only rarely do the two coincide precisely.

Brockweir was once the most important port of the River Wye. Together with the River Severn, the River Wye was the main trade route serving the Forest of Dean. Timber, iron and coal from the Forest were brought to Brockweir, loaded at the wharf and shipped downstream to Chepstow. A horse-drawn tram that brought the goods from the mines also served the port. Brockweir became a centre of shipbuilding. All of this came to an end with the arrival of the railway in the late 19th century.

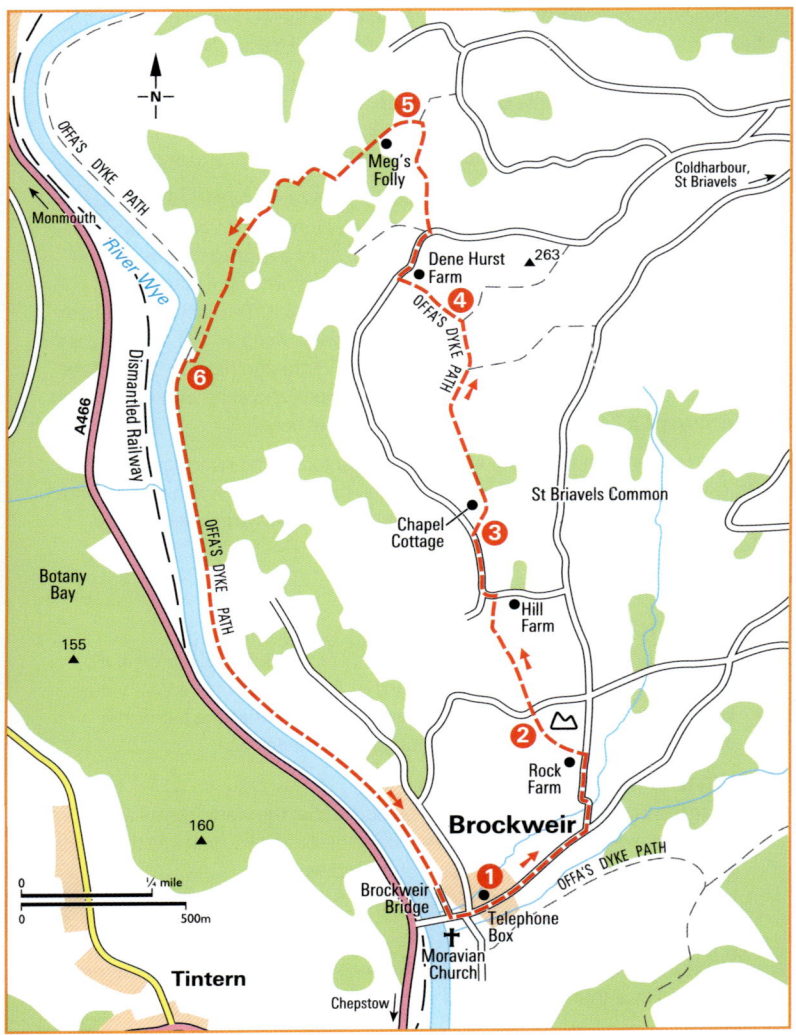

1. Walk uphill out of Brockweir until you reach a junction on your left, signposted 'Coldharbour'. Turn left along this narrow lane for about 200yds (183m). At a bend beside Rock Farm turn left onto a track, marked 'Offa's Dyke Path', which narrows and climbs to a lane.

2. Cross this and continue your ascent to reach another lane. Turn left here and follow the lane for 200yds (183m) to pass a cottage on the right, followed by some ruined stone buildings. Turn right along a lane.

3. Keep to the right of Chapel Cottage onto a path, still ascending. Further up, still on the path, keep left at a waymarked junction. Continue to climb until it brings you to another track. Turn left again.

4. After 50yds (46m), before a gate, fork right to a metal kissing gate into a field. Cross the field to a similar gate, to the left of a house. In the next field stay to the left of a farm and come to a third kissing gate at a lane. Turn right to climb gently. It levels out and then, where it starts to climb again at a corner, turn left onto the right-hand track, heading towards Oak Cottage (handpainted sign). Descend until you arrive at a lane with a gate on the left.

5. Turn left here to follow a track that descends to a house called Meg's Folly. Continue down, to the right of the house, alongside its garden boundary, ignoring a signposted path after 25yds (23m). After a further 250yds (229m) this time fork right to take the signposted path, descending more steeply. In 80yds (73m), at a low wooden marker post, turn left. This waymarked path now zig-zags down beside slabbed dry-stone walls. Keep an eye out for loose pebbles among the forest debris on the path. Eventually the path straightens and steepens, and you reach the edge of the woods and another metal kissing gate. Beyond it flows the River Wye, which is tidal here.

6. Turn left through the metal kissing gate and follow the river back to Brockweir. As you approach the village keep close to the river to enter a path that will bring you onto a lane leading up to the road at Brockweir Bridge. Turn left to return to the start.

Where to eat and drink
Over the bridge and a little downstream is The Old Station (see Walk 49), where a café is open from April to October. A little further The Wye Valley Hotel serves a range of snacks to hearty meals in either the bar or the dining room or weather permitting outside on the terrace.

What to see
Near the bridge in Brockweir you may notice that the water swirls and ruffles for no obvious reason. Look more closely and you will see that beneath the water are the remains of the old wharf.

While you're there
In St Briavels village is St Briavels Castle, built in 1131 by the Earl of Hereford. The castle is not a typical Norman construction as it was never intended as a frontline defensive structure. It is now a youth hostel.

49 BROCKWEIR TO TINTERN ABBEY

DISTANCE/TIME	4.25 miles (6.8km) / 2hrs 30min
ASCENT/GRADIENT	740ft (226m) / ▲▲
PATHS	Steep climb through fields to woodland, paths and tracks descending to the river; several stiles
LANDSCAPE	Hanging woods and meadow
SUGGESTED MAP	OS Explorer OL14 Wye Valley & Forest of Dean
START/FINISH	Grid reference: SO540011
DOG FRIENDLINESS	Off lead for long stretches, but on lead around livestock and in Moravian churchyard
PARKING	Lay-by in Brockweir or roadside further up
PUBLIC TOILETS	At Tintern Abbey

The Cistercian abbey of Tintern is one of the region's greatest monastic ruins, situated just over the border between Gloucestershire and Wales. Studying it today, a timeless landmark in a timeless, spectacularly beautiful setting on the wooded banks of the River Wye, it is not hard to understand why William Wordsworth appreciated it so much and how he came to immortalise it in his famous poem, 'Lines written a few miles above Tintern Abbey'.

What is left today is the defiantly noble shell of the abbey church, built in English Gothic style between 1270 and 1325. Tintern Abbey was only the second Cistercian foundation in Britain and the first in Wales. It was founded in May 1131 by Walter de Clare, Lord of Chepstow, and it soon prospered – largely thanks to various endowments of land in Gwent and Gloucestershire. Buildings were added, updated and restored thereafter until its dissolution in 1537.

Though grand and majestic in appearance, it was never particularly important or significant, and its history was largely quiet and uneventful. The abbey, which was best appreciated from the Wye until a new turnpike road cut through the scenic valley, was eventually purchased by the Crown from the Duke of Beaufort in 1901 for the sum of £15,000.

Near to Tintern Abbey is a landmark from more recent history. The Old Station, on the banks of the Wye, is also one of the region's most popular tourist attractions, and – given our love of steam trains and disused railway lines – it's not hard to see why. The original railway station, which opened in 1876 and closed to passengers in 1959 and freight in 1964, was purchased by the local council and now operates as a visitor attraction. There are three railway carriages to admire, two of which contain a souvenir and gift shop. The third carriage is smaller and includes railway memorabilia – among the displays are fascinating old photographs of Tintern station in bygone years.

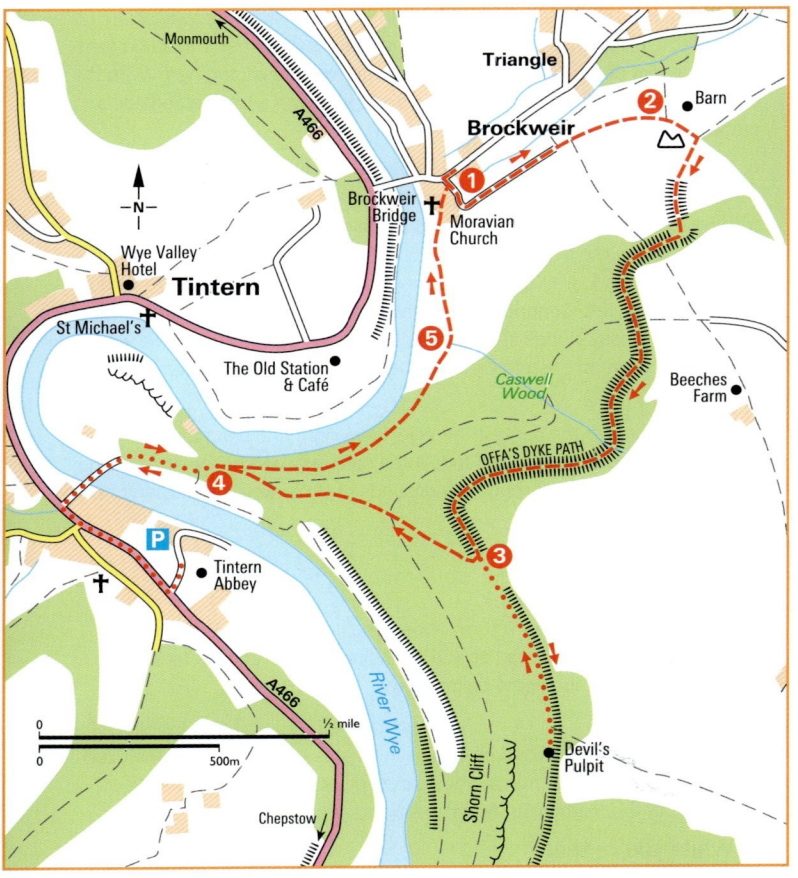

1. From the lay-by walk down the road for a few paces and turn left. Pass some outbuildings on the left and turn left, signposted 'Offa's Dyke'. Keep alongside buildings and barns and continue on the trail. Continue heading uphill to a gate and enter a field. On the right are trees and hedging. Ahead is a large barn.

2. Bear right before it and follow an enclosed path uphill, running to the right of a field. Make for a stile and gate in the top right corner and continue in the next field for several paces to a fork. Keep right and follow the path up the grassy slope towards trees. On reaching them head diagonally up the steep, stony path. At the top, opposite a stile, turn right, following the Offa's Dyke Path through trees. Stay on the trail, passing over stones and tree roots. At one point a wooded dell can be seen falling away to the right, and to the left fields are visible close by between the trees.

3. On reaching a path junction you have a choice. To visit the Devil's Pulpit (a look-out point) 0.5 miles (800m) off, keep ahead and then return to this intersection. The main walk turns right, signposted to Tintern. Descend through the trees to emerge from the cover at a T-junction. Turn right, and within 50yds (46m) bear left, again signed 'Tintern'. Pick your way down through the trees on a rocky path, and on reaching another T-junction turn right. The foot of the valley is visible through the trees along here. With the sound of traffic audible now, make for a junction with a track alongside a stone parapet.

4. To visit Tintern Abbey and the Old Station turn left here, following the track out of the woods to a bridge, crossing over the River Wye into Wales and turning left, briefly following the A466 in the direction of Chepstow. Otherwise, turn right along the track in the direction of Brockweir. This is a spectacular stretch of the walk, with the meandering River Wye seen and heard through the trees to the left. Continue on the obvious track to the point where the trees give way to grassy slopes and bracken, and along this stretch of the walk a stile can be seen on the left. Cross it and follow the grassy path down towards the river.

5. As you approach the bank of the Wye, keep right and head towards Brockweir. Make for a stile and follow the path between hedge and fencing, then stone walls. Pass through the grounds of Brockweir's Moravian Church and return to the lay-by.

Where to eat and drink
Across the bridge, near Tintern Abbey, you'll find the Old Station Café, open from April until October and providing a good range of freshly prepared meals and home-baked cakes.

What to see
The Moravian Church had its origins in what is now a region of the Czech Republic. It is a free church whose precepts influenced John Wesley, creator of the Methodist Church.

While you're there
Clearwell Caves is a natural cave system which has been extensively mined for iron ore over the years. The caves, formed by underground streams around 330 million years ago, are now part of a mining museum. Clearwell is about 7miles (11km) to the northeast of Brockweir.

STAUNTON AND THE FOREST OF DEAN

DISTANCE/TIME	6.25 miles (10.1km) / 3hrs
ASCENT/GRADIENT	655ft (200m) / ▲▲
PATHS	Forest tracks and paths
LANDSCAPE	Woodland, hills and village
SUGGESTED MAP	OS Explorer OL14 Wye Valley & Forest of Dean
START/FINISH	Grid reference: SO541125
DOG FRIENDLINESS	Very good
PARKING	Parking apron on forestry road beside main road, or on disused road section 400yds (366m) west
PUBLIC TOILETS	None on route

The Forest of Dean is all that remains of the primeval woodland that sprouted at the end of the ice age. It stands on a roughly a triangular plateau, bounded by the River Wye to the west and north, the River Severn to the south and Gloucester to the east.

Clearance began in about 4000 BC, as farmers established settlements. By the Iron Age the Forest had become an important source of minerals. The Romans mined here and evidence of these so-called 'scowles' can sometimes be discovered beneath small green mounds.

Before 1066 a large area of the forest was designated a royal hunting ground, and it remained the second largest Crown forest in England. In the 17th century the Forest was opened to private individuals and soon there were only a few hundred oaks left. Charles II ordered 11,000 acres (4,455ha) of oak to be planted and the Court of Verderers was set up to manage them. There are now some 27,000 acres (10,935ha) of oak, chestnut and other native trees. Today, the people who reside hereabouts are known as Foresters, and they maintain and preserve the ancient customs and privileges.

Several giant stones can be found on this spectacular walk. Composed of a quartz conglomerate – a mixture of quartz and Old Red Sandstone – they have mostly been formed by natural weathering over millions of years. The Suck Stone is thought to be one of the largest single boulders in the country, with estimates of its weight varying from 4,000 to 14,000 tons. From Near Hearkening Rock, keen-eared listeners are supposed to be able to hear messages whispered from the Buck Stone, which can be seen later in the walk. The Buck Stone used to be celebrated as the 'rocking stone', poised on its 3ft (90cm) apex, but in 1885 some lads heaved it over. The Long Stone is artificial, and probably created during the Bronze Age – some 7ft (2.1m) high, it is thought to have been part of an ancient cemetery.

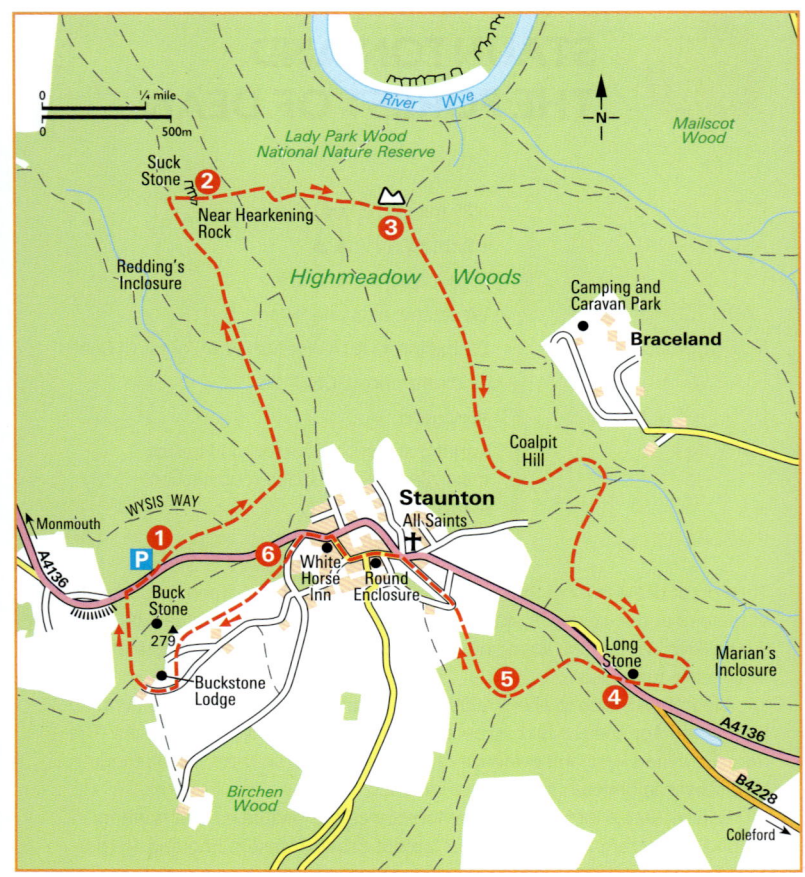

1. From the parking area, head along a track into the woods. Where the track curves sharp left, keep right to join another track. Follow this for just under 0.75 miles (1.2km), until you see large boulders on your right. Turn right to follow a waymarked path steeply up the slope, passing first the Suck Stone and then, at the top, Near Hearkening Rock (not the smaller slab to the left). These are just two of the many giant stones that you will pass on this walk.

2. Go up behind Near Hearkening Rock and, with your back to it, follow an initially graveled path through the trees for 150yds (137m) to a forest track. Turn left and immediately right, onto a path. Follow it through trees to a track. Keep right and take the next left path. Go right at a fork to reach a forest track. Cross this diagonally to walk with a high wire fence on your left. When the fence turns left veer right, following a path steeply to the valley bottom.

3. Turn right for just under 1 mile (1.6km). At a crossroads, by a sign on the left for campsites, turn right. After 100yds (91m), just before a telegraph pole, turn left onto a rising path, which you follow. Cross a major path and keep ahead to a track at a bend. You will hear traffic to your right. Turn left and follow this for 550yds (503m). At another crossways of tracks turn right onto a grassy path

(signed 'Highmeadow Trail') for 120yds (110m). Turn right along a path and continue to the Long Stone beside the A4136.

4. Turn right for a few paces and then cross the road to enter the woods on another path. Follow this to emerge at a junction of forest tracks. Turn left to follow the rising track. Bear right onto another track as you approach gates prohibiting public access, and keep ahead until just before the next intersection of tracks.

5. Turn sharp right to follow a broad path down to a farm track and onwards to Staunton. At a junction turn left, away from the main road, and go through the old village. Bend right, up to the White Horse Inn, and turn left along the pavement. Take the curving 'No Through Road' on the left, and at the stile and '15mph' sign ascend to follow a climbing path towards the Buck Stone.

6. Pass it and keep the wall closely on your right. Emerge left of Buckstone Lodge after 150yds (137m). Go down to a track and turn right, keeping right again on a falling path. Where the path divides, just before a telegraph pole, go right at a fork in front of you. Descend, passing a path running in from the left, and take the next left path alongside a fenced plantation. At the road turn right to return to the start.

Where to eat and drink
The only place on the route is the White Horse Inn in Staunton. Otherwise the nearest town of any size is Coleford, about 4 miles (6.4km) to the southeast, where there are several options.

What to see
In the village of Staunton look out for the curious round enclosure on your left as you pass through the village. This is the local pound where animals were kept before being sent to market, and where strays were secured for their owners to collect them – on payment of a fine.

While you're there
Nearby Coleford has an attractive marketplace and the Great Western Railway Museum, with railway memorabilia dating back to the late 19th century.

Explore the UK at RatedTrips.com